AF516090

REFRESHED ◆ REVISED ◆ UPDATED

Hachette CHILDREN'S Yearbook & Infopedia 2023

hachette INDIA

First published in 2022 by Hachette India
(Registered name: Hachette Book Publishing India Pvt Ltd)
An Hachette UK company
www.hachetteindia.com

1

This edition copyright © 2022 Hachette India

IMAGE COPYRIGHT INFORMATION: FRONT COVER: BORIS JOHNSON: Wikimedia Commons United Kingdom Open Government Licence v3.0; DROUPADI MURMU: Wikimedia Commons: GODL-India: https://commons.wikimedia.org/wiki/File:Droupadi_Murmu_official_portrait,_2022.jpg; Author: President's Secretariat; EKNATH SHINDE: Wikimedia Commons: GODL-India: https://en.m.wikipedia.org/wiki/File:Eknath_Shinde_with_PM_Narendra_Modi_Cropped.jpg; Author: Prime Minister's Office; ELON MUSK; Attribution: The Royal Society, https://en.wikipedia.org/wiki/Elon_Musk#/media/File:Elon_Musk_Royal_Society_(crop2).jpg; LOVLINA BORGOHAIN: Wikimedia Commons: GODL-India: Author: Ministry of Youth Affairs and Sports: https://ru.wikipedia.org/wiki/Felicitation_of_Tokyo_Olympics_Bronze_Medalist_Lovlina_Borgohain_(cropped).JPG; NEERAJ CHOPRA: Athletics Federation of India - Odisha2017.games/Odisha2017.games/CC-SA 4.0 International license; MAMATA BANERJEE: Wikimedia Commons: GODL-India/Published by Press Information Bureau on behalf of Ministry of Finance, Government of India under the ID 128738 and CNR 116171; PRIME MINISTER NARENDRA MODI: Wikimedia Commons: GODL-India: Official Photograph; https://www.pmindia.gov.in/en/image-gallery/; RAHUL GANDHI: Wikimedia Commons: GODL-India: http://164.100.47.194/Loksabha/Members/MemberBioprofile.aspx?mpsno=4074; UDDHAV THACKERAY: Wikimedia Commons: GODL-India: File:The Chief Minister of Maharashtra, Shri Uddhav Thackeray calling on the Prime Minister, Shri Narendra Modi, in New Delhi on February 21, 2020.jpg; Author: Prime Minister's Office; S. KIDAMBI: CCA-SA 4.0 International license. Attribution: Pierre-Yves Beaudouin; MITHALI RAJ: Wikimedia Commons: GODL-India: This file or its source was published by Press Information Bureau on behalf of President's Secretariat, Government of India under the ID 63953 and CNR 66639; Author: President's Secretariat; NIRMALA SITHARAMAN: Wikimedia Commons: GODL-India: This file or its source was published by Press Information Bureau on behalf of Ministry of Finance, Government of India under the ID 165766 and CNR 147174; Author: Ministry of Finance; VLADIMIR PUTIN: Wikimedia CC Attribution 4.0 License. Attribution: www.kremlin.ru; The Presidential Press and Information Office; VOLODYMYR ZELENSKYY: Wikimedia CC Attribution 4.0 International license; Attribution: President.gov.ua; https://www.president.gov.ua/en/president/biografiya; YOGI ADITYANATH: Wikimedia Commons: GODL-India: Author: President's Secretariat; This file or its source was published by Press Information Bureau on behalf of President's Secretariat, Government of India under the ID 121923 and CNR 109383; PIXABAY: astronomy; bacteria; bitcoin; blockchain; climate change; corona, drone; flood; helix nebula; iceberg; plastic; Marines in Afghanistan; metaverse; mobile phone; robot; rocket; Taj Mahal; windmill; **BACK COVER:** PIXABAY: Bitcoin, man-with-copy-space-futuristic-device, plastic; SOPHIA THE ROBOT: Wikimedia Commons: cropped from CC Attribution 4.0 International license. Attribution: President.az; The remaining photographs are from the public domain.

The copyright details and credits for the photographs in the book are on page 223, which is to be considered as an extension of the copyright page.

RESEARCH AND CONTENT WRITING: Chitrani Pandey; Diya Varkey

Caricatures on pgs 24–32 and 47; illustrations on pgs 141, 201 and 202: Mistunee Chowdhury, copyright © 2022 Hachette India

All rights reserved. No part of the publication may be reproduced, stored in a retrieval system (including but not limited to computers, disks, external drives, electronic or digital devices, e-readers, websites), or transmitted in any form or by any means (including but not limited to cyclostyling, photocopying, docutech or other reprographic reproductions, mechanical, recording, electronic, digital versions) without the prior written permission of the publisher, nor be otherwise circulated in any form of binding or cover other than that in which it is published and without a similar condition being imposed on the subsequent purchaser.

All maps in this work are pictorial representations, not to scale, and are not meant to represent exact political boundaries. They are for general illustration only, and are not intended to be used for reference purposes or reproduction elsewhere. It is clarified that the representation of a particular theme, or data set across regions with line/colour or other demarcations do not reflect political boundaries. It is also reiterated that such pictorial maps do not either represent or contradict India's national sovereignty, jurisdiction or the recognition of political regions as mandated by the Surveyor General of India for maps showing political boundaries.

All information has been updated till 1 July 2022 unless mentioned otherwise. All efforts have been made to verify the copyright ownership of photographs as well as the correctness of the information included in this edition. Any omissions are unintentional and regretted, and, following written communication, will be rectified in the next edition.

ISBN 978-93-93701-10-7

Hachette Book Publishing India Pvt. Ltd
4th & 5th Floors, Corporate Centre
Plot No. 94, Sector 44; Gurugram 122003, India

Printed and bound in India
by Manipal Technologies Limited, Manipal

CONTENTS

CONTENTS

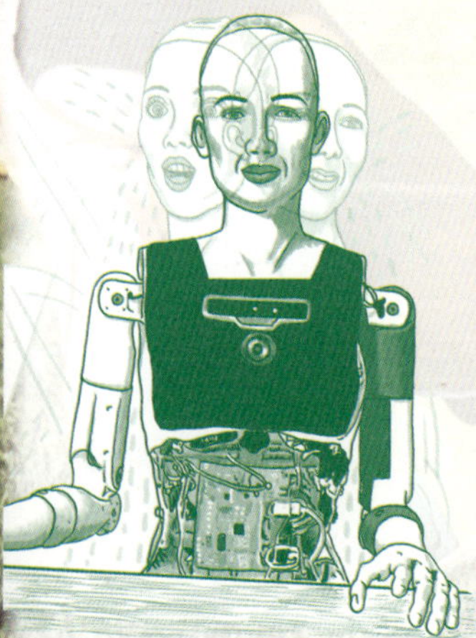

Diplomatic talks between Kyrgyzstan and India

On 26 October 2022, the Kyrgyz Republic's Security Council secretary visited India to hold the first diplomatic dialogue between the National Security Council Secretariats. Kyrgyzstan's representative Lieutenant General Marat Imankulov and India's National Security Adviser Ajit Doval discussed the challenges, threats and solutions for both Kyrgyzstan and India regarding regional and national security.

Commemorating Satyajit Ray

The Directorate of Film Festivals honoured iconic film-maker Satyajit Ray with a 'special retrospective' to commemorate his birth centennial. With a view to honouring the legacy of Satyajit Ray, a prize called the 'Satyajit Ray Lifetime Achievement Award for Excellence in Cinema' was initiated to be given at the International Film Festival of India (IFFI) annually, starting from 2021. The Award comprises a cash prize of ₹10 lakh, a certificate and a shawl, along with a Silver Peacock medal and scroll. The first award went to Hungarian film-maker Istvan Szabo and Hollywood film-maker Martin Scorsese.

Indian entrepreneur wins Earthshot Prize

The Earthshot Prize, awarded by the Royal Foundation of the Duke and Duchess of Cambridge, UK, recognizes the efforts of people working to make a positive change in the Earth's environment and facilitate the repair of our planet during the next ten years. The £1 million prize is oriented around five 'Earthshots': nature, world, ocean, climate and air. This year, Takachar, led by Indian engineer and entrepreneur Vidyut Mohan, was awarded the prize for its low-cost technological breakthrough to transform crop leftovers and waste biomass into fuels, fertilizers and speciality chemicals to reduce air pollution.

First IVF buffalo calf

On 23 October 2021, India's first IVF calf of the Banni breed was born. The calf was birthed from one of six IVF pregnancies at Vinay L. Vala's Sushila Agro farms in Dhanej village in Gir Somnath, Gujarat. Banni buffaloes are known for their higher milk yield in dry-climate conditions. The process was conducted by JKBovagenix of JK Trust, a non-governmental social initiative of the Raymond Group, to increase the number of genetically stronger buffaloes for enhancing milk production.

Andhra holds Maha Padayatra

Farmers and other landowners from the Thullur and Tadikonda mandals of Amaravati, Andhra Pradesh, started a 45-day Maha Padayatra demanding to maintain Amaravati as the only capital of Andhra Pradesh. During the tenure of Chandrababu Naidu, former chief minister of Andhra Pradesh (2014–19), 33,000 farmers donated their land as part of a Land Pooling Scheme (LPS) for this objective. After the Yuvajana Shramika Rythu Congress Party came to power, the construction stopped. In December 2019, Chief Minister Y.S. Jagan Mohan Reddy declared that the state would have three capitals: the executive capital at Visakhapatnam, the legislative capital at Amaravati and the judicial capital at Kurnool to ensure development for all regions equally.

India joins UNESCO World Heritage Committee

On 25 November 2021, India was elected as a member of the UNESCO World Heritage Committee for a period of four years. The decision came after India was re-elected to the UNESCO Executive Board. The UNESCO World Heritage Committee is responsible for implementing the World Heritage Convention, and allocates financial aid on requests by its member states. It also takes decisions about sites to be included on the World Heritage Sites list.

A web portal on EVs

At the COP26 Summit in Glasgow, UK, India unveiled 'e-Amrit' (Accelerated e-Mobility Revolution for India's Transportation), a web platform comprising all information about electric vehicles (EVs), including dispelling misconceptions about purchases, investment opportunities, regulations, subsidies and other topics. The portal was created and is maintained by the NITI Aayog as part of the UK–India Joint Roadmap 2030. The NITI Aayog aims to improve the site by adding more features and creative tools to make the portal user-friendly, interactive and attractive.

India's first food security museum

India's first food security museum was established in Thanjavur, Tamil Nadu, by the Food Corporation of India in collaboration with the Visvesvaraya Industrial and Technological Museum (VITM). Covering the history of agriculture and the evolution of food in India, the museum also includes cuisines and food distribution systems in India. It uses touchscreens, virtual reality sets, and other innovative technologies.

DECEMBER 2021

Prepping for cyber warfare

The Quantum Lab at the Military College of Telecommunication Engineering (MCET) in Mhow, Madhya Pradesh, was recently built by the Indian Army with assistance from the National Security Council Secretariat (NSCS) to lead research and teaching in this important emerging sector. With the help of this institute, students are being trained for cyber warfare through a cyber range and cyber security labs.

Chandrayaan-3 gets launch-ready

India's third lunar mission, Chandrayaan-3, has reached advanced stages of realization. All the systems in the propulsion and rover module have been integrated and tested. The module is being prepared to be launched in the first quarter of 2023. Chandrayaan-3 is a sort of repeat mission of Chandrayaan-2, but unlike the latter it will not have an orbiter. Instead, it has a propulsion module that will mimic a communications relay satellite.

JANUARY 2022

Air India back at Tata

After being in debt for seven decades, the airline was bought by the Tata Group, who had first established the airline. The airline had a debt of ₹61,562 crore as of 31 August 2021. The company also carried liability of up to ₹15,000 crore. The Tata Group bought the airlines with a ₹18,000 crore bid and took over ₹15,300 crore of the debt as well.

India gets new chief economic adviser

Dr V. Anantha Nageswaran was appointed as the new chief economic adviser (CEA) ahead of the tabling of the 2022–23 Union Budget. The scholar and earlier executive with Credit Suisse Group AG and Julius Baer Group will advise on new strategies for administering growth, investments and curbing fiscal deficit. He will also be an adviser to the finance minister and a lead author on the annual Economic Survey. Additionally, issues of income disparity and employment due to the COVID-19 pandemic will also be overseen by the new CEA.

Daughters to inherit property without a will

The Supreme Court declared a verdict allowing daughters to inherit their father's property in case a will is absent, under the Hindu Succession Act. Justices S. Abdul Nazeer and Krishna Murari declared their statement for daughters getting a preference for their father's property over other collaterals such as sons/daughters of brothers of the deceased father.

PM Modi's first India–Central Asian Summit

On 27 January, Narendra Modi held his first India–Central Asian Summit. The summit is a platform for the leaders of Asia to deliberate over issues of regional security and work towards strengthening relations between their countries. The virtual summit was attended by presidents of five countries: Kazakhstan, Uzbekistan, Tajikistan, the Kyrgyz Republic and Turkmenistan.

FEBRUARY 2022

National strategy on additive manufacturing

Ashwini Vaishnaw, Union Minister of Electronics and Information Technology, Communications and Railways, and Rajeev Chandrasekhar, Minister of State for Electronics and Information Technology and Skill Development and Entrepreneurship, introduced the National Strategy on Additive Manufacturing (AM), which aims to minimize the immediate disadvantages faced by local firms by accounting for next-generation digital manufacturing. The government believes that AM has enormous potential to change India's manufacturing and industrial production sector, and be a key mover in future economic strategy.

MAY 2022

Asani marks first cyclone of 2022

According to the India Meteorological Department (IMD), the first cyclone of 2022, Asani, developed in the Bay of Bengal and Arabian Sea area of the north Indian Ocean. The name Asani was given by Sri Lanka and translates as 'rage' in Sinhalese. The severe cyclone travelled at a speed of roughly 25 kmph toward the coast of Andhra Pradesh and Odisha. On 6 May, a low-pressure system, the precursor to the cyclone, developed over the south-east Bay of Bengal near the Andaman Sea. Less than 24 hours later, this system had become intense.

India becomes a part of First Movers Coalition

In an effort to de-carbonize the heavy industries and long-distance transportation sectors, India has joined the First Movers Coalition. At COP26, US President Joe Biden and the World Economic Forum introduced the First Movers Coalition as a model public–private cooperation to clean up the most carbon-intensive industries. Along with India, the USA has partnered with Denmark, Italy, Japan, Norway, Singapore, Sweden and the UK to develop early markets for clean technologies through legislative and private sector initiatives. In order to commercialize green technologies that corporate members agree to purchase, these government partners urge businesses from their nations to join the alliance and seek change in public policies.

Agnipath scheme launched for the Indian Army

The Central Government launched the Indian Army Agnipath (or Agneepath) Entry Scheme, under which Indian youth between the ages of 17.5 and 23 years will be recruited for the Indian Armed Forces to serve a short-service commission that lasts for a total of four years with a training period of six months and will be known as 'Agniveers'. After the completion of the four-year tenure, 25 per cent of the recruits from each batch will be offered regular service, and others will be given preference for jobs with the CAPF, Assam Rifles and state police. However, protestors against the scheme argued that the scheme provides no guarantee of recruitment after the four years of service and that Agniveers will not be eligible for gratuity or pension.

Maharashtra's political crisis

The crisis in the Maharashtra government peaked on 21 June 2022 when Eknath Shinde and several other Members of the Legislative Council of the Maha Vikas Aghadi (MVA) coalition moved to Surat in BJP-governed Gujarat, following their demand to Shiv Sena president Uddhav Thackeray to break the MVA alliance due to differences with the Congress Party and Nationalist Congress Party (NCP). Shinde rallied two-thirds of the members of the Shiv Sena to support him. On 28 June 2022, Uddhav Thackeray announced his retirement from his position as the chief minister of Maharashtra. He said that he would give up his position as a member of the Legislative Council. Shinde re-established ties with the BJP and was sworn in as the 20th chief minister of Maharashtra, with BJP's Devendra Fadnavis as the deputy chief minister.

The Flag Code is amended

In view of the celebrations of 75 years of Indian Independence and the 'Har Ghar Tiranga Abhiyan' under which PM Modi urged all citizens to hoist the tricolour at their homes between 13–15 August, the Centre amended the Flag Code of India to allow the national flag of India to be displayed in the open and on houses and buildings during both 'day and night'.

India gets its 15th president

On 25 July, BJP member Droupadi Murmu took oath as the 15th president of India, becoming only the second woman to hold the post and the first from the tribal community. Prime Minister Narendra Modi termed it as a milestone, saying, '...Her assuming the presidency is a watershed moment for India especially for the poor, marginalized and downtrodden.'

STOP PRESS

Monkeypox cases confirmed

On 2 August, India had eight confirmed cases of monkeypox cases. The Union Health Ministry issued guidelines to prevent its spread.

The world's largest floating solar power plant

Planned to be constructed in Khandwa district in Madhya Pradesh on Omkareshwar Dam on the River Narmada, this plant will generate 600 MW of power by 2022–23. This will make the district the only one in the state to have all three modes of power generation – thermal, hydel and solar.

Government withdraws Personal Data Protection Bill

On 4 August 2022, this Bill was withdrawn from Parliament, following 81 changes proposed to the Bill by the Parliament Panel after three years of review and deliberations.

First woman director general of CSIR

Dr N. Kalaiselvi became the first woman director-general of the Council of Scientific and Industrial Research (CSIR), India's largest research organization.

JUSTICE UDAY UMESH LALIT

Justice U.U. Lalit to be the 49th Chief Justice of India

The current Chief Justice of India N.V. Ramana, scheduled to retire on 8 November 2022, recommended Justice Uday Umesh Lalit as the next Chief Justice of India.

VICE-PRESIDENT JAGDEEP DHANKHAR

India gets new vice-president

Jagdeep Dhankhar has been elected as the 14th vice-president of India. He had earlier served as the governor of West Bengal. He was elected with 528 votes as opposed to Opposition candidate Margaret Alva, who garnered 182 votes.

French honour for Member of Parliament Shashi Tharoor

The Government of France has bestowed the highest French civilian honour – the Chevalier de la Legion d'Honneur – on senior Congress leader and Thiruvananthapuram Member of Parliament Shashi Tharoor for his written works and speeches.

SHASHI THAROOR

OCTOBER 2021

Military coup in Sudan destabilizes the country

On 25 October 2021, the military coup in Sudan overthrew Prime Minister Abdalla Hamdok and his cabinet ministers. Thousands of people protested the military takeover in the streets, resulting in 12 deaths and 280 people injured. After General Abdel-Fattah al-Burhan dissolved the transitional government that was moving towards structural reform, the military has become powerful once again. A state of emergency was declared by General al-Burhan, who rescheduled the 2022 elections to 2023 to ensure easy transfer of power. On 21 November, former prime minister Abdalla Hamdok was reinstated, but on 2 January 2022, he resigned after a massive civilian protest. Thousands of people including women and children have been detained for opposing the coup.

NOVEMBER 2021

New COVID-19 strain detected

With the COVID-19 virus evolving and mutating rapidly, an independent group of experts were gathered by the World health Organization (WHO) to monitor and evaluate the factors affecting the behaviour of the virus. The Technical Advisory Group on SARS-CoV-2 Virus Evolution (TAG-VE) convened to evaluate the new variant of Sars-Cov-2 virus – B.1.1.529 variant or Omicron. The first case of the new variant, Omicron, was reported to the WHO on 24 November 2021.

JANUARY 2022

First South Asian vice-president of the USA

On 20 January 2022, Kamala Harris, the current vice-president of the USA in the Joe Biden government, became the first woman, the first Black American, and the first South Asian American to hold a presidential position in the history of the USA. She was born in Oakland, California, to parents of Indian and Jamaican origin.

The meta year begins

2022 is being called the 'World of Meta' as companies focus on expanding the meta market by releasing the latest gadgets and technologies that will allow citizens easier access to the metaverse. Microsoft is spending on cloud services, which will hold together the digital worlds that will be available to the general public in 2022. The company launched Mesh, an initiative that enables

software developers to design programs that let various devices share the same virtual world. Mesh operates similarly to a video call only with the exception of three-dimensional holograms. In 2021, Facebook changed its name to Meta to indicate its focus on the metaverse.

Pig's heart transplanted in a human

On 10 January 2022, surgeons transplanted the genetically modified heart of a pig in a person at the University of Maryland School of Medicine, Baltimore, Maryland, USA. The patient, David Bennett, was ineligible for a human heart transplant. In an effort to save his life, the doctors transplanted the genetically modified pig heart into his body. This was the first time in history where animal organs have been used in place of human organs. The heart was accepted by Bennett's body and the procedure was successful. However, two months later, the 57-year-old Bennett died due to deteriorating health conditions.

China manipulates Earth's gravity

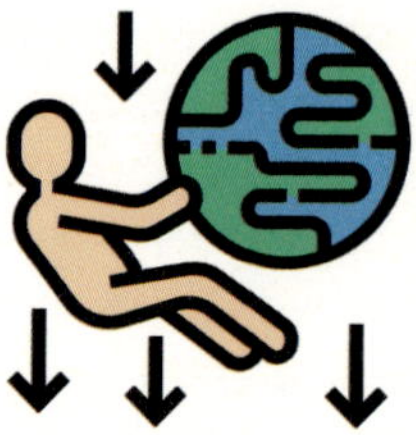

China has built a low-gravity research facility that has the ability to regulate the gravity of Earth's Moon, which has one-sixth of the Earth's gravity. Scientists can use powerful magnets at levels sufficient to manipulate the Moon's gravity and make Earth's gravitational pull completely 'disappear' by creating a 'vacuum' chamber of 60 cm diameter. This is an important achievement that can help scientists and astronauts in upcoming missions to the Moon.

Underwater volcano causes disruption

Tonga, a Polynesian island in the South Pacific Ocean, experienced an underwater volcanic eruption whose effects were felt all across the globe. A warning was declared when tsunami waves were noticed crashing on the shores of the Pacific coastline as well as Japan, Australia, New Zealand, Fiji, Russia, Chile and the USA. The eruption also led to severe damage to Tonga's capital Nuku'alofa, filling it with volcanic dust and cutting off communication lines.

Diplomatic boycott of Winter Beijing Games

In February 2022, the USA, followed by Australia, Britain and Canada, declared a diplomatic boycott of the Beijing Winter Olympics, i.e., government officials did not attend the event. Their reason: 'genocide and war against humanity inflicted by China on the Uyghurs and other predominantly Muslim ethnic minorities in the Xinjiang region'.

The Russia-Ukraine war

On 24 February 2022, Russia invaded Ukraine in what is known as the Russo-Ukrainian War. The Russian Federation, under President Vladimir Putin, had been stationing its troops on the Ukraine border since early 2021, and made numerous demands for prohibitions against Ukraine joining NATO, a military alliance that was founded in 1949 to counter Soviet expansion in Europe after the Second World War.

The roots of the conflict can be traced back to 2014 when the then Ukrainian president Viktor Yanukovych was overthrown by Ukrainian protesters. Russia annexed the Crimean Peninsula, declared control over the Luhansk region, previously part of Ukraine, and attacked the Donbas region (a war in which more than 14,000 were killed).

Putin declared that the aim of the invasion was to 'demilitarize and de-Nazify Ukraine'. However, the Russian president has denied all claims of invasion and declares Europe's biggest war since 1945 a 'special military operation'.

The war, however, has lasted longer than Russia expected and after failing to take control of the capital Kyiv, the Russian forces have turned their attention to the Donbas region again, where Russian-supported separatists have been fighting since 2014. The Ukrainians, with the backing of Western allies, have held off Russia for more than 100 days.

While the Indian government stayed neutral on the conflict, it launched Operation Ganga at its own cost to evacuate Indian students in Ukraine caught in the middle of the conflict. By 6 March, about 16,000 Indians had been flown to India in 76 flights after using various transportation corridors with the help of countries such as Romania, Hungary, Poland, Moldova and Slovakia, which are Ukraine's neighbours.

MARCH 2022

X-marker passports for gender-neutral citizens in the USA

The US Department of State announced that passport applicants will now have the opportunity to select their gender without submission of medical documentation, starting 11 April 2022. No inquiries will be initiated in case of gender disparity between their chosen gender on the passport and other citizenship and identity documents. Citizens may select option X as their gender marker on applications for their US passport. This option is meant to be available on other documentation papers from next year. In 2015, Dana Zzyym, a US Navy veteran, requested a different marker for gender other than M or F and was denied it. Zzyym received the X-marker passport after a six-year-long legal battle with the US Department.

Mercury and geomagnetic storms

Scientists have discovered that Mercury, the smallest planet in the solar system, experiences geomagnetic storms similar to those on Earth. The research's findings, published in the journal *Nature Communications*, established the existence of a ring current, a field of charged particles moving laterally around the globe, proving the presence of geomagnetic storms brought on by ring currents. The research was made possible by the accidental crashing of NASA's Messenger Space probe on Mercury in 2015.

Furthest galaxy discovered 13.5 billion years away

Researchers have discovered a celestial object, HD1, a possible galaxy that they estimate to be 13.5 billion light years away. HD1 is 100 million light years further away from the current farthest galaxy, GN-z11. HD1 is incredibly bright, pointing towards intense activity in the galaxy. Scientists first postulated that the object might be a starburst galaxy, or a galaxy that creates stars fast. They finally found that the galaxy was creating more than 100 stars every year, which is a rate ten times greater than that of ordinary starburst galaxies.

Second country adopts Bitcoin as legal currency

The Central African Republic adopted bitcoin as legal tender, making it the second country in the world (after El Salvador in Central America, which adopted it in April 2022) and the first African country to accept Bitcoin as a currency. While no official announcement regarding the currency was made, its parliament had passed a bill initiating regulations to govern the use of cryptocurrency.

Denmark is the first country to stop COVID-19 immunization

In April 2022, Denmark became the first nation to stop the COVID-19 immunization campaign as a result of their success in restricting the viral outbreak. The vaccination centres would stay open and the public can opt for booster shots if they like, but from 15 May 2022 they would not be asked to take the vaccine unless the evolutionary nature of the virus demands it.

NASA's fifth SpaceX journey

NASA's Crew-4 astronauts from SpaceX launched to the International Space Station in a brand-new Dragon spacecraft named Freedom, along with a Falcon 9 rocket booster on its fourth space mission. SpaceX's mission control facility in Hawthorne, California, will be used to track a series of automatic spacecraft manoeuvres during Dragon's flight, and NASA teams will use their mission control facility at the Johnson Space Center in Houston, Texas, to check on space station operations throughout the flight. The Crew-4 astronauts will spend months in space undertaking novel scientific studies in different fields, including plant science, health technology and materials science, all geared towards improving life on Earth. Additionally, they will conduct scientific studies that will aid NASA in getting ready for extended stays on the Moon and, eventually, Mars.

Russia banned from UNHRC

In response to Russia's military actions in Ukraine, the United Nations suspended the Russian Federation from its position on the UN Human Rights Council. The proposal was submitted by the US ambassador to the UN, Linda Thomas-Greenfield, in response to allegations that Russian troops had killed and tortured Ukrainian citizens in Bucha, a neighbourhood close to Kyiv. With 93 votes in favour, 24 against and 58 abstentions, the motion to remove Russia from the Human Rights Council was approved.

Meta-community on its way

The World Economic Forum, in partnership with Accenture and Microsoft, is creating a Global Collaboration Village as a digital model for future public–private cooperation. It aims to offer immersive environments where stakeholders can come together to promote global interactivity, impact and collaboration. In order to create governance and socioeconomic policy frameworks for the metaverse, the Forum is also launching an initiative on 'Defining and Building the Metaverse' with over 60 leading companies from technology and other sectors as well as experts from governments, academia and civil society.

Digital foreign direct investment (FDI)

At the World Economic Forum Annual Meeting 2022, a novel initiative to encourage international investment in the digital economy was introduced, named the 'Digital FDI Initiative'. It will implement projects in numerous nations to support the expansion of digital FDI on a national level. Nigeria will host the first FDI project in the digital sector. Through public–private partnerships, the Digital FDI programme will execute essential reforms in emerging markets and developing nations. By encouraging laws, rules and procedures adapted for specific nations, it plans to create digital-friendly investment climates.

World's longest pedestrian bridge

The world's longest pedestrian suspension bridge has been opened to the public in a mountain resort in the Czech Republic. The 721 m long Sky Bridge 721 is constructed more than 1,100 m (3,610 ft) above sea level. The structure, built over two years with an estimated cost of US $8.3 million, connects two mountain ranges and hangs 97.84 m (312 ft) above a valley. The bridge can accommodate up to 500 people at a time. For safety reasons, it will stay closed if winds reach a speed of above 135 kmph.

UN multilingualism at India's behest

The United Nations General Assembly (UNGA) passed an India-sponsored plan on multilingualism that mentions Hindi , Bangla and Urdu for the first time. The adopted resolution requested the UN to keep distributing important information and messages in both official and non-official languages. As part of these efforts, the 'Hindi@UN' project had been introduced in 2018, with the aim of expanding the UN's community outreach in Hindi and among the millions of Hindi-speaking people.

South Korea launches first indigenously made rocket

On 21 June, South Korea launched its first 'home'-made space rocket, Nuri. The rocket lifted off in the second attempt. In the first attempt, the rocket reached an altitude of 700 km and was successful in detaching the payload. However, it was unable to launch a mock satellite into orbit due to the burnout of the third engine earlier than expected. With its successful second attempt, the country became the 10th nation in the world to lift off a satellite into space. South Korea had earlier sent satellites into orbit but it was with the help of foreign launchers or foreign technology.

Elon Musk pulls away from Twitter deal

Elon Musk had offered to buy Twitter for $44 billion in April 2022. However, in July, Elon Musk withdrew his offer, stating that Twitter had failed to adhere to his demand of removing fake and spam accounts, which persisted on the platform. He also claimed that Twitter had breached the agreement and fired two top-level managers without consulting Musk as required by the agreement.

STOP PRESS

UK PM Boris Johnson resigns

On 7 July, UK Prime Minister Boris Johnson announced his pending resignation as leader of Conservative Party. At the time of going to press, Liz Truss, Secretary of State for Foreign, Commonwealth and Development Affairs, and Rishi Sunak, who served as chancellor of the exchequer from 2020 to 2022, were in the race for the post, with Truss emerging as the favourite.

Sri Lanka gets new leadership

On 21 July, Ranil Wickremesinghe, the leader of the centre-right United National Party since 1994, took oath as the new Sri Lankan president, following former president Gotabaya Rajapaksa fleeing the country and the declaration of a state of emergency amid a worsening economic crisis. Dinesh Gunawardena, a former cabinet minister, member of parliament and the leader of the house in the Sri Lankan Parliament, became prime minister.

RANIL WICKREMESINGHE

Earth has a record shortest day

Earth set a shortest-day record by completing its full spin in a duration that was 1.59 milliseconds less than 24 hours, on 29 July 2022. Scientists have been observing that Earth has been rotating faster than before.

Serena Williams announces retirement

On 9 August, American tennis champion Serena Williams announced her retirement from the game after the US Open (scheduled between 29 August and 11 September).

Salman Rushdie attacked

On 12 August, acclaimed author of 13 novels (including 1981 Booker winner *Midnight's Children*), among other works of fiction and non-fiction, Salman Rushdie was stabbed on stage just before he was to deliver a lecture at an event in Chautauqua, New York, by a 24-year-old New Jersey man. Rushdie has long faced death threats since the publication of his book, *The Satanic Verses*, in 1994.

PEOPLE TO REMEMBER

GENERAL BIPIN RAWAT (16 March 1958–8 December 2021): The first Chief of Defence Staff of the Indian Armed Forces died in a helicopter crash in December 2021 near Coonoor in Tamil Nadu.

SINDHUTAI SAPKAL (14 November 1948–4 January 2022): This social worker and activist worked for orphans in India. She received the Padma Shri in 2021.

LATA MANGESHKAR: (28 September 1929–6 February 2022): This legendary playback singer in Indian cinema had an eight-decade-long career and was known as the 'Nightingale of India' and the 'Queen of Melody'.

PANDIT BIRJU MAHARAJ (4 February 1938– 16 January 2022): This Indian dancer, composer and singer, introduced the Kathak dance form to the world.

SIDNEY POITIER (20 February 1927–6 January 2022): Remembered for his role in *To Sir with Love*, he was the first African American actor to win an Oscar for Best Actor (*Lilies of the Field*, 1963).

BAPPI LAHIRI (27 November 1952 –15 February 2022): This Indian singer and composer pioneered the use of disco music in Bollywood and related music industries.

DR RAMA KANT SHUKLA (24 December 1940 –11 May 2022): An eminent Hindi and Sanskrit scholar, this Padma Shri recipient was the founder-editor of the Sanskrit quarterly journal, *Arvacinasamskrtam*.

YURI AVERBAKH (8 February 1922–7 May 2022): The world's oldest living (and legendary) Grandmaster, this chess player received the title in 1952.

PANDIT SHIVKUMAR SHARMA (13 January 1938–10 May 2022): This acclaimed santoor player adapted the musical instrument for Hindustani classical music.

SIDDHU MOOSE WALA (11 June 1993–29 May 2022): This young rapper, singer, songwriter and actor's songs featured on Billboard Canadian, UK Asian and Global YouTube music charts.

KRISHNAKUMAR KUNNATH (23 August 1968–31 May 2022): Popularly known as KK, he was an Indian playback singer.

PANDIT BHAJAN SOPORI (22 June 1948– 2 June 2022): This santoor maestro studied and later taught music at Washington University, USA.

PALLONJI MISTRY (1 June 1929–28 June 2022): The India-born Irish-citizen chairman of the Shapoorji Pallonji Group was awarded the Padma Bhushan in 2016.

BHUPINDER SINGH (6 February 1940–18 July 2022): This ghazal and playback singer sang memorable songs such as 'Dil Dhoondta Hai', 'Naam Gum Jayega' and 'Karoge Yaad Toh'.

RAKESH JHUNJHUNWALA (5 July 1960–14 August 2022): Veteran Indian investor and stock trader, and founder of Akasa Air, he was referred to as the 'Big Bull of India'.

PADMA SHRI, 2022

Art: Ajita Srivastava, A.K.C. Natarajan, Arjun Singh Dhurve, Chandraprakash Dwivedi, Darshanam Mogilaiah, Durga Bai Vyam, Gosaveedu Shaik Hassan (Posthumous), H.R. Keshavamurthy, Kaajee Singh, Kamalini Asthana and Nalini Asthana (Duo), Khandu Wangchuk Bhutia, Kongampattu A.V. Murugaiyan, Konsam Ibomcha Singh, Lalita Vakil, Lourembam Bino Devi, Madhuri Barthwal, Padmaja Reddy, Ramachandraiah, Ram Dayal Sharma, Ram Sahay Panday, S. Ballesh Bhajantri, Sheesh Ram, Shyamamani Devi, Shivnath Mishra, Sonu Nigam, Sowcar Sankaramanchi Janaki, Sulochana Chavan, Thavil R. Muthukannammal, Tsering Namgyal

Civil Service: Guruprasad Mohapatra

Grassroots Innovation: Abdul Khader Nadakattin

Literature and Education: Avadh Kishore Jadia, Sirpi Balasubramaniam, Akhone Asgar Ali Basharat, Badaplin War, Chirapat Prapandavidya, Dhaneswar Engti, Dilip Shahani, Girdhari Ram Ghonju (Posthumous), Harmohinder Singh Bedi, Khalil Dhantejvi (Posthumous), J.K. Bajaj, Kali Pada Saren, Maria Christopher Byrski, Prof. Najma Akhtar, Narasimha Rao Garikapati, Narasingha Prasad Guru, P. Narayana Kurup, Raghuvendra Tanwar, Rutger Kortenhorst, Siddhalingaiah (Posthumous), Shaibal Gupta (Posthumous), Tara Jauhar, Tatiana Lvovna Shaumyan, T. Senka Ao, Vidyanand Sarek, Vishwamurti Shastri, V.L. Nghaka, Vidya Vindu Singh

Medicine: Dr Balaji Tambe (Posthumous), Dr Bhimsen Singhal, Dr Himmatrao Bawaskar, Dr Kamlakar Tripathi, Dr Lata Desai, Dr Narendra Prasad Misra (Posthumous), Dr Prokar Dasgupta, Dr Sunkara Venkata Adinarayana Rao, Dr Veeraswamy Seshiah, Dr Vijaykumar Vinayak Dongre

Public Affairs: Malji Bhai Desai

Science and engineering: Aditya Prasad Dash, Ajay Kumar Sonkar, Anil Kumar Rajvanshi, Jyantkumar Maganlal Vyas, Moti Lal Madan, Sanghamitra Bandyopadhyay, Subbanna Ayyappan

Social work: Acharya Chandanaji, Baba Iqbal Singh Ji, Basanti Devi, Gamit Ramilaben Raysingbhai, K.V. Rabiya, Om Prakash Gandhi, Prabhaben Shah, Prem Singh, Savaji Bhai Dholakia, Shakuntala Choudhary, S. Damodaran, Srimad Baba Balia

Sports: Avani Lekhara, Brahmanand Sankhwalkar, Faisal Ali Dar, Neeraj Chopra, Pramod Bhagat, Sankaranarayana Menon Chundayil, Sumit Antil, Vandana Kataria

Trade and Industry: Jagjit Singh Dardi, Muktamani Devi, Prahlad Rai Agarwala, Ryuko Hira

Others: Animal Husbandry: Sosamma Iype; **Agriculture:** Amai Mahalinga Naik, Seth Pal Singh; **Spiritualism:** Guru Tulku Rinpoche, Sadguru Brahmeshanand Acharya Swami; **Yoga:** Sivananda

PADMA VIBHUSHAN, 2022

Art: Prabha Atre
Civil Service: General Bipin Rawat (Posthumous)
Literature and Education: Radheyshyam Khemka (Posthumous)
Public Affairs: Kalyan Singh (Posthumous)

PADMA BHUSHAN, 2022

Art: Gurmeet Bawa (Posthumous), Rashid Khan, Victor Banerjee,
Civil Service: Rajiv Mehrishi
Literature and Education: Pratibha Ray, Swami Sachidanand, Vashishth Tripathi
Public Affairs: Buddhadeb Bhattacharjee, Ghulam Nabi Azad,
Sports: Devendra Jhajharia
Trade and Industry: Cyrus Poonawalla, Krishna Ella and Suchitra Ella (Duo), Natarajan Chandrasekaran, Satya Narayana Nadella, Sundararajan Pichai
Science and Engineering: Sanjaya Rajaram (Posthumous)
Others (Culinary: Madhur Jaffery

GRAMMY AWARDS, 2022

Record of the Year: 'Leave the Door Open by Silk Sonic
Album of the Year: *We Are* by Jon Batiste
Song of the Year: 'Leave the Door Open' by Silk Sonic
Best New Artiste: Olivia Rodrigo
Best Pop Vocal Album: *Sour* by Olivia Rodrigo
Best Rap Album: *Call Me If You Get Lost* by Tyler, the Creator
Best Rock Album: *Medicine at Midnight* by Foo Fighters
Best Jazz Vocal Album: *Generations* by The Baylor Project
Best R&B Album: *Heaux Tales* by Jazmine Sullivan
Best Country Album: *Starting Over* by Chris Stapleton

93RD ACADEMY AWARDS, 2022

Best Picture: *Coda* – Philippe Rousselet, Fabrice Gianfermi and Patrick Wachsberger (producers)
Best Actor in a Leading R ole: Will Smith for *King Richard*
Best Actress in a Leading Role: Jessica Chastain for *The Eyes of Tammy Faye*
Best Actor in a Supporting Role: Troy Kotsur for *Coda*
Best Actress in a Supporting Role: Ariana Debose for *West Side Story*
Best Animated Feature Film: *Encanto* – Jared Bush, Byron Howard (directors), Yvett Merino and Clark Spencer (producers)
Best Cinematography: *Dune* – Greig Fraser
Best Costume Design: *Cruella* – Jenny Beavan
Best Direction: *The Power of the Dog* – Jane Campion
Best International Feature Film: *Drive My Car* – Japan
Best Short Film (Animated): *The Windshield Wiper* – Alberto Mielgo and Leo Sanchez
Best Short Film (Live Action): *The Long Goodbye* – Aneil Karia and Riz Ahmed
Best Documentary (Feature): *Summer of soul (...Or, When the Revolution Could Not Be Televised)* – Ahmir 'Questlove' Thompson (director), Joseph Patel, Robert Fyvolent and David Dinerstein (producers)
Best Documentary (Short Subject): *The Queen of Basketball* – Ben Proudfoot (director)
Best Film Editing: *Dune* – Joe Walker
Best Writing (Adapted Screenplay): *Coda* – Sian Heder
Best Writing (Original Screenplay): *Belfast* – Kenneth Branagh
Best Production Design: *Dune* – Patrice Vermette; Set Decoration: Zsuzsanna Sipos

68TH NATIONAL FILM AWARDS, 2022

Best Feature Film: *Soorarai Pottru* (Tamil); director: Sudha Kongara

Best Direction: *Ayyappanum Koshiyum* (Malayalam); director: Sachidanandan K.R.

Best Debut Film of a Director: *Mandela* (Tamil); director: Madonne Ashwin

Best Popular Film Providing Wholesome Entertainment: *Tanhaji* (Hindi); director: Om Raut

Best Children's Film: *Sumi* (Marathi); director: Amol Vasant Gole

Best Film on National Integration: *Three Sisters* (Bengali); director: Putul Rafey Mahmood

Best Film on Social Issues: *Justice Delayed, But Delivered* (Hindi) – director: Kamakhya Narayan Singh; *Funeral* (Marathi) – director: Vivek Dubey

Best Film on Environment Conservation/ Preservation: *Taledanda* (Kannada); director: Praveen Krupakar

Best Actor: Suriya for *Soorarai Pottru*; Ajay Devgn for *Tanhaji;*

Best Actress: Aparna Balamurali for *Soorarai Pottru*

Best Supporting Actor: Biju Menon for *Ayyappanum Koshiyum*

Best Supporting Actress: Lakshmi Priyaa Chandramouli for *Sivaranjiniyum Innum Sila Pengalum* (Tamil)

Best Child Artist: Anish Mangesh Gosavi for *Tak Tak* (Marathi); Akanksha Pingle and Divyesh Indulkar for *Sumi*

Best Playback Singer (Male): Rahul Deshpande for *Mi Vasantrao* (Marathi); **(Female):** Nanjiyamma for song 'Kalakkatha' in *Ayyappanum Koshiyum*

Best Cinematography: Supratim Bhol for *Avijatrik* (Bengali)

Best Screenplay (Original): Sudha Kongara and Shalini for *Soorarai Pottru;* **(Dialogue Writer):** Madonne Ashwin for *Mandela*

Best Editing: A. Sreekar Prasad for *Sivaranjiniyum Innum Sila Pengalum*

Best Audiography: (Location Sound Recordist): Jobin Jayan for *Dollu* (Kannada); **(Sound Designer):** Anmol Bhave for *Mi Vasantrao*

Best Production Design: Anees Nadodi for *Kappela* (Malayalam)

Best Make-up Artist: T.V. Rambabu for *Natyam* (Telugu)

Best Costumes: Nachiket Barve and Mahesh Sherla for *Tanhaji*

Best Music Direction: S. Thaman for *Ala Vaikunthapurramuloo* (Telugu); **(Background Score):** G.V. Prakash Kumar for *Soorarai Pottru*

Best Lyrics: Manoj Muntashir for *Saina* (Hindi)

Best Stunts Choreography: Rajasekhar, Mafia Sasi and Supreme Sundar for *Ayyappanum Koshiyum*

Best Choreography: Sandhya Raju for *Maharishi* (Telugu)

Special Jury Award: *Admitted* (Hindi and English) – director: Ojaswee Sharma; *Semkhor* (Dimasa) – director: Aimee Baruah; *Vaanku* (Malayalam) – director: Kavya Prakash; *June* (Marathi) – director: Siddharth Menon

PULITZER PRIZES, 2021

JOURNALISM

Public Service: *The Washington Post*

Breaking News Reporting: The staff of *The Miami Herald*

Investigative Reporting: Corey G. Johnson, Rebecca Woolington and Eli Murray of the *Tampa Bay Times*

Explanatory Reporting: Staff of *Quanta* Magazine, notably Natalie Wolchover

International Reporting: The staff of *The New York Times*

Feature Writing: Jennifer Senior of *The Atlantic*

Commentary: Melinda Henneberger of the *Kansas City Star*

Criticism: Salamishah Tillet, contributing for *The New York Times*

Editorial Writing: Lisa Falkenberg, Michael Lindenberger, Joe Holley and Luis Carrasco

Breaking News Photography: Marcus Yam of the *Los Angeles Times*, Win McNamee, Drew Angerer, Spencer Platt, Samuel Corum and Jon Cherry of Getty Images

Feature Photography: Adnan Abidi, Sanna Irshad Mattoo, Amit Dave and the late Danish Siddiqui of Reuters

BOOKS, DRAMA AND MUSIC

Fiction: *The Netanyahus: An Account of a Minor and Ultimately Even Negligible Episode in the History of a Very Famous Family* by Joshua Cohen

Drama: *Fat Ham*, by James Ijames

History: *Covered with Night by Nicole Eustace and Cuba: An American History* by Ada Ferrer

Biography: *Chasing Me to My Grave: An Artist's Memoir of the Jim Crow South* by the late Winfred Rembert, as told to Erin I. Kelly

Poetry: *Frank: Sonnets* by Diane Seuss

General Nonfiction: *Invisible Child: Poverty, Survival and Hope in an American City* by Andrea Elliott

Music: *Voiceless Mass* by Raven Chacon

OTHER IMPORTANT AWARDS

Zishaan A. Latif	Ramnath Goenka Award in the Photojournalism category for his photo-essay work
Diebedo Francis Kere	Pritzker Architecture Prize
Mirabai Chanu	BBC Indian Sportswoman of the Year award
The Last Cuentista by Donna Barba Higuera	The John Newbery Medal by the Association for Library Service to Children, a division of the American Library Association
The Book of Form and Emptiness by Ruth Ozeki	Women's Prize for Fiction, UK
Emma Raducanu (US Open 2021 tennis, women's singles' winner)	Laureus World Breakthrough of the Year Award 2022
Sir Clive Lloyd	Knighthood by Prince William, the Duke of Cambridge at Windsor Castle
Aarefa Johari	Chameli Devi Jain Award for an Outstanding Woman Mediaperson 2021
Shaylyn Ford (Mrs America)	Mrs World 2022
Navdeep Kaur (Mrs India World 2021)	Best National Costume award at the Mrs World 2022 Pageant
Sumit Bhale (Lavni artiste from Maharashtra)	Gold medal at the International Folk Art Festival in Dubai
Prajakta Koli (Indian Youtuber and Actor)	Named 'Youth Climate Champion' by the United Nations Development Programme
Shinzo Abe (Former Japan Prime Minister, assassinated in July 2022)	Netaji Award 2022 by Netaji Research Bureau
Sathyamangalam Tiger Reserve (Tamil Nadu, India) and Bardiya National Park (Bansagadhi, Nepal)	(Joint) TX2 award for doubling their tiger populations since 2010
B.V. Doshi	Royal Gold Medal 2022 by the Royal Institute of British Architects (RIBA)
Kishore Kumar Das (founder of educational charity 'Bidyanando'	Commonwealth Points Of Light Award, UK
Ukrainian President Volodymyr Zelensky	John F. Kennedy Award
Cynthia Rosenzweig, a Nasa climate research scientist	World Food Prize 2022
Sir David Attenborough	UN Champion of the Earth Lifetime Achievement Award
Kerala Arts and Crafts Village Organization	International Craft Award 2021 by World Crafts Council International as the best crafts village in the world

ABDUL KHADER NADAKATTIN

In the news for: Agricultural innovations and winning the Padma Shri; Where: India

A grassroots agricultural innovator from Dharwad in Karnataka, Nadakattin was honoured with the Padma Shri

in 2022. He was awarded for his many agricultural discoveries, such as a ploughing blade manufacturing machine, a seed-cum-fertilizer and a water-heating boiler, among others. His innovations are based on the enduring principles of sustainability, cost-effectiveness, eco-friendliness and social acceptance.

CAPTAIN ABHILASHA BARAK

In the news for: Being the first woman combat aviator in the Indian Army; Where: India

Twenty-six-year-old Captain Abhilasha Barak from Haryana became the first woman to join the Indian Army's Aviation Corps as a combat aviator. She was awarded her 'wings', alongside 36 army pilots, at a ceremony after her year-long training at the Combat Army Aviation Training School at Nashik in Maharashtra. She comes from a family of army officers and her father is Col S. Om Singh (Retd).

ADITYA CHOPRA

In the news for: Launching the 'Saathi Card' to help daily-wage earners; Where: India

Bollywood filmmaker Aditya Chopra launched the 'Saathi Card' for daily-wage earners in September 2021 for a long-term and sustainable benefit for daily-wage earners working in the Hindi film industry. This card will provide health insurance, school-fee allowance, ration supply and other facilities to daily-wage earners and their families. The card holders will receive a health insurance benefit of up to two lakh rupees, free annual check-ups and discount on medical treatments. The eligibility criteria for being a card holder is to be a registered member of the Hindi Film Federation, be 35 years old and above, and to have at least one dependent member.

ANJU BOBBY GEORGE

In the news for: Winning the WA 'Woman of the Year' Award; Where: India
On 1 December 2021, World Athletics (WA) honoured Indian track legend Anju Bobby George with the 'Woman of the Year' award. She received this for her efforts to inspire women to represent India in international sports. She had won a gold medal in the IAAF World Athletics Final in Monaco in 2005, which was India's first gold medal in the long jump event.

ANWAR HUSSAIN SHAIK

In the news for: Heading the WTO Committee on Technical Barriers of Trade; Where: India
Anwar Hussain Shaik, an Indian government officer (Indian Railway Traffic Service), has been appointed to chair the World Trade Organization's committee on Technical Barriers to Trade. The Technical Barriers Committee is tasked with resolving barriers to trade by reviewing and strengthening the implementation of trade rules and regulations.

BAD BUNNY

In the news for: Being the first Latino to lead a live-action Marvel movie; Where: USA
Bad Bunny (Benito Antonio Martínez Ocasio), a Puerto Rican rapper, will be the first Latino to lead a live-action Marvel movie. He will play the title character of 'the dead one' in Marvel's film *El Muerto*. It will be the first time in the Marvel universe that a Latin actor has their own live-action superhero movie.

B.V. DOSHI

In the news for: Receiving the Royal Gold Medal 2022 for architecture; Where: India
Iconic architect Balkrishna Vithaldas Doshi, 94, has completed over 100 buildings in his career of more than 70 years. For his noteworthy contribution, he was awarded one of the world's highest honour in architecture, the Royal Gold Medal for 2022 by the Royal Institute of British Architects. Doshi's key projects include Atira Guest House, Ahmedabad (1958), Aranya Low Cost Housing in Indore (1989), the Institute of Indology, Ahmedabad (1962), the Indian Institute of Management Bangalore (1977–92) and Amdavad Ni Gufa, Ahmedabad (1994), among others.

CAMPBELL WILSON

In the news for: Becoming Air India's new CEO; Where: India

Air India's first foreign boss, Wilson was appointed as the new chief executive officer (CEO) and managing director (MD) of Air India, which was taken over by the Tata Group in January 2022, sixty-nine years after they had relinquished their stake in the airline to the Indian government. Wilson was previously the founding CEO of Scoot, a subsidiary of Singapore Airlines, and later senior vice president, sales and marketing, at Singapore Airlines. He returned to Scoot as CEO in April 2020 before becoming the CEO and MD of Air India in June 2022.

CHANGPENG ZHAO

In the news for: Being the world's richest cryptocurrency holder; Where: Singapore

The founder of Binance, Changpeng Zhao is the richest cryptocurrency holder. Of Chinese origin, Zhao was born in Canada, and resides in Singapore. He has facilitated trades of over US $9.5 trillion, which were two-thirds more than those traded by centralized cryptocurrency exchanges. His company, founded in 2017, has attained the position of being the largest cryptocurrency exchange in the world by daily trading volume and currently deals in more than 600 cryptocurrencies.

DEEPIKA PADUKONE

In the news for: Being the first Indian to be honoured twice by *Time* magazine; Where: India

A popular Indian actor, well known for her performance in the film industry, Padukone is the first Indian to be honoured twice by *Time* magazine. This year, she shared the '2022 *Time* 100 Impact Awards' with world leaders including singers, activists and politicians, among others. In 2018, she was in *Time*'s list of the world's 100 most influential people.

DENNIS SULLIVAN

In the news for: Winning the Abel Prize; Where: USA

The 2022 Abel Prize, given by the Norwegian Academy of Science and Letters, was awarded to American mathematician Dennis Sullivan on 28 March 2022. The prize is an accolade awarded to mathematicians who have made outstanding contributions. The prestigious award, often referred to as the Nobel Prize for mathematicians, is given out annually and is named after the acclaimed 19th-century Norwegian mathematician Niels Henrik Abel. Sullivan was given this award for his contribution in algebra, geometry and topology.

DEVASAHAYAM PILLAI

In the news for: Being canonized; Where: India

St. Devasahayam Pillai is the first Indian layman to be declared a saint by Pope Francis of the Vatican City. Pillai was born in 1712 in the Kanyakumari district of the then Travancore state. In the 18th century, he converted to Christianity and took on the name 'Lazarus'. He is among five Indians who have been canonized.

ELON MUSK

In the news for: *Time's* 2021 'Person of the Year'; Where : USA

On 15 December 2021, *Time* magazine awarded the prestigious 'Person of the Year' title to Elon Musk, the CEO of Tesla, and the founder and CEO of the space exploration company, SpaceX. The magazine recognized Musk's participation as influential in various events of the year, calling him variously a '...genius, edgelord, visionary, industrialist, and showman.'

GAUTAM ADANI

In the news for: Becoming the richest Asian 2022; Where: India

Gautam Adani became the fourth richest person in the world – coming right behind Elon Musk, Bernard Arnault & family, and Jeff Bezos and displacing Microsoft co-founder Bill Gates – with a net worth of US $116.4 billion in *Forbes*'s real-time billionaires list on 21 July 2022.

The founder and chairman of the Adani Group, with businesses spanning a wide variety of fields such as mining, port management and energy, Adani was the only Indian to claim a position on Bloomberg's Top10 Billionaires list in February 2022.

FALGUNI NAYAR

In the news for: Winning the 'Entrepreneur of the Year 2021' award; Where: India

The founder of Nykaa, who started the company at the age of 49, Falguni Nayar was declared India's richest self-made woman billionaire on the Forbes Billionaires List 2022. A former investment banker, she gave up her job to start Nykaa, a beauty and fashion retailer e-commerce website and one of the most well-known business start-ups in the country. She won the 'EY Entrepreneur of the Year 2021' award.

GITA GOPINATH

In the news for: Becoming the first Indian-origin first deputy managing director of the International Monetary Fund; Where: USA

Indian American economist Gita Gopinath was assigned the position of first deputy managing director of the International Monetary Fund (IMF) in January 2022. From 2019 to 2022, Gopinath was the fund's chief economist. She will be the second-ranking official at the world body. She has also received the Pravasi Bharatiya Samman, the highest honour conferred on overseas Indians by the Government of India, and the Distinguished Alumnus Award from the University of Washington, USA.

HARNAAZ SANDHU

In the news for: Winning the title of Miss Universe 2021; Where: India

Harnaaz Sandhu was crowned Miss Universe 2021. The 21-year-old from Punjab represented India in the 70th Miss Universe held in Israel and won the title 21 years after another Indian, Lara Dutta, had won the title in 2000. Sandhu's journey began with winning the Times Fresh Face Contest in 2017. She is currently completing her studies.

KAILASH SATYARTHI

In the news for: Appointment as SDG Advocate; Where: The United Nations (UN)

Kailash Satyarthi, who received the Nobel Peace Prize in 2014. was appointed as the Sustainable Development Goals (SDG) Advocate on 17 September 2021 by UN chief Antonio Guterres. Satyarthi is expected to work on a vision to achieve sustainable development and help influence people to do so, as well as expand outreach to protect the planet.

KANE TANAKA

In the news for: Being the world's oldest person; Where: Japan

On 25 April 2022, the world's oldest person Kane Tanaka from Fukika, Japan, died at 119 years, passing on the title to Lucile Randon (or Sister Andre) of Ales, France. Tanaka was a Japanese supercentenarian, who became the last surviving person born before 1907. Born in 190l, she was declared the world's oldest person by Guinness World Records in 2019.

NEWSMAKERS

KAPIL SIBAL

In the news for: Resigning from the Congress; Where: India

Kapil Sibal, the well-known lawyer, resigned from the Congress Party after three decades of being associated with it, and filed his nomination to become a member of Parliament in the Rajya Sabha as an independent candidate. His decision was supported by the Samajwadi Party. Sibal is a successful lawyer who served as president of India's Supreme Court Bar Association. He was a Union minister under the Congress Party. He was elected unopposed to the Rajya Sabha.

MAYA ANGELOU

In the news for: Being the first black woman to be featured on the US quarter coin; Where: USA

Maya Angelou (4 April 1928–28 May 2014) became the first black woman to be featured on the US 25-cent coin. An iconic poet, writer and memoirist, she is known for her autobiographical style of writing. Her most famous book, *I Know Why the Caged Bird Sings,* brought her international recognition and several awards. Before her death, she was awarded more than 50 honorary degrees.

MUKESH AMBANI

In the news for: Joining the World's $100 Billion Club; Where: India

In October 2021, Reliance Industries chairman and managing director Mukesh Ambani joined the world's most exclusive wealth club with a worth of at least US $100 billion, as per the Bloomberg Index, after a reported US $23.8 billion increase in his wealth. According to the same index, he became Asia's richest man on 3 June 2022, after a record rally in shares.

NAMYA JOSHI

In the news for: Winning the Global Child Prodigy Award; Where: India

Namya Joshi, a student of class 9 of Sat Paul Mittal School in Ludhiana, Punjab. received the Global Child Prodigy Award 2022, from among the top 100 child prodigies of the world, in a ceremony held in Dubai. The prize acknowledged her use of technology for educational purposes. She used the famous video game, Minecraft, to design curriculum and convert conventional learning systems into educational gaming sessions. She had earlier also received the Pradhan Mantri Rashtriya Bal Puraskar in India for the same achievement.

NAND MULCHANDANI

In the news for: Being the first Indian-origin person to become Chief Technology Officer, CIA; Where: USA

The CIA appointed Nand Mulchandani as its chief technology officer in May 2022. A Cornell University graduate in computer science and mathematics, he is the first Indian-origin person to hold this post. He has been a co-founder of successful start-ups like Open DNS (acquired by Cisco), Oblix (acquired by Oracle), Determina (acquired by VMWare) and ScaleXtreme (acquired by Citrix). Earlier, he was the chief technical officer and acting director of the US Department of Defence's Joint Artificial Intelligence Center.

NAVJOT SINGH SIDHU

In the news for: Being jailed in road rage case; Where : India

Navjot Singh Sidhu, former cricketer and politician, was put behind bars for 'intentionally harming' Gurnam Singh, leading to the latter's death in 1988. The Supreme Court reviewed the petition filed by Gurnam Singh's family against the 2018 verdict, which had imposed only a fine of ₹1,000 without any jail term. Finally, in May 2022, the Supreme Court found Navjot Singh Sidhu guilty of voluntarily causing hurt, and sentenced the politician to one year of rigorous imprisonment.

NEERAJ CHOPRA

In the news for: Winning India's first Olympic gold medal in athletics; Where: Tokyo Olympics

Born in Khandra village in Panipat district, Haryana, Neeraj Chopra became the first Indian athlete to win an Olympics gold in athletics on 7 August 2021. His throw of 87.58 m got him first place in the men's javelin throw. He became India's second ever individual Olympic gold medallist after shooter Abhinav Bindra in the 2008 Beijing Olympics. In June 2022, Chopra threw 89.30 m at the Paavo Nurmi Games in Turku, Finland, second behind Finnish thrower Oliver Helander (who threw 89.93 m) while bettering his own national record by over a metre. In July, he won the silver medal in the World Athletics Championships in Eugene, Oregon, US, the first Indian athlete to do so.

DHANUSH

In the news for: Starring in the action thriller film – *The Gray Man;* Where: USA

Dhanush, the multifaceted star of Tamil cinema, who is an actor, director, producer, lyricist and playback singer, played the much anticipated role of a dangerous assassin called Avik San in the movie *The Gray Man*, directed by the Russo Brothers of Marvel fame. The film, featuring Ryan Gosling, Chris Evans and Ana De Armas, was much talked about since its premiere on Netflix on 22 July 2022. Soon after, Joe and Anthony Russo announced a sequel and a spin-off for *The Gray Man*. But will Dhanush, who has starred in over 46 films and won four National Film Awards, be part of those as well? Watch this space...

PARKASH SINGH BADAL

In the news for: Being the oldest election candidate; Where: India

An Indian politician who belongs to the Shiromani Akali Dal (SAD) and served five terms as the chief minister of Punjab, Parkash Singh Badal was also the oldest contestant to run for the Punjab assembly elections at the age of ninety-four. He lost to AAP's Gurmeet Singh Khudian from his long-time Lambi seat in Muktsar district. Before him, in 2016, the former chief minister of Kerala, V.S. Achuthanandan, at the age of ninety-two, contested the assembly elections as the country's oldest candidate.

RISHI SUNAK

In the news for: His bid for position of Conservative Party leader; Where: UK

The son-in-law of Infosys founder N.R. Narayana Murthy and Sudha Murty, British politician and MP for Richmond (Yorks), Rishi Sunak grabbed headlines after British prime minister Boris Johnson resigned and, in July, Sunak announced his candidacy to replace him in the Conservative Party leadership election. Sunak served as chancellor of the exchequer (2020–22) and chief secretary to the treasury (2019–20).

SAM BANKMAN-FRIED

In the news for: Being the youngest billionaire of cryptocurrency; Where: USA

With a real time net worth of US $19.8 billion, Sam Bankman-Fried (also referred to as SBF) from Stanford, California, is the youngest crypto billionaire. In 2019, he launched FTX, his own exchange that was created 'by traders, for traders'. The value of FTX was estimated to be US $18 billion in 2021, pushing SBF to be listed as one of the wealthiest people in the under-30 category.

NEWSMAKERS

SHIVANI MEENA

In the news for: First woman to be appointed as an excavation engineer; Where: India

An IIT Jodhpur alumnus, Shivani Meena, has become a part of the Rajrappa Open Cast Project in Jharkhand, which assesses coal mine overburden dumps, social forestry, agricultural wastelands and distribution of wastelands. Shivani Meena is the first woman excavation engineer in an open-cast mine in Coal India, in charge of repair and maintenance of heavy excavation machinery.

VIJAY SHEKHAR SHARMA

In the news for: Biggest IPP in corporate history; Where: India

In November 2021, founder and CEO of Paytm, Sharma took to the stock market the biggest IPO in corporate history. Paytm's ₹18,300 crore IPO was oversubscribed 1.89 times, which was greater than Coal India's ₹15,000 crore offer 10 years ago. However, it was also the day when Paytm's share crashed by 27 per cent.

VANITA GUPTA

In the news for: Being the first Indian American to hold the position of the associate attorney general of the USA; Where: USA

As the associate attorney general of the USA, Vanita Gupta is the first Indian-origin person to become the third-ranking official at the US Justice Department, and the 19th associate attorney general. She is the first civil rights lawyer to hold any of the posts at the US Justice Department and has previously held the title of president and CEO of the Leadership Conference on Civil and Human Rights, the country's oldest and largest coalition of non-partisan civil rights organizations. Gupta's parents are Indian immigrants and she was born in Philadelphia, Pennsylvania. She received her Bachelor of Arts degree from Yale University and her Juris Doctor from New York University School of Law, USA.

Here's a sneak peek at what will make news in 2023.

- **Eurozone adds a member:** In January, Croatia will adopt the euro as its currency and become the 20th member state of the eurozone. The last time a country joined the monetary union was in 2015, when Lithuania adopted the currency.
- **World University Games, winter edition:** In February, the Winter World University Games will be held in Lake Placid, New York, USA.
- **South Asian Games 2023:** In March, the South Asian Games are planned to be held in Pakistan.
- **Warner Bros centenary:** In April, Warner Bros Entertainment Inc. will celebrate its 100th anniversary.
- **SDG Summit 2023:** The United Nations High-level Political Forum (HLPF) on Sustainable Development Goals will meet at the level of heads of state and government under the UN General Assembly (UNGA) in September 2023.
- **Women's football:** In July, the FIFA Women's World Cup will be held in Australia and New Zealand.
- **Men's cricket:** In November, the much anticipated ICC Cricket World Cup will be held in India.

UN DAYS

3 March World Wildlife Day
8 March International Women's Day
20 March International Day of Happiness
21 March International Day of Forests
22 March World Water Day
7 April World Health Day
22 April Earth Day
3 May World Press Freedom Day
31 May World No Tobacco Day
8 June World Oceans Day
20 June World Refugee Day
21 June International Day of Yoga
11 July World Population Day
12 August International Youth Day
15 September International Day of Democracy
21 September International Day of Peace
2 October International Day of Non-violence
10 October World Mental Health Day
11 October International Day of the Girl Child
20 November Universal Children's Day
1 December World Aids Day
10 December Human Rights Day
11 December International Mountain Day

ANNIVERSARIES

9 January **100th death anniversary of SATYENDRANATH TAGORE**
(1 June 1842 – 9 January 1923)

The elder brother of Rabindranath Tagore, Satyendranath Tagore was the first Indian officer of the Indian Civil Service under British rule in 1864. Born into the illustrious Tagore family of Jorasanko in Calcutta (now Kolkata, West Bengal), to Debendranath Tagore and Sarada Devi, he was also a poet, writer, composer, polyglot and social reformer. After stints in Bombay Presidency and Ahmedabad, among others, he concluded his career as the first Indian sessions judge (Satara district). He wrote many songs, of which 'Mile Sabe Bharat Santan, Ektan Gaho Gaan' (Unite, India's children, sing in unison), was feted as an Indian anthem.

30 January **MAHATMA GANDHI was assassinated 75 years ago**
(2 October 1869–30 January 1948)

Mahatma Gandhi was a prominent Indian freedom fighter. On 30 January 1948, he was fatally shot by Nathuram Godse, a nationalist whose views differed from Gandhi's on several issues. Gandhi was on his way to a multi-faith prayer meeting in Birla House (now Gandhi Smriti) in Delhi, when Godse came out of the crowd and shot him at point-blank range. This was a turning point in Indian history politically. The day is observed as Martyrs' Day in India and as the International School Day of Non-Violence and Peace worldwide.

'Be the change you wish to see.'

5 March **70th death anniversary of JOSEPH STALIN**
(18 December 1878–5 March 1953)

Joseph Stalin was the secretary-general of the Communist Party of the Soviet Union (1922–53) and premier of the Soviet state (1941–53). Under his dictatorial rule, he put a halt to all private trade and created a completely state-run economy, eliminating all rival trade that could compete with the government. Though under him the Soviet Union became an industrial and military superpower, his reign of terror cruelly stamped out millions of his own countrymen including all who dared oppose him.

23 March **100th birth anniversary of HEMU KALANI**
(23 March 1923–21 January 1943)

A freedom fighter in the Indian movement for independence, Hemu Kalani was the leader of the Swaraj Sena in Sindh (now in Pakistan), a student-led organization affiliated with the All India Students Federation. The British sent army detachments after this revolutionary supporter of the Swadeshi movement. Kalani and his associates decided to derail the train the troops were travelling on, but were caught. Kalani was hanged to death when he was only nineteen. His Martyrdom Day is observed by the Sindhi community to honour his memory and inspire young people.

7 April **200th death anniversary of JACQUES ALEXANDER CHARLES**
(12 November 1746–7 April 1823)

Jacques Charles was a French physicist who, along with two brothers – Anne-Jean Robert (1758–1820) and Nicolas-Louis Robert (1760–1820) – launched the world's first unmanned hydrogen balloon in August 1783. In December the same year, Charles and his co-pilot Nicolas-Louis ascended to about 1,800 ft (550 m) in a manned gas balloon. Charles' Law, which states how gases expand when heated, was formulated by Joseph Louis Gay-Lussac in 1802, who credited it to Jacques Charles.

'Nothing will ever equal that moment of joyous excitement which filled my whole being when I felt myself flying away from the earth.'

8 April **50th death anniversary of PABLO PICASSO**
(25 October 1881–8 April 1973)

Picasso, a Spanish painter, sculptor, printmaker and ceramicist, was an influential artist known for his distinct eye and artistic creations. It is believed that he created more than 20,000 paintings, drawings, ceramics and sculptures in his lifetime. He co-founded the cubist art movement (with Georges Braque), which had a ripple effect on music, literature and architecture. Picasso is also recognized for his collage art.

'The purpose of art is washing the dust of daily life off our souls.'

20 April **150th death anniversary of JUSTUS VON LIEBIG**
(12 May 1803–20 April 1873)

Liebig was a German chemist recognized for his major contributions to organic chemistry and agricultural chemistry. He is said to have laid the foundations of modern chemistry and trained a number of students in the field. Liebig popularized German botanist Carl Spengel's 'Law of the Minimum' as a scientific concept, which states that the growth of a crop is dictated by the nutrient least available and not by the total number of nutrients available to it. He is also known as the founder of the theory of mineral nutrition of plants.

2 May **102nd birth anniversary of SATYAJIT RAY**
(2 May 1921–23 April 1992)

'Cinema's characteristic forte is the ability to capture and communicate the intimacies of the human mind.'

Satyajit Ray was a well-known Indian filmmaker born to an affluent family in Kolkata. A recipient of the Padma Bhushan (1965), the Padma Shri (1958), and the National Award for the Best Director six times, he was the first Indian to win an Oscar for cinematography in 1992. He was an inspiration to international directors like Christopher Nolan and Martin Scorsese, who attributed their interest in Indian cinema to Ray's films. His best known works include *Pather Panchali* (1955), *Aparajito* (1956) and *Charulata* (1964).

8 May **150th death anniversary of JOHN STUART MILL**
(20 May 1806–8 May 1873)

John Stuart Mill was an English political economist and philosopher. He was an influential thinker who contributed significantly to social and political theories. A few of his famous works include *System of Logic* (1843), *On Liberty* (1859) and *Utilitarianism (1861)*. His work also extended to the moral sciences and religion. He believed in a moral theory called 'utilitarianism', which said that right actions result in happiness and wrong ones produce suffering. He was also the pioneer of the 'harm principle". It ideated that people should have the liberty to act without restrictions, which should only be applied to prevent actions causing harm to others.

'A man who has nothing for which he is willing to fight, nothing which is more important than his own personal safety, is a miserable creature and has no chance of being free unless made and kept so by the exertions of better men than himself.'

23 June 70th death anniversary of DR SYAMA PRASAD MUKHERJEE (6 July 1901–23 June 1953)

An Indian lawyer, academician and politician, Dr Syama Prasad Mukherjee was born in Calcutta (now Kolkata, West Bengal). At 33, he became the youngest vice-chancellor of Calcutta University. He joined the Hindu Mahasabha and became its president in 1944. In 1946, he wrote to the viceroy Lord Mountbatten, demanding the partition of Bengal. He became free India's first minister of industry and supply in Prime Minister Jawaharlal Nehru's cabinet, but resigned a year later due to differences of opinion with Nehru. On 21 October 1951, he founded the Bharatiya Jana Sangh, a precursor of the Bharatiya Janata Party. In 1953, protesting against Kashmir's special status, he entered it without permission, and was taken into custody. He died in detention.

'The achievement of unity amidst adversity has always been India's aim.'

5 June 300th birth anniversary of ADAM SMITH (5 June 1723–17 July 1790)

Adam Smith was a Scottish economist and philosopher who played a significant role in the Scottish and European Enlightenment. He believed that if people were given the right to produce and exchange goods as they wanted, the economy would prosper greatly as opposed to markets under strict governmental rules. He argued that opening up trade to local and international competitors would encourage the flow of income and wealth in the country. He was known for his work – *An Inquiry into the Nature and Causes of the Wealth of Nations* (or simply, *The Wealth of Nations*) – which describes a system of market-defined wages due to free trade in contrast to government-restricted wages.

19 June 400th birth anniversary of BLAISE PASCAL (19 June 1623–19 August 1662)

Blaise Pascal was a French mathematician who invented the Pascaline, a calculator, in the early 1640s – the first 'digital' calculator (it could add and subtract integers) to be mass produced. In 1653, he established Pascal's Law of Pressure, which stated that when pressure was applied to fluid in a closed container, the fluid flowed equally in all directions in the container. This law laid the foundation for hydraulics and was one of the most significant developments in modern mechanical technology.

22 June **125th birth anniversary of**

ERICH MARIA REMARQUE

(22 June 1898–25 September 1970)

Erich Remarque was a well-known German author who wrote screenplays, stories and novels. At the age of 18, he was sent to the Western front to fight in the First World War. He was wounded on the battlefield and later changed his career to education. In the following years, Remarque worked in a variety of professions including business, editing, freelance writing, accounting, sales and journalism. His most famous work – *All Quiet on the Western Front* – iterates the challenges faced by soldiers in the World War.

'Heaven has no favourites.'

26 June **150th birth anniversary of GAUHAR JAAN**

(26 June 1873–17 January 1930)

Gauhar Jaan was an Indian dancer and singer, who studied various kinds of music and dance under the most respected ustads of her time, including Hindustani pure and light classical vocal music, Dhrupad, Rabindra Sangeet and Kathak. On 11 November 1902, she became one of the earliest Indian voices to be recorded. Her announcing her name at the end of the record by saying, 'My name is Gauhar Jaan'. became her signature. She is known to have sung around 600 songs in more than 10 languages, befitting her sobriquet: 'Gramophone Girl'.

27 June **125th death anniversary of DWARKANATH GANGULY**

(20 April 1844 –27 June 1898)

Dwarkanath Ganguly was a schoolteacher in 19th-century Kolkata in British-ruled India. As a young student, he was inspired by the writings of Akshay Kumar Dutta, a leader of the Bengal Renaissance, on the plight of Indian women. Ganguly took up the editorship of *Abalabandhab* ('Friend of Women'), the world's first magazine for women's liberation. Through it, he spread awareness about the problems of Indian women. Ganguly was also a part of the Brahmo Samaj, and husband to one of India's first practising female doctors, Kadambini Ganguly.

15 August **151st birth anniversary of SRI AUROBINDO GHOSE (15 August 1872–5 December 1950)**

Born in Calcutta (now Kolkata), Sri Aurobindo was an Indian nationalist, poet and philosopher. He is recognized as the first leader to actively declare complete independence as the goal of the freedom struggle through *Bande Mataram,* a newspaper he edited. Later, he withdrew from politics, moved to Pondicherry (now Puducherry) and built an ashram there. He believed that there is a chance for every individual to attain a higher level of consciousness that would lead to the transformation of the body, mind and life. A few of his many writings include *The Life Divine, The Synthesis of Yoga* and *Savitri.*

'When the mind is still, then truth gets her chance to be heard in the purity of silence.'

29 August **100th birth anniversary of SIR RICHARD ATTENBOROUGH (29 August 1923–24 August 2014)**

Sir Richard was an iconic British director, entrepreneur and actor. He held the presidency of the Royal Academy of Dramatic Art, the British Academy of Film and Television Arts and Chelsea Football Club (for life). He won eight Oscars from 12 Academy Award nominations for his film *Gandhi* (1982) in 1983. As a producer, he worked on projects such as *The League of Gentlemen* (1960), *The Angry Silence* (1960) and *Whistle Down the Wind* (1961). He was a UNICEF Goodwill Ambassador for 17 years.

'I believe we need heroes... we need certain people who we can measure our own shortcomings by.'

31 August **50th death anniversary of JOHN FORD (1 February 1894–31 August 1973)**

John Ford was an American naval officer and film-maker. He is recognized as one of the greatest film-makers of all time, who won six Academy Awards and four New York Film Critics' awards. Ford was known for his films of the Western genre. He made 136 movies in his career spanning 50 years, out of which 54 were westerns. Interestingly, all of his films that won him the Academy Awards – *The Informer* (1935), *The Grapes of Wrath* (1940), *How Green Was My Valley* (1941) and *The Quiet Man* (1952) – were not Westerns.

THE YEAR AHEAD

3 October 100th death anniversary of KADAMBINI BOSE GANGULY
(18 July 1861–3 October 1923)

One of the first Indian female graduates in British-ruled India, Kadambini Bose Ganguly was also one of the first Indian practitioners of Western medicine in the country, and one who was educated in India. She went to the UK in 1892 to obtain more qualifications in her field and came back to work as a gynaecologist at the Lady Dufferin Hospital, and later started her own private practice. She became one of six representatives in the first female delegation of the 1889 Indian National Congress, and in 1906, she helped organize the Women's Conference in Calcutta after the partition of Bengal.

21 November 125th birth anniversary of RENE MAGRITTE
(21 November 1898–15 August 1967)

Rene Magritte was a Belgian painter who was famous for his thought-provoking and witty art. He responded to the surrealist art movement, crafting paintings with unexpected images; for instance: In his work, *The Memoirs of a Saint*, he painted the sky with a curtain. His famous works include *The Treachery of Images* (1929) and *The Son of Man* (1946).

'Everything we see hides another thing, we always want to see what is hidden by what we see.'

24 December 50th death anniversary of E.V. RAMASAMY PERIYAR
(17 September 1879–24 December 1973)

Popularly known as Periyar, E.V. Ramasamy was a reformer and a social activist who opposed the caste system and initiated reforms to help remove caste rigidities. He worked for the Indian National Congress for a few years and later headed the Justice Party. He supported the use of khadi and Swadeshi goods, and protested against untouchability and discrimination against certain castes. He is well known for launching the Self-Respect or Dravidian Movement, which called for erasing distinctions between non-Brahmins and Brahmins.

'Everyone has the right to refute any opinion. But no one has the right to prevent its expression.'

2 UPDATES

2022: 1,020 women for 1,000 men

2015–16: 991 women for 1,000 men

Women in India outnumber men, says a new report

According to the findings of the fifth edition of the National Family Health Survey (NFHS-5), there has been a significant demographic shift with **1,020** women reported for every **1,000** men. Since the survey's inception in 1992, this is the first time such a statistic has been recorded. The last survey (2015-16) stated that there were **991** women for every **1,000** men.

The decadal census is the only census accepted as the official information on population trends in India and is watched more closely through a surveillance programme. NFHS surveys are smaller and conducted at district levels. They are considered pointers to the future.

In 23 states and Union Territories the sex ratio was greater than 1,000, i.e., women made up more of the total population than men. **In six states and Union Territories, it was found that the sex ratio was less than 950.** Delhi and Punjab came under this category.

2015–16: 919 females per 1,000 males

2019–20: 929 women for 1,000 men

A closer look at sex ratio at birth with regard to children born in the last five years showed that boys, on average, continue to have better chances and opportunities for survival than girls. The improvement shown was minimal, with only **919** females per **1,000** males in 2015–16 to **929** per **1,000** in 2019–20.

A state-wise analysis of the NFHS data also indicates that India is on track to stabilizing its population. According to this data, most states and UTs have a Total Fertility Rate (TFR) of less than two. A TFR of less than **2.1** occurs when a woman, on average, bears two children over a lifetime.

FUN FACT

As per the NFHS-5 results, the state/UT with the **highest child sex ratio** is **Ladakh** (1,125 females per 1,000 males) and the **lowest child sex ratios** are recorded in **Chandigarh** and **Goa** (both with 838 females per 1,000 males).

INDIAN AI'S BRIGHT FUTURE

In a report published by International Data Corporation (IDC), India's Artificial Intelligence (AI) market is projected to hit US **$7.8 billion by 2025**, growing at a Compound Annual Growth Rate (CAGR) of **20.2 per cent**. It reported that the applications under the software (AI) category brought in the highest share of revenue, displaying a **52 per cent** growth over the course of 2020. Organizations are now using **multiple AI applications** such as **ERM** (enterprise risk management) and **CRM** (customer relationship management), among others, to perform their work, expand supply chains in response to projected or current demands, and save costs and enhance their ROI (return on investment).

It is estimated that the market will be led by the AI software segment and is estimated to grow from US $2.8 billion in 2020 at a CAGR of 18.1 per cent by the end of 2025. One of the earliest uses of **AI in India was in the healthcare field**. In 1986, H.N. Mahabala and a team at IIT Madras were involved in a project as part of India's Knowledge Based Computing Systems initiative. The knowledge-based programme named **Eklavya** was designed to support community health workers in dealing with symptoms of illnesses in toddlers.

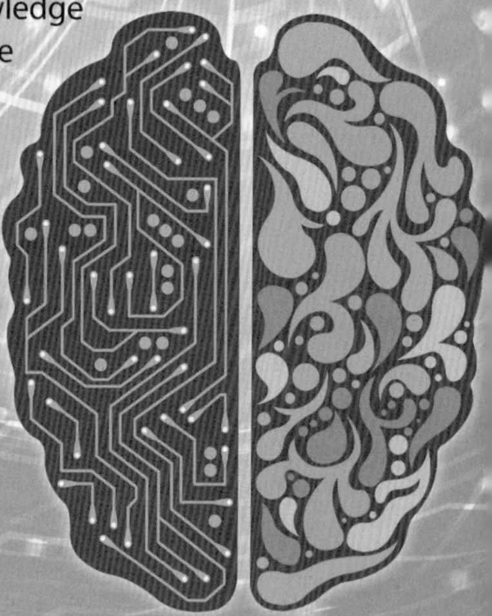

India cracks down on VPNs and cloud services

On 28 April 2022, the Indian Computer Emergency Response team (Cert-In), India's nodal cybersecurity agency, directed that all VPN (virtual private network) companies operating in India must maintain a record of their customers' personal details. A VPN expands a private network across a public network, and facilitates users to send and receive data across shared or public networks in a manner as if they are directly connected to the private network. Under this new law, all VPN companies operating in India are required to log and store the following data for at least five years:

- The email address, username and phone number;
- The subscriber's purpose of use;
- The IP addresses allotted by the VPN service and the IP address used by the subscriber to sign up; and
- The patterns of usage, timestamps, and subscription.

The mandate was issued just a few days after **Surfshark, ExpressVPN** and **NordVPN** announced they would stop offering their services to India. It urged government employees to **not save sensitive data**, including internal, restricted or confidential data files onto any non-government cloud services such as **Google Drive** or **Dropbox**. The NIC also asked them to not 'root' or 'jailbreak' their mobile phones, which are ways of bypassing limitations, and doing things manufacturers and carriers don't allow. The mandate also prohibits the use of external mobile-based scanner services to scan internal government documents. The most widely used mobile-app scanner service has been **CamScanner**, which came under fire along with other **Chinese apps banned** by the Indian government in June 2020.

At a meeting of the **UN Ad Hoc Committee**, India made its stance on this issue clear. The UN committee debated a comprehensive global convention to counter the use of communication technologies and information for criminal purposes.

India has the highest number of digital transactions in the world

With **48 billion** transactions, India accounted for the highest number of global real-time transactions in 2021. To put this in a global perspective, according to ACI Worldwide, this is close to three times those of China **(18 billion)**, the closest competitor, and six-and-a-half-times more than the USA, France, Canada, UK and Germany combined.

In 2020, India was the place for **41 million** transactions a day and witnessed a reported growth rate of **213 percent**, according to a report published by FIS, Inc., USA, a multinational corporation offering financial products and services.

The reasons for the increase include the growing popularity of payment apps that utilize UPI-based systems and QR code payments among merchants, along with an escalation in the use of digital payments during the COVID-19 pandemic. All these factors added up to real-time payments making up **31.3 per cent** of the total payments' transaction volume in 2021. 'Prime-Time for Real Time', a worldwide report that analyses the volume of real-time payments and growth in over 48 markets, estimated that by 2024 the percentage of volume of real-time payments in overall electronic transactions will cross **50 per cent**.

FUN FACT

UPI (Unified Payments Interface) was launched in India by former Reserve Bank governor Raghuram Rajan in April 2016, but became popular following demonetization in November 2016 and the Central Government's emphasis on cashless transactions. Currently, more than 200 banks are actively providing UPI Services, as of December 2020.

UPDATES

The keys to the kingdom – Mukesh Amabani's successors

In June 2022, Mukesh Ambani put in motion his succession plan. **Akash Ambani**, his 30-year-old firstborn, will succeed him as chairman at **Reliance Jio Infocomm Ltd**, India's leading wireless carrier. Mukesh Ambani will, however, continue to head Jio Platform Ltd, the umbrella that owns all digital assets, including the one he plans to leave to his son.

Meanwhile, **Isha Ambani**, Akash's twin, is expected to head India's largest network of stores, **Reliance Retail**. The youngest of the three siblings, **Anant**, is expected to take the reins of the legacy **oil-to-chemicals** business.

Upon taking over the business, Anant will certainly have his work cut out for him, with the aim to move way from polluting hydrocarbons to cleaner, more sustainable energy sources like sodium-ion batteries, solar panels and green hydrogen for less than US$1 per 1 kilogram. He has been given a decade to reach these goals. Mukesh Ambani calls this the **1-1-1 target**.

Indian production house buys land in the metaverse

The Indian production house **Pooja Entertainment** announced in 2022 that it had acquired **virtual land** in the metaverse, a space in which users interact with a virtual (computer generated) environment as well as other users.

Virtual real estate seems to be gaining traction, with American celebrities such as Justin Bieber, Ariana Grande and DJ Marshemello owning space and performing in the metaverse while using their digital avatars.

The 'land', named '**Poojaverse**', aims at providing a space for creators to produce immersive experiences that are the first of their kind. The initial step in this direction came in the form of the announcement of a movie, '**Bade Miyan Chote Miyan**', a project starring household Bollywood names such as Akshay Kumar and Tiger Shroff. The film is set to be released around Christmas in 2023 in many languages including Hindi, Malayalam, Tamil, Kannada and Telugu.

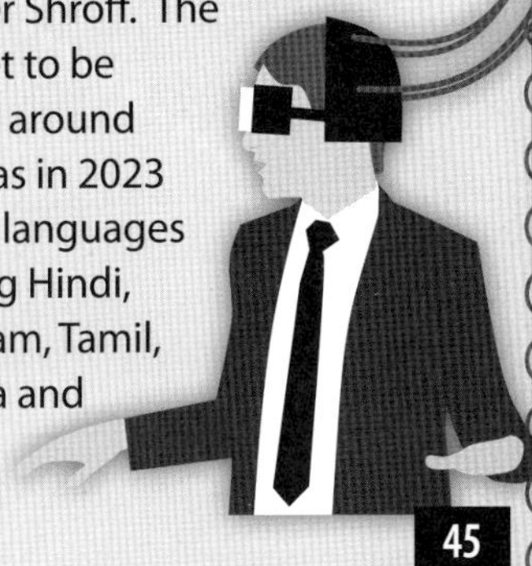

THE ARCHIES

In a partnership between **Netflix** and **Archie Comics**, a film based on the beloved characters and their antics is all set to hit screens soon. Zoya Akhtar, known for films such as *Zindagi Na Milegi Dobara, Dil Dhadakne Do* and *Gully Boy*, is all set to direct a new take on the iconic Archie comics. The film's promotions faced a mixed reception, with accusations of nepotism due to the cast members' star-studded family trees.

The cast : The Archies ensemble cast is composed of **seven actors**, three of whom hail from the dazzling world of Bollywood. Veronica Lodge is played by **Suhana Khan** (Shah Rukh Khan's daughter), Archibald 'Archie' Andrews by **Agastya Nanda** (Amitabh Bachchan's grandson) and **Khushi Kapoor** (Sridevi's younger daughter) plays Elizabeth 'Betty' Cooper. The three other cast members are Dot (singer and songwriter) as Midge, Yuvraj Menda as Dilton Donald Doiley, Vedang Raina as Reginald 'Reggie' Mantle and Mihir Ahuja as Jughead Jones.

The film is shot in **Ootacamand** and will be released on Netflix in 2023.

Ms MARVEL

On 8 June 8 2022, *Ms Marvel* premiered on **Disney+**. Looking at a vast range of subjects from the effects of intergenerational post-Partition trauma among Pakistanis and Indians as well as the duality of the Muslim American, Ms Marvel follows **Kamala Khan**, a teenager. Since childhood, she has hero-worshipped the Avengers only to discover that she too has powers. The character, played by newcomer **Iman Vellani**, is the first Muslim superhero in the Marvel Cinematic Universe (MCU).

The comics, written and created by **Sana Amanat** and **Willow Wilson**, shot to the top of the charts upon their release in 2014.

A.R. Rahman's directorial debut

Rahman's first foray into the directorial space comes in the form of **Le Musk**, a tale of a girl on the hunt for the men who orphaned her 20 years ago, with only the memory of their scent. The idea of doing a virtual-reality film using perfumes was initially suggested to him by his wife, Saira Banu, and he developed it.

The film is a **virtual-reality film** and premiered at **Cannes XR**, Marche du Film's programme dedicated to virtual and augmented reality. The film itself utilizes **aroma** and **motion** in order to engage the viewer.

While on the red carpet at Cannes, Rahman also hinted at more projects to come.

India's first original cinematic universe

On 15 June 2022, the first trailer of **Ayan Mukerji**'s new film *Brahmastra Part One: Shiva* aired to a wide viewership with over 72 million views on YouTube. The film, which has been seven years in the making, is said to be India's biggest cinematic experience yet. With reports of its monumental budget (over ₹300 crore), its star cast (**Amitabh Bachchan, Ranbir Kapoor** and **Alia Bhatt**, to name a few) and top production houses (Dharma Productions and Fox Star Studios), the film has gained fame as India's first original cinematic universe. Slated to be the first in a trilogy, the film was initially announced in 2014.

The film is scheduled to premiere on 9 September 2022. Courtesy of Disney, the film will get a global release. The studio has added **Brahmastra Part One: Shiva** to its domestic (North American) repertoire. This means the film will rub shoulders with other Disney blockbusters such as **Thor: Love and Thunder**, **Black Panther: Wakanda Forever** and **Avatar: The Way of Water**.

India's themed-tourism trains

On 14 June 2022 at 6 p.m. India's first private train under the **Bharat Gaurav Scheme** took off on its maiden journey from **Coimbatore North Station** in **Tamil Nadu** to **Sainagar Shirdi** in **Maharashtra**. The train reached Shirdi on 16 June 2022 at 7:25 a.m.

The operator of this private train is a firm named **South Star Rail**. The maintenance of the train will be undertaken by housekeeping service providers, who will clean the train's utility areas at frequent intervals. Not only this, the train will provide a traditional vegetarian menu prepared by expert caterers.

The route

According to an official release, this train will stop at **Tiruppur, Erode, Salem, Yelahanka, Dharmavaram, Mantralayam** and **Wadi**.

THE FACILITIES

The fare to travel on board the service gives customers two options. Passengers can opt either for a **train ticket fare** or a **package**. Customers who choose the package fare can reap the benefits of offers such as:

1. Transportation to Shirdi from Coimbatore and back;
2. A VIP *darshan;*
3. Bus arrangements;
4. Air-conditioned accommodation;
5. Facilitation by a tour guide; and
6. Travel insurance.

The Bharat Gaurav Scheme

The Bharat Gaurav Scheme was launched in November 2021. The scheme has created a third segment of the Indian Railways dedicated to tourism. Before this the Railways had two segments: passengers and goods.

The scheme aims to provide theme-based tourist circuit trains. The application process is open to a wide number of people such as trusts, societies and even state governments, all of whom can apply to run the trains on themed tourism routes. The scheme seeks to promote India's cultural heritage and history among people in India and around the world.

Shri Ramayana Yatra

Starting on 21 June 2022, the Shri Ramayana Yatra, a **Bharat Gaurav Tourist** train, became the first Indian tourist train to cross an international border, when it entered Nepal.

The train follows the Ramayana Circuit identified by the Ministry of Tourism under their Swadesh Darshan Scheme. It covers the prominent places associated with the life of Lord Ram in 19 nights/20 days.

The Bharat Gaurav Train's first stop will be **Ayodhya**, where tourists will visit the Hanuman Mandir, the Ram Janmabhoomi Temple and the Bharat Mandir at Nandigram.

After this, the train will go to **Buxar** in Bihar, to visit Ramrekha Ghat on the River Ganga and the hermitage of Vishwamitra.

In Nepal, the train will reach **Janakpur**, where tourists will stay in hotels overnight. Tourists will then visit the Ram-Janaki Temple in the town.

Following Janakpur, the train will return to India and move to **Sitamarhi** in Bihar, believed to be Sita's birthplace. The next stop will be **Varanasi**, where tourists will visit ancient temples and travel to Shringverpur, where it is believed that Ram, Sita and Lakshman crossed the River Ganga and travelled across Chitrakoot on foot.

The train will then go west, to **Nashik** in Maharashtra, where tourists will visit Trayambakeshwar Temple and Panchavati. It will then go south, to the birthplace of Lord Hanuman – Kishkindha in **Hampi**, Karnataka.

After Hampi, the next destination is **Rameswaram** in Tamil Nadu, so tourists can visit the Ramanathaswamy Temple and Dhanushkodi. Then, the train will head for a day's excursion to Kanchipuram to the Shiva Kanchi, Kamakshi and Vishnu Kanchi temples.

For its last destination, the train will head to **Telangana**, to what is called the 'Ayodhya of the South', Bhadrachalam. The train will end its **8,000 km** journey in Delhi.

INDIA AT THE 75TH CANNES FILM FESTIVAL AS THE COUNTRY OF HONOUR

For the first time in the festival's history, Cannes announced a **Country of Honour** at the Marche du Film – India. As Cannes celebrates its 75th anniversary, India celebrates 75 years of Independence. Marche du Film (Market of Film) is one of the largest international business centres.

Headed by **Anurag Singh Thakur**, Minister for Information and Broadcasting, the Indian delegation also walked the red carpet.

Deepika Padukone, who was on the official jury, joined the India Pavilion to unveil a poster from the International Film Festival of Goa.

Befittingly, **Shaunak Sen** won the L'Oeil d'Or (Golden Eye) at the 75th Cannes Film Festival. His documentary film **'All That Breathes'**, which was an audience-favourite, won the prestigious **2022 Golden Eye for Best Documentary** at the festival. It follows the lives of Nadeem and Saud, two brothers from Delhi. Nadeem and Saud persist and persevere in their efforts to rescue migratory black kites. The film is set against the backdrop of worsening air quality and social issues. The film had won the **World Cinema Grand Jury Prize** at the **Sundance Film Festival** earlier in 2022.

Cannes Classics

Thamp (1978), a Malayalam film directed by G. Aravindan, was screened at the Cannes Classics section of the festival, alongside a tribute to the late filmmaker Satyajit Ray's film *Pratidwandi* (1970).

FUN FACT

2022 is the **second year** in a row when India has won the Golden Eye for Best Documentary. In **2021, Payal Kapadia** won it for her film, ***A Night of Knowing Nothing***.

UPDATES

Geetanjali Shree wins the International Booker Prize

On 27 May 2022, **Geetanjali Shree** made history as the first Indian to win the International Booker Prize for a novel originally written in Hindi. ***Tomb of Sand*** or ***Ret Samadhi*** (its title in the original Hindi) is also the first novel translated from any **Indian language to win the award**.

The £50,000 (US $63,000) prize money is to be divided between the author and the translator **Daisy Rockwell**, who lives in Vermont, USA.

The book, called an 'irresistible novel' and a 'joyous cacophony' by the Booker judges, follows an 80-year-old woman's journey to Pakistan in a bid to face the unresolved trauma of her experiences of Partition as a teenager. Geetanjali Shree has written three novels and several story collections, which have been translated into English, French, German, Serbian and Korean.

FUN FACT The first graphic novel on the Booker longlist was **Nick Dsarno's *Sabrina*** in 2018.

About the International Booker Prize

The International Booker Prize is awarded annually for a single book, translated into English and published in the UK or Ireland. The International Booker Prize originated in 2005 and was initially called the Man Booker International Prize. At the time of its inception, it was a biennial prize for a body of work. Additionally, there was no rule that the work should be in a language other than English.

In 2015, the rules of the original Booker Prize expanded, allowing writers of all nationalities to enter – as long as their books were published in the UK and written in English. Post this change, the International Prize adjusted its rules to mirror the English-language prize. It has since been awarded annually for a single book, written in another language and translated into English.

Odisha's Shreya Lanka joins K-pop band, Blackswan

After global auditions that spanned six months, record label **DR Music** announced that 18-year-old **Shreya Lanka** would be the **fifth member of Blackswan**, a South Korean pop band. Lanka, who goes by the stage name '**Sriya**', will join the group along with **Gabriela Dalcin** (Gabi), a Brazilian teen, as a new member. The band, which consists of members Youngheun, Fatou, Judy and Leia, will now have these two add-on members. Both the new members were selected as part of DR Music's **Cygnus talent search programme**. The programme was so named as it claimed to find more stars to add to the constellation 'Cygnus' -- which derives its name from the Latinized Greek word for swan.

As part of a rigorous training programme that started in December, both girls had to rehearse and hone their vocal, Korean language and dance skills. Shreya was one of 23 finalists shortlisted from among more than 4,000 girls who had auditioned for the position in the Korean band.

After being introduced to the world of K-pop by a friend, Lenka, who grew up in Rourkela, Odisha, took to the unique and catchy choreographies. Looking up to bands like EXO, Stray Kidz and BTS, she grew to appreciate their style, and Korean culture and language.

International Year of Millets: 2023

A proposal to declare 2023 as the 'International Year of Millets' put forward by the Indian government has been approved by the United Nations General Assembly (UNGA). The proposal was supported by 72 countries and was approved on 5 March 2021. India produces more than 170 tonnes of millets, and it contributes to 80 per cent of Asia's production and 20 per cent of global production.

In preparation, the Indian government has taken steps:

1. The formation of a core committee;
2. The International Trade Fair (New Delhi, Nov 2021) displayed and promoted the consumption of millets; and
3. A book of recipes utilizing millets has been sent to all cabinet ministers, chief ministers, governors, lieutenant governors and ministers of state.

To bring millets into the public eye, further initiatives will be launched:

1. The organization of a Monthly Millet Challenge;
2. Hotel buffets to focus on millet-based dishes in 2023;
3. Online platforms and delivery agents to popularize millets; and
4. Encouragement of the promotion of millets in print, social and electronic media.

CGI: In the news

Computer Generated Information (CGI) is the use of computer software to create still or animated visual content. It is also called **3D imaging** or **3D Rendering**. It is used to create scenes and characters in movies, shows and games. Applied across a wide range of fields such as architecture, advertising, virtual reality, art and engineering, CGI is used to create digital elements on either pre-existing subjects or blank canvases.

The first use of CGI in films was probably in **Vertigo** (1958), Alfred Hitchcock's thriller film. **John Whitney** and American graphic designer **Saul Bass** collaborated to produce the never-seen-before opening credits of the film. The special effects were achieved by a simple spiral animation, depicting the feeling of vertigo, achieved by using a gun director (an anti-aircraft targeting computer) that would rotate, a pendulum and a pen attached to it.

In 1972, a short film, **A Computer Animated Hand**, depicted computer-generated faces and hands. The world had never seen this style of animation before, one that involved the drawing of **350 polygons** and **triangles**, followed by digitization through an animation program.

In the 1990s, several films used CGI, most notably **Fight Club**, **Toy Story** and **Jurassic Park**. The path-breaking blockbuster *Jurassic Park* featured extensive 'physical' CGI, used to add texture to the dinosaurs in a way that made them look incredibly lifelike. With the release of **Toy Story** in 1995, the world saw the first entirely CGI movie.

FUN FACT

In recent years, most science-fiction blockbusters have used CGI extensively, so much so that 90 per cent of what one may see on screen is CGI, including sets, characters and technology.

Cryptocurrency: What's the fuss about?

Cryptocurrency can be explained simply by breaking the word into two – Crypto refers to encryption, meaning that all information is converted into a secret code, so that outsiders cannot access it unless they crack the code or have the key. Currency refers to money, or what the market calls an '**asset**'. Therefore, we can say that cryptocurrency is a **digital asset**. **Bitcoin** was the first cryptocurrency, formed in 2009.

Cryptocurrency is finite. This means that like gold and silver, cryptocurrency is limited. It is created through mining, which is when very powerful computers solve powerful problems. When people buy and sell using cryptocurrency, these records are stored in high security logs known as "**blockchains**".

A blockchain **consists of information** that has been collected in groups. Each group is called a block. Each block has a certain storage capacity. Once that capacity has been reached, the block closes so that no more information can be stored. Each closed block is linked to the previous closed block, thus forming a chain of data called a blockchain. Once a block has reached capacity, the information stored within it is immutable, which means it cannot be changed.

Why is cryptocurrency bad for the environment?

The amount of energy needed to solve the mathematical problems associated with the mining of cryptocurrencies is immense, more than what is used by some countries.

A cryptocurrency analytics site **Digiconimist** stated that per transaction, Bitcoin uses the same amount of power that is used over **74.01 days** in the average American household.

Annually, about **37 kilotonnes** of electronic waste are produced in the process of Bitcoin mining.

Wordle mania

A word game that took the world by storm was created by Brooklyn-based American programmer **Josh Wardle** as a gift for his partner, Palak Shah. The duo had spent a large amount of time playing online word games created by *The Times* newspaper, before taking a shot at creating one of their own.

How to play: Upon opening the app or the website, a five-box wide by six-box long grid is displayed. Each box can hold a single letter. One must type in their guess for the five-letter word and then press 'Enter'.

As there is no starting clue, any five-letter word will function as a first guess. After hitting Enter, the game reveals clues as to how to find the correct word. It does this by responding in the following ways –

a. A green box indicates that you have filled the letter correctly and in the right position;
b. A yellow box indicates that you have filled in the correct letter, but it is in the wrong place;
c. A grey box indicates the letter isn't in the word at all.

Why did it become so popular?

Post its initial launch in October 2021 as a game anyone could play for free, the game did not rise to fame immediately. It only exploded once the addition of the '**Share**' feature in mid-December made it easy to post and flaunt one's success online.

'An enterprise created for refugees, by refugees...'

Chatterbox is an online language learning platform that trains and employs refugees as tutors. The app combines AI to host self-study classes as well as native language coaches from the refugee community. It was founded by **Mursal Hedayat**, an Afghan refugee living in the UK and an engineer by profession, who decided to create something that would utilize skills among refugees and other marginalized professionals. The platform aims at filling the gap between refugees with qualifications and the professional market. It does so by creating pathways into potential careers for displaced professionals.

NASA's microwave-sized spaceship

On 30 June 2022, American space agency NASA launched the Cislunar Autonomous Positioning System Technology Operations and Navigation Experiment (CAPSTONE). CAPSTONE is a **CubeSat** the size of a microwave oven and weighs only **25 kg**. The satellite was launched on Rocket Lab's Electron rocket from the Rocket Lab Launch Complex 1 on the Mahia Peninsula in New Zealand.

CAPSTONE lift-off (Photo: Rocket Lab/NASA)

The satellite is testing a new **elliptical lunar orbit**, heading towards the orbit that Gateway, a future **moon-orbiting outpost**, will be utilizing. **Gateway** is part of NASA's Artemis programme. CAPSTONE will function as a pathfinder, to help reduce risk for future spacecraft by verifying the dynamics of the halo-shaped orbit as well as testing new navigation technologies. The spacecraft is currently in **low-Earth orbit**, and will take about four months to reach the targeted lunar orbit.

Follow CAPSTONE's progress

NASA has invited the general public to watch and follow CAPSTONE's journey in real-time, using **Eyes on the Solar System, which is an interactive** 3D data visualization. It will also post updates about when CAPSTONE will be available to view on NASA's Ames Research Centre's home page, and social media channels such as Twitter and Facebook.

FUN FACT

According to NASA, CubeSats are a class of research spacecraft called 'nanosatellites'.

The Artemis Accords

'The Artemis Accords' are a global agreement between governments joining the Artemis Program, a US-led initiative to take humans to the Moon by 2025, following a set of principles to guide space exploration cooperation among nations. In July 2022, Saudi Arabia became the 21st country to sign the Artemis Accords.

METAVERSE

THE NEW REALITY?

Technology has come a long way from stone tools to building a global network that allows people to share data and information with just a click. Technological innovations today also hold the ability to transport individuals into a digitally crafted universe, famously known as the 'metaverse' – a network of 3D virtual worlds focused on connecting socially.

The metaverse is a concept of an online **3D digital world** with virtual land and objects. Online and video games such as Axie Infinity and The Sandbox, and 3D virtual world browser-based platforms such as Decentraland already include aspects of the metaverse in their online worlds. Daily transactions like socialization, activities for leisure, such as sports and movies, and business transactions will all be held in this artificially crafted world. While ethical issues such as privacy and piracy are going to impact its users, there is no denying that the metaverse is the way forward.

What Is the Metaverse?

Defined as a virtual-reality space in which users can interact with a computer-generated environment and other users, the metaverse is an artificial digital space fabricated for users to experience reality in a virtual place. It is a **digital space**, a 3D interactive digitally crafted universe where one can connect with people, and interact and socialize with them in a digital environment.

Navigation in the meta world is dependent on **avatars**. An avatar is a **graphical representation** of the participating individual's persona or character in the digital world and you have the freedom to customize your avatar. It can have characteristics similar to your own, or be something completely different, like an animal or even an object. Currently, the concept of avatar is used in apps such as Snapchat; Apple also launched Animojis, where you can choose how you want to be represented in this world.

More about the Metaverse

The concept of the metaverse was initially introduced to us by fictional texts. The 2018 adaption of Ernest Cline's novel, *Ready Player One*, directed by Stephen Spielberg, is the most common reference to the meta world. The book and the movie design a virtual reality where people go to escape the real world. Our metaverse is similar. Interactive technologies such as virtual headgear form a simple framework to create a simulation, integrating various faculties of vision, hearing and sensing, thereby fabricating a lifelike experience of a virtual 3D world. The simulated world allows humans to carry out a variety of activities such as business transactions, events, shopping and socializing, among others.

With the introduction of blockchain technology, business transactions through NFTs (non-fungible tokens) will form the backbone of the metaverse. Blockchains are shared and immutable collections of data records of transactions between parties. The business assets recorded can be tangible such as a house, car, cash and so on, or non-tangible such as patents, branding and copyrights. The blockchains protect the data and distribute it, but they cannot alter or edit the data. These blockchains will form an important source of income in the meta world.

NFT stands for non-fungible token, and NFTs are tokens that we can use to represent ownership of unique items. They let us tokenize things like art, collectibles and even real estate. They can only have one official owner at a time and they are secured by the blockchain – no one can modify the record of ownership or copy-paste a new NFT into existence. 'Non-fungible' is an economics term that describes things like your furniture, a song file or your computer. These things are not interchangeable for other items because they have unique properties. In contrast, money is a fungible item, where a ₹100 note can be converted into four ₹20 notes or two ₹50 notes and so on.

Other technologies that can improve the experience of the meta world

KEY TECHNOLOGIES FOR THE METAVERSE

Blockchain and cryptocurrency: Blockchain technology provides decentralized systems for digital proof of ownership, digital collectability, transfer of value, governance and accessibility. Cryptocurrencies enable users to transfer value, like buying land in a virtual world, while they work and socialize in the 3D digital world.

Artificial intelligence (AI): AI can be applied to the non-player characters (NPCs) in different scenarios, such as placing them across 3D spaces to facilitate lifelike conversations with users or perform other specific tasks. Another application is to create metaverse avatars, by analysing 2D images or 3D scans to generate realistic and accurate avatars.

Augmented reality (AR) and virtual reality (VR): Augmented reality (AR) and virtual reality (VR) can give us an immersive and engaging 3D experience. AR uses digital visual elements and characters to morph the real world. It's more accessible than VR and can be used

comprise hardware such as haptic gloves (a wearable that imitates the feeling of handling real objects in the virtual world), motion detectors and VR treadmills, among many others.

However, the artificial world presents a conflict with our form of reality. When data is easily accessible via the Internet, what is the need to construct an augmented reality, which will support the same functions that can be well conducted in a way similar to the non-digital world?

Creators argue that the way we retrieve information fails to account for the experience and visual perception that can be provided in the digital world. The metaverse provides us with the ability to create out-of-the-world experiences that help us in understanding reality.

Currently, to extract data about, say, the Moon, we simply research the information and are able to retrieve the required data easily. However, imagine if you were able to step on a digitally crafted Moon and have a first-hand experience of how things work on the Moon. Imagine being able to feel the texture of the surface of the Moon and taking a step on it. It is the presence of this real-life experience that makes the metaverse an exciting and important element of technology.

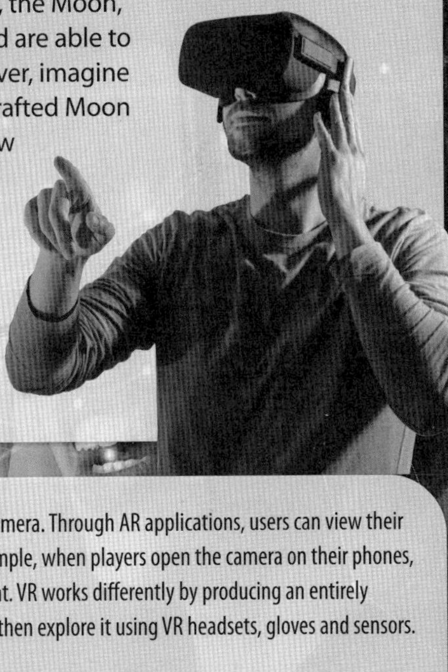

on almost any smartphone or digital device with a camera. Through AR applications, users can view their surroundings with interactive digital visuals. For example, when players open the camera on their phones, they can see Pokémons in the real-world environment. VR works differently by producing an entirely computer-generated virtual environment. Users can then explore it using VR headsets, gloves and sensors.

3D reconstruction: One of the challenges for the metaverse is to create a digital environment that appears as close to our real world as possible. With the help of 3D reconstruction, it can create realistic and natural-looking spaces. These virtual replicas of physical world objects can also be referred to as digital twins.

Internet of things (IoT): IoT is a system that can connect everything in our physical world to the Internet through sensors and devices. Implementing IoT can seamlessly connect the 3D world to a large number of real-life devices. This enables the creation of real-time simulations in the metaverse.

UPDATES

While the concept of a creatively crafted world sounds exciting, it comes with ethical concerns about the rules and regulations of the community. The society we live in today is guided by a fixed set of rules and guidelines. Will the same laws be applicable in this artificial world of ours? Or will there be a different set? If so, who is mandated with creating these laws? And what should be the basis for the formulations of these laws? Another major threat to the metaverse includes the concern for privacy. The issue of tracking data through web browsers is a valid concern in the present world. This would be multifold in the metaverse. The technology we use to position ourselves in the metaverse will allow the respective companies to access our experiences and alter our digital world according to our needs.

The metaverse will further emphasize the inequalities in society as only people from the richer sections will be able to access the technology with greater efficiency. However, the metaverse is still a work-in-progress. It could be one big all-encompassing metaverse or multiple metaverses you can travel around. Wait and watch!

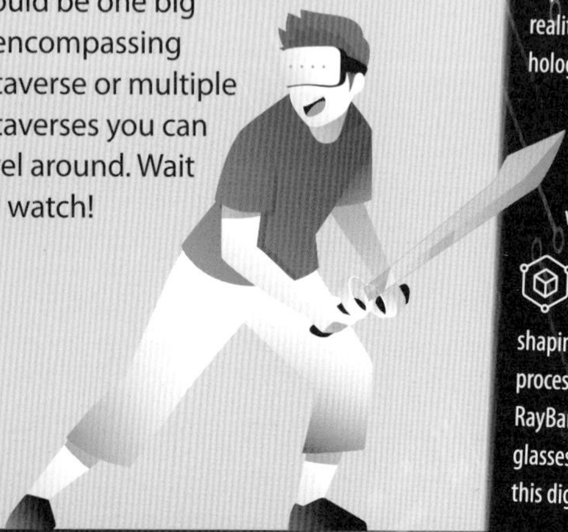

TIMELINE OF THE METAVERSE

- Metaverse technology was simply a plot for a sci-fi novel. The term was first used by Neal Stephenson in *Snow Crash* in **1982**.
- In the **1990s**, Sega pioneered virtual-reality arcade devices, such as the SEGA VR-1 motion simulators.
- Sportsvision broadcast the first live NFL game in **1998** with the virtual 1st & Ten graphic system, known as the yellow yard marker. The technology displays a yellow line on top of the feed for viewers to see where the team advances to get a first touchdown. After this, overlaying graphics became popular.
- In **2010**, Palmer Luckey, an 18-year-old entrepreneur and inventor, fabricated a prototype of the Oculus Rift VR headset, a virtual-reality head-mounted display with a 90-degree field of vision and computer processing power. It is credited with reviving VR.
- In **2014**, Sony and Samsung both announced their VR headsets. In the same year, the Google released its first Cardboard device and AR glasses. The Cardboard is a low-cost VR viewer for smartphones.
- **2016** was the boom year for metaverse technology. Microsoft launched the HoloLens headsets to provide a mixed experience of augmented as well as virtual reality. The HoloLens allowed users to project a hologram and manipulate it in the real world. The mobile game Pokémon Go also used a similar technological combination to project Pokémons on roads around the world using augmented reality.
- In **2021**, Facebook changed its name to Meta, indicating a shift in the vision in shaping the metaverse. They are also in the process of launching smart glasses, called RayBan Stories, which are augmented reality glasses that would change the way we perceive this digital universe.

3 LITERATURE

The word 'literature' means 'acquaintance with letters', from the Latin 'lettera' or letter. Literature is broadly divided into two categories: fiction, which is imaginary, and non-fiction, which is factual. Here are the common types of literature:

Autobiography: A narration of a person's life that they tell themselves.

Biography: A factual narration of a person's life, told by somebody else.

Drama: A piece of writing, with dialogue and action, meant to be performed on stage.

Essay: A written discussion of a topic from an individual's viewpoint.

Fable: A moral story in which the characters are typically animals.

Fairy tale: A fictional story with central themes of fantasy and magic.

Folk tale: Traditional stories, circulated orally among people of a specific community, region or country.

Journal or Diary: The day-to-day recordings of someone's life, usually autobiographical in nature, but often fictional too.

Legend: A story about an important individual or event popularly regarded as historical although not verifiable.

Memoir: An autobiographical account of the writer's memories, emotions and views.

Myth: An ancient religious, spiritual or traditional story describing how the world or humankind came to be.

Novel: A full-length piece of fiction, written in prose. A **novella** is a short novel.

Poetry: A piece written in verse, in which lines may or may not rhyme or stick to a specific meter.

Short story: A narrative in prose, much shorter than a novel, and usually, but not always, about the size of a chapter in a novel.

E-literature: Electronic literature is created in digital environments. It includes conversational characters or 'chatterbots'; interactive fiction, novels in the form of emails, SMS messages or blogs; and poems and stories generated by computers. An e-book is an electronic version of a print book, to be read on a computer, or a device such as a tablet, a smartphone or an e-reader.

FEMOIR A MEMOIR WRITTEN BY A WELL-KNOWN FEMALE ACTOR OR COMEDIAN, EMBRACING BODY POSITIVITY, PROFESSIONAL ADVANCEMENT AND A SUPPORTIVE FEMALE COMMUNITY.

TYPES OF FICTION

Fiction includes novels, short stories, fables, folk tales, fairy tales, plays, poetry, and comic books. Here are the main types of fiction genres.

Campus novel: A novel in which the main action takes place around the campus of a university, college or school.

Children's: A book written primarily for children is listed in this genre. This includes fiction written in many formats, such as picture books, graphic fiction, short stories and full-length novels. A category higher than children's fiction is young adult (YA) fiction. It broadly includes books for adolescents and young adults in the age group of 14 to 19 years.

Comedy: Fiction that intends to amuse readers and provoke laughter.

Crime: Fiction written about crime and detection. There are several subgenres, such as detective fiction, legal thrillers and courtroom drama.

Fantasy: This genre looks at magic and other forms of the supernatural as its primary inspiration. 'Fantastic' elements may be hidden in a semi-real world setting (like the Harry Potter series); or they may occur in a fantastical world.

MAGICAL REALISM IS A GENRE IN WHICH MAGICAL EVENTS ARE A PART OF ORDINARY LIFE.

Graphic fiction: This genre covers a huge range from picture books and comic books to graphic novels and manga, in which a series of images and word or speech balloons convey a narrative.

Horror: Fiction that primarily aims to scare and incite fear in the reader. Although they largely use supernatural elements, books with gruesome, frightening or suspenseful themes are also part of the genre.

Romance: Novels in this genre are centred on a romantic relationship. This genre extends from classics to Mills & Boon romances.

Spy: Born of the political climate in Europe prior to the First World War, spy fiction began around the time the first modern intelligence services were formed and swiftly became popular through the Second World War.

Thriller: This eventful genre involves suspense and exciting action. It typically follows a hero pitted against a villain who aims to destroy the hero, his country or even the world.

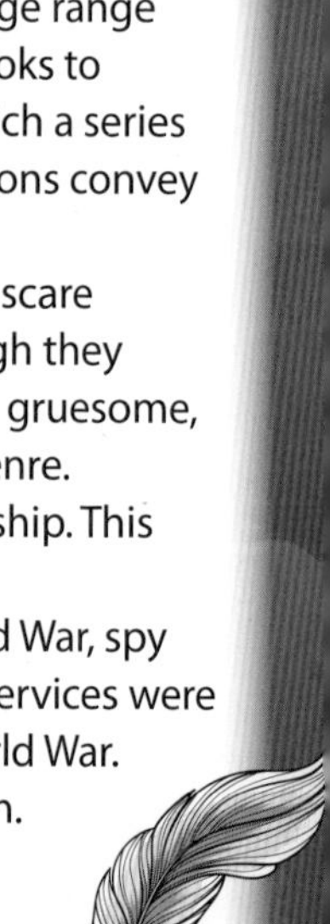

Satire: When an author ridicules or derides a vice or a folly through humour and wit, it is called satire. It is marked by irony, sarcasm, parody and exaggeration.

Wild West Fiction: This genre originated in the American Wild West, cowboy heroism and Native American life.

TYPES OF POETRY

Here are the main forms of poetry:

Acrostic: The first letter, syllable or word of each line or stanza spells out a word/message.

Ballad: A poem that tells a story similar to a folk tale or legend.

Blank/free verse: A poem that does not rhyme, or follow a meter.

Burlesque poetry: In this a serious subject is treated with humour.

Couplet: A poem of two consecutive lines that rhyme.

Elegy: A sad poetic reflection about the death of a person.

Epic: A long serious poem, telling the story of a heroic figure.

Epitaph: A commemorative poem praising the deceased.

Haiku: A Japanese poem of three unrhymed lines of five, seven, and five syllables, usually with a reference to a 'season'.

Limerick: A short, humorous five-line poem.

Lyric: A poem that expresses the thoughts/feelings of the poet.

Narrative: A poem that tells a story.

Ode: A long meditative lyric, with a formal stanzaic structure.

Pastoral: It depicts rural life.

Rhyme: This repeats same or similar sounds in words at the end of lines.

Romantic: Poetry of nature and love.

Shape: A poem written in the shape of an object.

Sonnet: A lyric 14-line poem, with a formal rhyme scheme.

TYPES OF DRAMA

Drama is a work of fiction that is meant to be performed on stage, or acted out.

Epic: A long poem about heroism and events significant for a culture or nation. Oral or primary epics are handed down through the spoken word and written down after centuries. Examples are Greek epics, such as *The Iliad* and Indian epics like the Mahabharata. Literary epics are modern works such as John Milton's *Paradise Lost* .

Romance: Also known as chivalric romance, this deals with the courageous quests and adventures of a heroic individual, often a brave knight.

Tragicomedy: This describes work that blends elements of tragedy and comedy. Black (or serious/dark) comedy is also part of it.

Comedy: This includes parody, satire, burlesque, clowning and romantic comedy, among other types of comedy.

Tragedy: Coming from the poetic and religious traditions of ancient Greece, tragedy takes its inspiration from human suffering. Shakespeare's *Hamlet* and Sophocles's *Antigone* are examples.

CLI-FI OR CLIMATE FICTION IS A SUBGENRE OF SCIENCE FICTION THAT DEALS WITH THE GROWING CONCERN OVER GLOBAL WARMING.

BOOKS TO SCREEN

Coming soon to a screen, all these films are based on books!

- ***The Bad Guys (2022):*** Pierre Perifel's cinematic take on the wildly popular 'Bad Guys' books, written by Aaron Blabey, is set to hit screens in 2022. Starring Sam Rockwell and Richard Ayoade, the film follows several former criminal animals in their quest to become good and the disastrous results that follow.
- ***Lockwood & Co. (2022):*** Based on Jonathan Stroud's series of the same name, Lockwood & Co. follows three teenagers as they unravel a mystery that will change the course of history. With Joe Cornish directing the pilot, the series stars Ruby Stokes alongside Morven Christie.
- ***Paper Girls (2022):*** Based on the graphic novel series by Brian Vaughan, and starring Sofia Rosinsky and Ali Wong, the Amazon Prime Original show will follow four 12-year-old girls from 1988 on a time- travelling adventure. The series premiered on 29 July 2022.
- ***The Ballad of Songbirds and Snakes (2023):*** Starring Rachel Zegler, Hunter Schafer and Tom Blyth, Francis Lawrence's adaptation of Suzanne Collins's book is one of the most highly anticipated films of 2023. The film is a prequel to The Hunger Games trilogy and follows 18-year-old Coriolanus Snow years before his rise to power, as he is chosen to mentor the female tribute of District 12, Lucy Gray Baird.
- ***Anansi Boys (2023):*** Based on Neil Gaiman's book of the same name, *Anansi Boys* follows the sons of Anansi, a spider god. The movie will star Whoopi Goldberg, Malachi Kirby and Fiona Shaw.
- ***Are You There God? It's Me, Margaret (2023):*** The on-screen adaptation of Judy Blume's iconic novel, directed by Kelly Fremon Craig, is set to hit screens by 2023. Starring Rachel McAdams and Kathy Bates, the film tells the tale of 11-year-old Margaret and her family's move from the bustling city to the seemingly boring suburbs.
- ***Percy Jackson and the Olympians (2023):*** Rick Riordan's global phenomenon. Percy Jackson. is all set to hit screens with the Disney+ production starring Walker Scobell and Jason Mantzoukas, with James Bobin slated to direct the pilot. The show will follow Percy Jackson, a 12-year-old New Yorker, whose life is thrown into absolute chaos when he discovers that he is a demigod.

4 COUNTRIES

Important International Organizations

- **ACP:** African, Caribbean and Pacific Group of States
- **ADB:** Asian Development Bank
- **AI:** Amnesty International
- **APEC:** Asia-Pacific Economic Cooperation
- **ASEAN:** Association of South-East Asian Nations
- **EU:** European Union
- **IFAD:** International Fund for Agricultural Development
- **IFRC:** International Federation of Red Cross and Red Crescent Societies
- **IMSO:** International Mobile Satellite Organization
- **INTERPOL:** International Criminal Police Organization
- **IOC:** International Olympic Committee
- **ISO:** International Organization for Standardization
- **ITSO:** International Telecommunications Satellite Organization
- **ITU:** International Telecom Union
- **NAM:** Non-Aligned Movement
- **NATO:** North Atlantic Treaty Organization
- **OECD:** Organization for Economic Cooperation and Development
- **OPEC:** Organization of Petroleum Exporting Countries
- **SAARC:** South Asian Association for Regional Cooperation
- **WMO:** World Meteorological Organization
- **WWF:** World Wide Fund for Nature

UN: The United Nations

UN Specialized Agencies:

- **ESCAP:** Economic and Social Commission for Asia and the Pacific
- **FAO:** Food and Agricultural Organization
- **IBRD:** International Bank for Reconstruction and Development
- **IDA:** International Development Association
- **ILO:** International Labour Organization
- **IMF:** International Monetary Fund
- **UNESCO:** United Nations Educational, Scientific and Cultural Organization
- **UNICEF:** United Nations Children's Fund
- **WHO:** World Health Organization
- **WIPO:** World Intellectual Property

NOTE: Includes sovereign states in the United Nations System. Time zones are calculated from the Greenwich Mean Time (GMT) and are mentioned in hours and minutes; GDP per capita is is approximate, in US dollars and based on the last figures available; Population figures are based on each country's last national census; Life expectancy figures are in years; Internet TLD stands for Internet Top Level Domain; Flags may not match exact proportions. All information updated up to 30 July 2022.

AFGHANISTAN

LOCATION: South-central Asia

CAPITAL: Kabul

AREA: 652,230 sq. km

LANGUAGES: Pashto, Dari

MAIN RELIGION: Islam

CURRENCY: Afghani

LITERACY RATE: 37.3%

LIFE EXPECTANCY: 53.65 years

TIME ZONE: +4.30

TYPE OF GOVERNMENT: Islamic Emirate

HEAD OF STATE AND GOVT: (Interim) Prime Minister Mullah Mohammad Hasan Akhund

GDP PER CAPITA: $2,000

POPULATION: 37,466,414

ISD CODE: 93 **INTERNET TLD:** .af

The Minaret of Jam in the Hari River Valley is a UNESCO World Heritage Site.

ALBANIA

LOCATION: South-east Europe

CAPITAL: Tirana

AREA: 28,748 sq. km

LANGUAGE: Albanian

MAIN RELIGION: Islam

CURRENCY: Lek

LITERACY RATE: 98.1%

LIFE EXPECTANCY: 79.47 years

TIME ZONE: +1

TYPE OF GOVERNMENT: Parliamentary Republic

HEAD OF STATE: President Ilir Meta

HEAD OF GOVT: Prime Minister Edi Rama

GDP PER CAPITA: $13,300

POPULATION: 3,095,344

ISD CODE: 355

INTERNET TLD: .al

Albania produces all of its electricity through hydropower or the use of water resources.

ALGERIA

LOCATION: North Africa

CAPITAL: Algiers

AREA: 2,381,741 sq. km

LANGUAGES: Arabic, French, Berber

MAIN RELIGION: Islam

CURRENCY: Algerian Dinar

LITERACY RATE: 81.4%

LIFE EXPECTANCY: 78.03 years

TIME ZONE: +1

TYPE OF GOVERNMENT: Presidential Republic

HEAD OF STATE: President Abdelmadjid Tebboune

HEAD OF GOVT: Prime Minister Ayman Benabderrahmane

GDP PER CAPITA: $10,700

POPULATION: 44,178,884

ISD CODE: 213 **INTERNET TLD:** .dz

The Djamaa El Djazair Mosque is the world third largest mosque and holds the world's tallest minaret, which stands at 265 m (87 ft).

Background: Algeria

ANDORRA

LOCATION: West Europe

CAPITAL: Andorra la Vella

AREA: 468 sq. km

LANGUAGES: Catalan, French, Castilian, Portuguese

MAIN RELIGION: Christianity

CURRENCY: Euro

LITERACY RATE: 100%

LIFE EXPECTANCY: 83.42 years

TIME ZONE: +1

TYPE OF GOVERNMENT: Parliamentary Democracy and Co-principality

HEAD OF STATE: Co-prince Emmanuel Macron and Co-prince Archbishop Joan-Enric Vives Sicilia

HEAD OF GOVT: Executive Council President Xavier Espot Zamora

GDP PER CAPITA: $49,900

POPULATION: 85,560

ISD CODE: 376

INTERNET TLD: .ad

Andorra has a small volunteer ceremonial army. Spain and France defend it with their armies.

ANGOLA

LOCATION: South-central Africa

CAPITAL: Luanda

AREA: 1,246,700 sq. km

LANGUAGES: Portuguese, Bantu, other African languages

MAIN RELIGIONS: Indigenous faiths, Christianity

CURRENCY: Kwanza

LITERACY RATE: 71.1%

LIFE EXPECTANCY: 62.11 years

TIME ZONE: +1

TYPE OF GOVERNMENT: Presidential Republic

HEAD OF STATE AND GOVT: President Joao Manuel Goncalves Lourenco

GDP PER CAPITA: $6,200

POPULATION: 34,795,287

ISD CODE: 244

INTERNET TLD: .ao

After its independence from Portugal in 1975, Angola went through a civil war for 27 years.

ANTIGUA AND BARBUDA

LOCATION: Central America

CAPITAL: Saint John's

AREA: 442.6 sq. km

LANGUAGE: English

MAIN RELIGION: Christianity

CURRENCY: East Caribbean Dollar

LITERACY RATE: 99%

LIFE EXPECTANCY: 77.8 years

TIME ZONE: –4

TYPE OF GOVERNMENT: Constitutional Monarchy and Parliamentary Democracy

HEAD OF STATE: Queen Elizabeth II

HEAD OF GOVT: Prime Minister Gaston Browne

GDP PER CAPITA: $18,000

POPULATION: 100,335

ISD CODE: 1-268

INTERNET TLD: .ag

Antigua and Barbuda is often called the land of 365 beaches due to the beautiful and long coastline.

Background: Andorra

ARGENTINA

LOCATION: South America

CAPITAL: Buenos Aires

AREA: 2,780,400 sq. km

LANGUAGE: Spanish

MAIN RELIGION: Christianity

CURRENCY: Argentine Peso

LITERACY RATE: 99%

LIFE EXPECTANCY: 78.31 years

TIME ZONE: –3

TYPE OF GOVERNMENT: Federal Presidential Republic

HEAD OF STATE AND GOVT: President Alberto Fernandez

GDP PER CAPITA: $19,700

POPULATION: 46,245,668

ISD CODE: 54 **INTERNET TLD:** .ar

The country is named after the Latin word *argentum*, which means 'silver' in English.

ARMENIA

LOCATION: South-western Asia, east of Turkey

CAPITAL: Yerevan

AREA: 29,743 sq. km

LANGUAGE: Armenian

MAIN RELIGION: Christianity

CURRENCY: Dram

LITERACY RATE: 99.8%

LIFE EXPECTANCY: 76.13 years

TIME ZONE: +4

TYPE OF GOVERNMENT: Parliamentary Democracy

HEAD OF STATE: President Vahagn Khachaturyan **HEAD OF GOVT:** Prime Minister Nikol Pashinyan

GDP PER CAPITA: $12,600

POPULATION: 3,000,756

ISD CODE: 374 **INTERNET TLD:** .am

One of the oldest centres of civilizations, Armenia was the first country in the world to officially embrace Christianity as its religion (c. 300 BCE).

AUSTRALIA

LOCATION: Between Indian Ocean and South Pacific Ocean

CAPITAL: Canberra

AREA: 7,741,220 sq. km

LANGUAGE: English

MAIN RELIGION: Christianity

CURRENCY: Australian Dollar

LITERACY RATE: 100%

LIFE EXPECTANCY: 83.09 years

TIME ZONE: +8 to +10.30

TYPE OF GOVERNMENT: Constitutional Monarchy and Federal Parliamentary Democracy

HEAD OF STATE: Queen Elizabeth II **HEAD OF GOVT:** Prime Minister Anthony Albanese

GDP PER CAPITA: $48,700

POPULATION: 24,141,369

ISD CODE: 61 **INTERNET TLD:** .au

Australia has the largest sand island: the 122 km long Fraser Island, just off its east coast.

Background: Australia

AUSTRIA

LOCATION: Central Europe

CAPITAL: Vienna

AREA: 83,871sq. km

LANGUAGE: German

MAIN RELIGION: Christianity

CURRENCY: Euro

LITERACY RATE: 99%

LIFE EXPECTANCY: 82.27 years

TIME ZONE: +1

TYPE OF GOVERNMENT: Federal Parliamentary Republic

HEAD OF STATE: President Alexander Van der Bellen

HEAD OF GOVT: Chancellor Sebastian Kurz

GDP PER CAPITA: $51,900

POPULATION: 8,913,088

ISD CODE: 43 **INTERNET TLD:** .at

The first woman to win the Nobel Peace Prize in 1905, Bertha von Suttner, was from Austria.

AZERBAIJAN

LOCATION: West Asia, bordering Caspian Sea

CAPITAL: Baku

AREA: 86,600 sq. km

LANGUAGE: Azerbaijani

MAIN RELIGION: Islam

CURRENCY: Azerbaijani Manat

LITERACY RATE: 99.8%

LIFE EXPECTANCY: 74.15 years

TIME ZONE: +4

TYPE OF GOVERNMENT: Presidential Republic

HEAD OF STATE: President Ilham Aliyev

HEAD OF GOVT: Prime Minister Ali Hidayat oglu Asadov

GDP PER CAPITA: $13,700

POPULATION: 10,353,296

ISD CODE: 994 **INTERNET TLD:** .az

The 'burning mountain' is a rare natural wonder in the Absheron Peninsula. It 'burns' all year due to natural gas escaping from the ground.

(THE) BAHAMAS

LOCATION: Central America

CAPITAL: Nassau

AREA: 13,880 sq. km

LANGUAGES: English, Creole

MAIN RELIGION: Christianity

CURRENCY: Bahamian Dollar

LITERACY RATE: 99%*

LIFE EXPECTANCY: 76.13 years

TIME ZONE: –5

TYPE OF GOVERNMENT: Constitutional Monarchy and Parliamentary Democracy

HEAD OF STATE: Queen Elizabeth II

HEAD OF GOVT: Prime Minister Philip Davis

GDP PER CAPITA: $30,800

POPULATION: 355,608

ISD CODE: 1-242

INTERNET TLD: .bs

The word 'Bahamas' comes from the Spanish *bajamar*, meaning 'shallow water'. The archipelago has nearly 700 islands, with only about 30 inhabited ones.

BAHRAIN

LOCATION: South-central Asia

CAPITAL: Manama

AREA: 760 sq. km

LANGUAGES: Arabic, English, Farsi, Urdu

MAIN RELIGION: Islam

CURRENCY: Bahraini Dinar

LITERACY RATE: 97.5%

LIFE EXPECTANCY: 79.9 years

TIME ZONE: +3

TYPE OF GOVERNMENT: Constitutional Monarchy

HEAD OF STATE: King Hamad bin Isa Al Khalifah **HEAD OF GOVT:** Prime Minister Khalifah bin Salman Al Khalifah

GDP PER CAPITA: $40,900

POPULATION: 1,540,558

ISD CODE: 973 **INTERNET TLD:** .bh

The Bahraini dollar is the world's second highest valued currency after the American dollar.

BANGLADESH

LOCATION: South Asia

CAPITAL: Dhaka

AREA: 148,460 sq. km

LANGUAGE: Bangla (Bengali)

MAIN RELIGION: Islam

CURRENCY: Taka

LITERACY RATE: 74.9%

LIFE EXPECTANCY: 74.7 years

TIME ZONE: +6

TYPE OF GOVERNMENT: Parliamentary Republic

HEAD OF STATE: President Abdul Hamid **HEAD OF GOVT:** Prime Minister Sheikh Hasina Wajed

GDP PER CAPITA: $4,800

POPULATION: 164,098,818

ISD CODE: 880 **INTERNET TLD:** .bd

Bangladesh is blessed with deep, rich and fertile soil from the three rivers – the Ganga, the Brahmaputra and the Meghna – that form the deltaic plain upon which it sits.

BARBADOS

LOCATION: Caribbean Sea

CAPITAL: Bridgetown

AREA: 430 sq. km

LANGUAGE: English

MAIN RELIGION: Christianity

CURRENCY: Barbadian Dollar

LITERACY RATE: 99.6%

LIFE EXPECTANCY: 78.55 years

TIME ZONE: –4

TYPE OF GOVERNMENT: Parliamentary Republic

HEAD OF STATE: Sandra Mason **HEAD OF GOVT:** Prime Minister Mia Mottley

GDP PER CAPITA: $12,900

POPULATION: 302,674

ISD CODE: 1-246 **INTERNET TLD:** .bb

Local people frequently refer to their country as 'Bim' casually. The name comes from the Igbo word *bém*, which means 'my home' in English.

Background: Barbados

BELARUS

LOCATION: Eastern Europe

CAPITAL: Minsk

AREA: 207,600 sq. km

LANGUAGES: Belarusian, Russian

MAIN RELIGION: Christianity (Russian Orthodox Church)

CURRENCY: Belarusian Ruble

LITERACY RATE: 99.9%

LIFE EXPECTANCY: 74.28 years

TIME ZONE: +2

TYPE OF GOVERNMENT: Presidential Republic

HEAD OF STATE: President Alexander Lukashenko **HEAD OF GOVT:** Prime Minister Roman Golovchenko

GDP PER CAPITA: $19,100

POPULATION: 9,441,842

ISD CODE: 375 **INTERNET TLD:** .by

There are more than 20,000 rivers in Belarus.

BELGIUM

LOCATION: North-west Europe

CAPITAL: Brussels

AREA: 30,528 sq. km

LANGUAGES: Dutch, French, German

MAIN RELIGION: Christianity

CURRENCY: Euro

LITERACY RATE: 99%

LIFE EXPECTANCY: 81.6 years

TIME ZONE: +1

TYPE OF GOVERNMENT: Constitutional Monarchy and Parliamentary Democracy

HEAD OF STATE: King Philippe **HEAD OF GOVT:** Prime Minister Alexander De Croo

GDP PER CAPITA: $48,200

POPULATION: 11,847,338

ISD CODE: 32 **INTERNET TLD:** .be

Belgium produces nearly 220,000 tonnes of chocolate every year. The country is also famous for waffles.

BELIZE

LOCATION: Central America

CAPITAL: Belmopan

AREA: 22,966 sq. km

LANGUAGES: English, Creole, Spanish

MAIN RELIGION: Christianity

CURRENCY: Belize Dollar

LITERACY RATE: 82.7%

LIFE EXPECTANCY: 75.5 years

TIME ZONE: –6

TYPE OF GOVERNMENT: Constitutional Monarchy and Parliamentary Democracy

HEAD OF STATE: Queen Elizabeth II **HEAD OF GOVT:** Prime Minister Johnny Briceno

GDP PER CAPITA: $6,100

POPULATION: 412,387

ISD CODE: 501 **INTERNET TLD:** .bz

The motto of the country is 'Under the shade, I flourish' due to it being covered with rainforests.

Background: Belgium

BENIN

LOCATION: West Africa

CAPITAL: Porto Novo

AREA: 112,622 sq. km

LANGUAGES: French, Fon, other African languages

MAIN RELIGIONS: Indigenous faiths, Christianity, Islam

CURRENCY: CFA Franc

LITERACY RATE: 42.4%

LIFE EXPECTANCY: 62.21 years

TIME ZONE: +1

TYPE OF GOVERNMENT: Presidential Republic

HEAD OF STATE AND GOVT: President Patrice Talon

GDP PER CAPITA: $3,300

POPULATION: 13,754,688

ISD CODE: 229 **INTERNET TLD:** .bj

Benin's name comes from a large body of water called 'The Bight of Benin'.

BHUTAN

LOCATION: South Asia

CAPITAL: Thimphu

AREA: 38,394 sq. km

LANGUAGES: Dzongkha, Sharchhopka

MAIN RELIGION: Buddhism

CURRENCY: Ngultrum

LITERACY RATE: 66.6%

LIFE EXPECTANCY: 72.31 years

TIME ZONE: +6

TYPE OF GOVERNMENT: Constitutional Monarchy

HEAD OF STATE: King Jigme Khesar Namgyel Wangchuck **HEAD OF GOVT:** Prime Minister Lotay Tshering

GDP PER CAPITA: $10,900

POPULATION: 867,775

ISD CODE: 975 **INTERNET TLD:** .bt

Bhutan was one of the last countries to introduce television to its people. The government lifted the ban on TV in 1999.

BOLIVIA

LOCATION: Central South America

CAPITAL: La Paz

AREA: 1,098,581 sq. km

LANGUAGES: Spanish, Quechua, Aymara, Guarani

MAIN RELIGION: Christianity

CURRENCY: Boliviano

LITERACY RATE: 92.5%

LIFE EXPECTANCY: 72.5 years

TIME ZONE: –4

TYPE OF GOVERNMENT: Presidential Republic

HEAD OF STATE AND GOVT: President Luis Arce

GDP PER CAPITA: $7,900

POPULATION: 12,054,379

ISD CODE: 591 **INTERNET TLD:** .bo

Lake Titicaca in the Andes is the highest navigable lake in the world, at 3,810 m (12,500 ft) above sea level.

BOSNIA AND HERZEGOVINA

LOCATION: South-east Europe

CAPITAL: Sarajevo

AREA: 51,197 sq. km

LANGUAGES: Bosnian, Croatian, Serbian

MAIN RELIGIONS: Christianity, Islam

CURRENCY: Convertible Mark

LITERACY RATE: 98.5%

LIFE EXPECTANCY: 77.98 years

TIME ZONE: +1

TYPE OF GOVERNMENT: Parliamentary Republic

HEAD OF STATE: Chairman of Presidential Council Sejik Dzaferovic

HEAD OF GOVT: Chairman of Council of Ministers Zoran Tegeltija

GDP PER CAPITA: $14,300

POPULATION: 3,816,459

ISD CODE: 387 **INTERNET TLD:** .ba

The capital city Sarajevo was the first city in Europe with a full-time electric tram.

BOTSWANA

LOCATION: Southern Africa

CAPITAL: Gaborone

AREA: 581,730 sq. km

LANGUAGES: English, Setswana, Kalanga

MAIN RELIGION: Christianity

CURRENCY: Pula

LITERACY RATE: 88.5%

LIFE EXPECTANCY: 65.64 years

TIME ZONE: +2

TYPE OF GOVERNMENT: Parliamentary Republic

HEAD OF STATE AND GOVT: President Mokgweetsi Eric Masisi

GDP PER CAPITA: $16,000

POPULATION: 2,384,246

ISD CODE: 267

INTERNET TLD: .bw

The Okavango Delta was declared as one of the 7 Natural Wonders of Africa in 2013.

BRAZIL

LOCATION: North-east South America

CAPITAL: Brasilia

AREA: 8,515,710 sq. km

LANGUAGES: Portuguese

MAIN RELIGION: Christianity

CURRENCY: Real

LITERACY RATE: 93.2%

LIFE EXPECTANCY: 75.92 years

TIME ZONE: –3

TYPE OF GOVERNMENT: Presidential Federal Republic

HEAD OF STATE AND GOVT: President Jair Bolsonaro

GDP PER CAPITA: $14,100

POPULATION: 217,240,060

ISD CODE: 55

INTERNET TLD: .br

Brazil is home to 60 per cent of the Amazon rainforest.

BRUNEI

LOCATION: South-east Asia

CAPITAL: Bandar Seri Begawan

AREA: 5,765 sq. km

LANGUAGE: Malay

MAIN RELIGION: Islam

CURRENCY: Brunei Dollar

LITERACY RATE: 97.2%

LIFE EXPECTANCY: 78.38 years

TIME ZONE: +8

TYPE OF GOVERNMENT: Islamic Absolute Monarchy

HEAD OF STATE AND GOVT: Sultan Hassanal Bolkiah

GDP PER CAPITA: $62,200

POPULATION: 478,054

ISD CODE: 673 **INTERNET TLD:** .bn

The Istana Nurul Iman Palace in Brunei is reportedly the largest residential palace in the world, with 1,788 rooms and 257 bathrooms.

BULGARIA

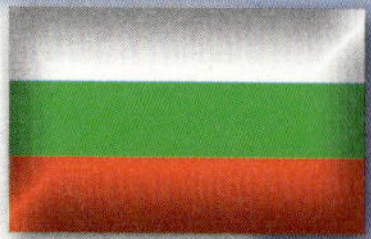

LOCATION: South-east Europe

CAPITAL: Sofia

AREA: 110,879 sq. km

LANGUAGE: Bulgarian

MAIN RELIGION: Christianity

CURRENCY: Lev

LITERACY RATE: 9847%

LIFE EXPECTANCY: 75.57 years

TIME ZONE: +2

TYPE OF GOVERNMENT: Parliamentary Republic

HEAD OF STATE: President Rumen Radev **HEAD OF GOVT:** Prime Minister Galab Donev

GDP PER CAPITA: $22,400

POPULATION: 6,813,253

ISD CODE: 359 **INTERNET TLD:** .bg

The first Bulgarian Empire was established in 681 CE, and the name 'Bulgaria' hasn't changed since, making it the only country in Europe to never have changed its name.

BURKINA FASO

LOCATION: West Africa

CAPITAL: Ouagadougou

AREA: 274,200 sq. km

LANGUAGES: French, indigenous African languages

MAIN RELIGION: Islam

CURRENCY: CFA Franc

LITERACY RATE: 41.2%

LIFE EXPECTANCY: 63.44 years

TIME ZONE: 0

TYPE OF GOVERNMENT: Presidential Republic

HEAD OF STATE: President Lt Col Paul-Henri Sandaogo Damiba **HEAD OF GOVT:** Prime Minister Albert Ouedraogo

GDP PER CAPITA: $2,200

POPULATION: 21,935,389

ISD CODE: 226

INTERNET TLD: .bf

The phrase 'Burkina Faso' means 'Land of the Honest (Incorruptible) Men.'

BURUNDI

LOCATION: Central Africa

CAPITAL: Bujumbura

AREA: 27,830 sq. km

LANGUAGES: Kirundi, French, Swahili

MAIN RELIGION: Christianity

CURRENCY: Burundi Franc

LITERACY RATE: 68.4%

LIFE EXPECTANCY: 67.42 years

TIME ZONE: +2

TYPE OF GOVERNMENT: Presidential Republic

HEAD OF STATE: President Evariste Ndayishimiye **HEAD OF GOVT:** Prime Minister Alain-Guillaume Bunyoni

GDP PER CAPITA: $700

POPULATION: 12,696,478

ISD CODE: 257 **INTERNET TLD:** .bi

The world's longest freshwater lake, Lake Tanganyika, is in Burundi. It stretches up to 673 km.

CABO VERDE

LOCATION: North Atlantic Ocean, off West Africa

CAPITAL: Praia

AREA: 4,033 sq. km

LANGUAGES: Portuguese, Creole

MAIN RELIGION: Christianity

CURRENCY: Cape Verdean Escudo

LITERACY RATE: 86.8%

LIFE EXPECTANCY: 73.75 years

TIME ZONE: –1

TYPE OF GOVERNMENT: Parliamentary Republic

HEAD OF STATE: President Jose Maria Neves **HEAD OF GOVT:** Prime Minister Ulisses Correia e Silva

GDP PER CAPITA: $6,000

POPULATION: 596,707

ISD CODE: 238 **INTERNET TLD:** .cv

Only four of Cabo Verde's 10 main islands have agriculture, producing over 90 per cent of the country's food.

CAMBODIA

LOCATION: South-east Asia

CAPITAL: Phnom Penh

AREA: 181,035 sq. km

LANGUAGES: Khmer, French

MAIN RELIGION: Theravada Buddhism

CURRENCY: Riel

LITERACY RATE: 80.5%

LIFE EXPECTANCY: 70.65 years

TIME ZONE: +7

TYPE OF GOVERNMENT: Parliamentary Constitutional Monarchy

HEAD OF STATE: King Norodom Sihamoni
HEAD OF GOVT: Prime Minister Hun Sen

GDP PER CAPITA: $4,389

POPULATION: 16,713,015

ISD CODE: 855 **INTERNET TLD:** .kh

The Cambodian flag is the only flag in the world to feature a building – the Angkor Wat Temple.

Background: Cabo Verde

CAMEROON

LOCATION: Central Africa

CAPITAL: Yaounde

AREA: 475,440 sq. km

LANGUAGES: French, English, African languages

MAIN RELIGIONS: Indigenous faiths, Christianity, Islam

CURRENCY: CFA Franc

LITERACY RATE: 77.1%

LIFE EXPECTANCY: 63.27 years

TIME ZONE: +1

TYPE OF GOVERNMENT: Multiparty Presidential Republic

HEAD OF STATE: President Paul Biya

HEAD OF GOVT: Prime Minister Joseph Dion Ngute

GDP PER CAPITA: $3,600

POPULATION: 29,321,637

ISD CODE: 237

INTERNET TLD: .cm

Cameroon is home to the Goliath frog, the world's largest frog, with a length of 33 cm and weighing up to 3.25 kg.

CANADA

LOCATION: North America

CAPITAL: Ottawa

AREA: 9,984,670 sq. km

LANGUAGES: English, French

MAIN RELIGION: Christianity

CURRENCY: Canadian Dollar

LITERACY RATE: 99%

LIFE EXPECTANCY: 83.8 years

TIME ZONE: –3.30 to –8

TYPE OF GOVERNMENT: Constitutional Monarchy and Federal Parliamentary Democracy

HEAD OF STATE: Queen Elizabeth II

HEAD OF GOVT Prime Minister Justin Trudeau

GDP PER CAPITA: $45,900

POPULATION: 38,232,593

ISD CODE: 1 **INTERNET TLD:** .ca

Canada is the second largest country in the world by area, after Russia.

CENTRAL AFRICAN REPUBLIC

LOCATION: Central Africa

CAPITAL: Bangui

AREA: 622,984 sq. km

LANGUAGES: French, Sangho, Arabic, Hansa

MAIN RELIGIONS: Indigenous faiths, Christianity, Islam

CURRENCY: CFA Franc

LITERACY RATE: 37.4%

LIFE EXPECTANCY: 55.54 years

TIME ZONE: +1

TYPE OF GOVERNMENT: Presidential Republic

HEAD OF STATE: President Faustin-Archange Touadera **HEAD OF GOVT:** Prime Minister Felix Moloua

GDP PER CAPITA: $900

POPULATION: 5,454,533

ISD CODE: 236 **INTERNET TLD:** .cf

In the 1880s, when the French colonized this area, they named it Oubangui-Chari as most of it is located in the Oubangui and Chari river basins.

CHAD

LOCATION: North-central Africa

CAPITAL: N'Djamena

AREA: 1,284,000 sq. km

LANGUAGES: French, Arabic

MAIN RELIGIONS: Islam, Christianity

CURRENCY: CFA Franc

LITERACY RATE: 22.3%

LIFE EXPECTANCY: 59.15 years

TIME ZONE: +1

TYPE OF GOVERNMENT: Presidential Republic

HEAD OF STATE: Interim President Mahamat Idriss Deby Itno (Chairman, Transitional Military Council)

HEAD OF GOVT: Prime Minister Albert Pahimi Padacke

GDP PER CAPITA: $1,500

POPULATION: 17,963,211

ISD CODE: 235 **INTERNET TLD:** .td

Chad is called the 'Dead Heart of Africa' because of its harsh and inhospitable climate.

CHILE

LOCATION: South America

CAPITAL: Santiago

AREA: 756,102 sq. km

LANGUAGE: Spanish

MAIN RELIGION: Christianity

CURRENCY: Chilean Peso

LITERACY RATE: 96.4%

LIFE EXPECTANCY: 79.5 years

TIME ZONE: –3

TYPE OF GOVERNMENT: Presidential Republic

HEAD OF STATE AND GOVT: President Gabriel Boric

GDP PER CAPITA: $23,300

POPULATION: 18,430,408

ISD CODE: 56 **INTERNET TLD:** .cl

Chile is the longest and narrowest country in the world. It is 4,300 km long and just 175 km wide (on average).

CHINA

LOCATION: East Asia

CAPITAL: Beijing

AREA: 9,596,961 sq. km

LANGUAGES: Mandarin, Cantonese

MAIN RELIGIONS: Atheism (official), Taoism, Buddhism

CURRENCY: Renminbi

LITERACY RATE: 96.8%

LIFE EXPECTANCY: 77.72 years

TIME ZONE: +8

TYPE OF GOVERNMENT: Communist/ Single-party Republic

HEAD OF STATE: President Xi Jinping

HEAD OF GOVT: Premier Li Keqiang

GDP PER CAPITA: $16,400

POPULATION: 1,410,539,758

ISD CODE: 86 **INTERNET TLD:** .cn

The Chinese invented the compass, gunpowder, ice cream and toilet paper. The last invention was used only by emperors.

Background: Chile

COLOMBIA

LOCATION: North-west South America

CAPITAL: Bogota

AREA: 1,138,910 sq. km

LANGUAGE: Spanish

MAIN RELIGION: Christianity

CURRENCY: Colombian Peso

LITERACY RATE: 95.6%

LIFE EXPECTANCY: 74.89 years

TIME ZONE: –5

TYPE OF GOVERNMENT: Presidential Republic

HEAD OF STATE AND GOVT: President Ivan Duque Marquez

GDP PER CAPITA: $13,400

POPULATION: 49,059,221

ISD CODE: 57 **INTERNET TLD:** .co

The river Cano Cristales in La Macarena is known to change colours. It is also called the 'Rainbow River'.

COMOROS

LOCATION: Southern Africa

CAPITAL: Moroni

AREA: 2,235 sq. km

LANGUAGES: Arabic, French, Shikomoro

MAIN RELIGION: Islam

CURRENCY: Comorian Franc

LITERACY RATE: 58.8%

LIFE EXPECTANCY: 67.2 years

TIME ZONE: +3

TYPE OF GOVERNMENT: Federal Presidential Republic

HEAD OF STATE AND GOVT: President Azali Assoumani

GDP PER CAPITA: $3,100

POPULATION: 864,335

ISD CODE: 269 **INTERNET TLD:** .km

Comoros is called the 'Perfume Isles' because of its fragrant ylang-ylang flower whose oil is a major export traditionally.

(DEMOCRATIC REPUBLIC OF THE) CONGO

LOCATION: Central Africa

CAPITAL: Kinshasa

AREA: 2,344,858 sq. km

LANGUAGE: French

MAIN RELIGION: Christianity

CURRENCY: Congolese Franc

LITERACY RATE: 77%

LIFE EXPECTANCY: 61.83 years

TIME ZONE: +1

TYPE OF GOVERNMENT: Semi-presidential Republic

HEAD OF STATE: Felix-Antoine Tshisekedi Tshilombo **HEAD OF GOVT:** Prime Minister Jean-Michel Sama Lukonde

GDP PER CAPITA: $1,098

POPULATION: 108,407,721

ISD CODE: 243 **INTERNET TLD:** .cd

The River Congo and its tributaries provide 12,800 km of waterway for transportation in the country. This is vital for the shipment of goods.

 Background: Comoros

(REPUBLIC OF THE) CONGO

LOCATION: Central Africa

CAPITAL: Brazzaville

AREA: 342,000 sq. km

LANGUAGES: French, Lingala, Monokutuba, other African languages

MAIN RELIGION: Christianity

CURRENCY: CFA Franc

LITERACY RATE: 80.3%

LIFE EXPECTANCY: 62.1 years

TIME ZONE: +2

TYPE OF GOVERNMENT: Presidential Republic

HEAD OF STATE: President Denis Sassou-Nguesso **HEAD OF GOVT:** Prime Minister Anatole Collinet Makosso

GDP PER CAPITA: $3,400

POPULATION: 5,546,307

ISD CODE: 242 **INTERNET TLD:** .cg

For its size, the Republic of Congo has a large number of languages, with up to 62 recognized spoken languages, and many more dialects.

COSTA RICA

LOCATION: Central America

CAPITAL: San Jose

AREA: 51,100 sq. km

LANGUAGE: Spanish

MAIN RELIGION: Christianity

CURRENCY: Costa Rican Colon

LITERACY RATE: 89.9%

LIFE EXPECTANCY: 62.26 years

TIME ZONE: –6

TYPE OF GOVERNMENT: Presidential Republic

HEAD OF STATE AND GOVT: President Rodrigo Chaves Robles

GDP PER CAPITA: $5,200

POPULATION: 5,151,140

ISD CODE: 506

INTERNET TLD: .cr

The 'yiguirro', a clay- coloured thrush, is Costa Rica's national symbol.

COTE D'IVOIRE

LOCATION: Western Africa

CAPITAL: Yamoussoukro

AREA: 322,463 sq. km

LANGUAGES: French, Dioula

MAIN RELIGIONS: Islam, Christianity

CURRENCY: CFA Franc

LITERACY RATE: 89.9%

LIFE EXPECTANCY: 62.26 years

TIME ZONE: 0

TYPE OF GOVERNMENT: Presidential Republic

HEAD OF STATE: President Alassane Ouattara **HEAD OF GOVT:** Prime Minister Patrick Jerome Achi

GDP PER CAPITA: $19,700

POPULATION: 5,204,211

ISD CODE: 225 **INTERNET TLD:** .ci

Elephants are facing extinction in Cote d'Ivoire, once famous for its ivory trade. Its national football team is known as 'Les Elephants', meaning 'The Elephants'.

Background: Costa Rica

CROATIA

LOCATION: South-east Europe

CAPITAL: Zagreb

AREA: 56,594 sq. km

LANGUAGE: Croatian

MAIN RELIGION: Christianity

CURRENCY: Croatian Kuna (Euro will be used from 1 January 2023)

LITERACY RATE: 99.3%

LIFE EXPECTANCY: 77.22 years

TIME ZONE: +1

TYPE OF GOVERNMENT: Parliamentary Republic

HEAD OF STATE: President Zoran Milanovic **HEAD OF GOVT:** Prime Minister Andrej Plenkovic

GDP PER CAPITA: $26,500

POPULATION: 4,188,853

ISD CODE: 385 **INTERNET TLD:** .hr

In 2019, Croatia became the youngest member of the European Parliament.

CUBA

LOCATION: Central America

CAPITAL: Havana

AREA: 110,860 sq. km

LANGUAGE: Spanish

MAIN RELIGION: Christianity

CURRENCY: Cuban Peso

LITERACY RATE: 99.8%

LIFE EXPECTANCY: 79.64 years

TIME ZONE: –5

TYPE OF GOVERNMENT: Communist/ Single-party Republic

HEAD OF STATE: President Miguel Diaz-Canel **HEAD OF GOVT** Manuel Marrero Cruz

GDP PER CAPITA: $12,300

POPULATION: 11,008,112

ISD CODE: 53 **INTERNET TLD:** .cu

Cubans refer to their island as 'El Cocodrilo' because when viewed from above, it resembles a crocodile.

CYPRUS

LOCATION: Mediterranean

CAPITAL: Nicosia

AREA: 9,251 sq. km

LANGUAGES: Greek, Turkish

MAIN RELIGION: Christianity (Greek Orthodox Church)

CURRENCY: Euro

LITERACY RATE: 99.1%

LIFE EXPECTANCY: 79.74 years

TIME ZONE: +2

TYPE OF GOVERNMENT: Presidential Democracy

HEAD OF STATE AND GOVT: President Nicos Anastasiades

GDP PER CAPITA: $37,700

POPULATION: 1,295,102

ISD CODE: 357 **INTERNET TLD:** .cy

The Cyprus mouflon is a kind of wild sheep that was originally found only in Cyprus.

Background: Croatia

CZECH REPUBLIC

LOCATION: Central Europe

CAPITAL: Prague

AREA: 78,867 sq. km

LANGUAGE: Czech

MAIN RELIGION: Christianity

CURRENCY: Czech Koruna

LITERACY RATE: 99%

LIFE EXPECTANCY: 79.73 years

TIME ZONE: +1

TYPE OF GOVERNMENT: Parliamentary Republic

HEAD OF STATE: President Milos Zeman **HEAD OF GOVT:** Prime Minister Petr Fiala

GDP PER CAPITA: $38,300

POPULATION: 10,705,384

ISD CODE: 420 **INTERNET TLD:** .cz

Prague is also called 'the city of a hundred spires'.

DENMARK

LOCATION: North Europe

CAPITAL: Copenhagen

AREA: 43,094 sq. km

LANGUAGE: Danish

MAIN RELIGION: Christianity (Evangelical Lutheran church)

CURRENCY: Danish Krone

LITERACY RATE: 99%

LIFE EXPECTANCY: 81.66 years

TIME ZONE: +1

TYPE OF GOVERNMENT: Parliamentary Constitutional Monarchy

HEAD OF STATE: Queen Margrethe II **HEAD OF GOVT:** Prime Minister Mette Frederiksen

GDP PER CAPITA: $55,900

POPULATION: 5,920,767

ISD CODE: 45 **INTERNET TLD:** .dk

There are 443 named islands in the Danish archipelago and only 76 of these are inhabited.

DJIBOUTI

LOCATION: East Africa

CAPITAL: Djibouti City

AREA: 23,200 sq. km

LANGUAGES: French, Arabic

MAIN RELIGION: Islam

CURRENCY: Djiboutian Franc

LITERACY RATE: 70%

LIFE EXPECTANCY: 65,3 years

TIME ZONE: +3

TYPE OF GOVERNMENT: Presidential Republic

HEAD OF STATE: President Ismail Omar Guelleh **HEAD OF GOVT:** Prime Minister Abdoulkader Kamil Mohamed

GDP PER CAPITA: $5,500

POPULATION: 957,273

ISD CODE: 253 **INTERNET TLD:** .dj

Background: Denmark

Lake Assal in Djibouti lies 156 m (512 ft) below sea level, making it the lowest point in Africa.

DOMINICA

LOCATION: Central America

CAPITAL: Roseau

AREA: 751 sq. km

LANGUAGES: English, French

MAIN RELIGION: Christianity

CURRENCY: East Caribbean Dollar

LITERACY RATE: 94%

LIFE EXPECTANCY: 78.21 years

TIME ZONE: –4

TYPE OF GOVERNMENT: Parliamentary Republic

HEAD OF STATE: President Charles Savarin **HEAD OF GOVT:** Prime Minister Roosevelt Skerrit

GDP PER CAPITA: $9,900

POPULATION: 74,629

ISD CODE: 1-767 **INTERNET TLD:** .dm

Christopher Columbus came to this island in 1493 on a Sunday. That's why he called it 'Dominica', meaning Sunday in Latin.

DOMINICAN REPUBLIC

LOCATION: Central America

CAPITAL: Santo Domingo

AREA: 48,670 sq. km

LANGUAGE: Spanish

MAIN RELIGION: Christianity

CURRENCY: Dominican Peso

LITERACY RATE: 93.8%

LIFE EXPECTANCY: 72.56 years

TIME ZONE: –4

TYPE OF GOVERNMENT: Presidential Republic

HEAD OF STATE AND GOVT: President Luis Abinader

GDP PER CAPITA: $17,000

POPULATION: 10,694,700

ISD CODE: 809 **INTERNET TLD:** .do

The oldest extant cathedral in the Americas is in Santo Domingo – the Cathedral of Santa Maria la Menor. Its construction began in 1512.

EAST TIMOR

LOCATION: South-east Asia

CAPITAL: Dili

AREA: 14,874 sq. km

LANGUAGES: Tetum, Portuguese

MAIN RELIGION: Christianity

CURRENCY: US Dollar

LITERACY RATE: 68.1%

LIFE EXPECTANCY: 69.92 years

TIME ZONE: +9

TYPE OF GOVERNMENT: Semi-presidential Republic

HEAD OF STATE: President Francisco Guterres **HEAD OF GOVT:** Prime Minister Taur Matan Ruak

GDP PER CAPITA: $3,200

POPULATION: 1,445,006

ISD CODE: 670 **INTERNET TLD:** .tl

Nine days after East Timor gained independence from Portugal in 1975, it was occupied by Indonesia. It became independent of Indonesian rule in 2002.

ECUADOR

LOCATION: Western South America

CAPITAL: Quito

AREA: 283,561 sq. km

LANGUAGE: Spanish

MAIN RELIGION: Christianity

CURRENCY: US Dollar

LITERACY RATE: 93.6%

LIFE EXPECTANCY: 78 years

TIME ZONE: –5

TYPE OF GOVERNMENT: Presidential Republic

HEAD OF STATE AND GOVT: President Guillermo Lasso

GDP PER CAPITA: $10,300

POPULATION: 17,289,554

ISD CODE: 593 **INTERNET TLD:** .ec

Ecuador is one of 13 countries through which the Equator passes.

EGYPT

LOCATION: North Africa

CAPITAL: Cairo

AREA: 1,001,450 sq. km

LANGUAGES: Arabic, English, French

MAIN RELIGION: Islam

CURRENCY: Egyptian Pound

LITERACY RATE: 71.2%

LIFE EXPECTANCY: 74.45 years

TIME ZONE: +2

TYPE OF GOVERNMENT: Presidential Republic

HEAD OF STATE: President Abdel Fattah el-Sisi **HEAD OF GOVT:** Prime Minister Mostafa Madbouly

GDP PER CAPITA: $12,200

POPULATION: 107,770,524

ISD CODE: 20 **INTERNET TLD:** .eg

The Great Pyramid of Giza in Egypt is the only existing ancient wonder of the world.

EL SALVADOR

LOCATION: Central America

CAPITAL: San Salvador

AREA: 21,041 sq. km

LANGUAGE: Spanish

MAIN RELIGION: Christianity

CURRENCY: US Dollar

LITERACY RATE: 89.1%

LIFE EXPECTANCY: 75.31 years

TIME ZONE: –6

TYPE OF GOVERNMENT: Presidential Republic

HEAD OF STATE AND GOVT: President Nayib Bukele

GDP PER CAPITA: $8,100

POPULATION: 6,568,745

ISD CODE: 503 **INTERNET TLD:** .sv

El Salvador, a country with 21 volcanoes, was in an infamous 100-hour war with neighbouring Honduras, over a soccer game in 1969.

Background: Egypt

EQUATORIAL GUINEA

LOCATION: Central Africa

CAPITAL: Malabo

AREA: 28,051 sq. km

LANGUAGES: Spanish, French

MAIN RELIGION: Christianity

CURRENCY: CFA Franc

LITERACY RATE: 95.3%

LIFE EXPECTANCY: 63.7 years

TIME ZONE: +1

TYPE OF GOVERNMENT: Presidential Republic

HEAD OF STATE: President Teodoro Obiang Nguema Mbasogo **HEAD OF GOVT:** Prime Minister Francisco Pascual Eyegue Obama Asue

GDP PER CAPITA: $17,000

POPULATION: 857,008

ISD CODE: 240 **INTERNET TLD:** .gq

Equatorial Guinea is the smallest African country that is a member of the United Nations.

ERITREA

LOCATION: East Africa

CAPITAL: Asmara

AREA: 117,600 sq. km

LANGUAGES: Tigrinya, Arabic, English

MAIN RELIGIONS: Islam, Christianity

CURRENCY: Eritrean Nakfa

LITERACY RATE: 76.6%

LIFE EXPECTANCY: 66.85 years

TIME ZONE: +3

TYPE OF GOVERNMENT: Presidential Republic

HEAD OF STATE AND GOVT: President Isaias Afwerki

GDP PER CAPITA: $1,600

POPULATION: 6,209,262

ISD CODE: 291 **INTERNET TLD:** .er

A one-party nation, the country has not held national or presidential elections since independence in 1993.

ESTONIA

LOCATION: East Europe

CAPITAL: Tallinn

AREA: 45,228 sq. km

LANGUAGE: Estonian, Russian

MAIN RELIGION: Christianity

CURRENCY: Euro

LITERACY RATE: 99.8%

LIFE EXPECTANCY: 77.6 years

TIME ZONE: +2

TYPE OF GOVERNMENT: Parliamentary Republic

HEAD OF STATE: President Alar Keris
HEAD OF GOVT: Prime Minister Kaja Kallas

GDP PER CAPITA: $35,600

POPULATION: 1,211,524

ISD CODE: 372 **INTERNET TLD:** .ee

Estonia has the highest number of meteorite craters per square kilometre in the world.

ESWATINI

LOCATION: Southern Africa

CAPITAL: Mbabane

AREA: 17,364 sq. km

LANGUAGES: English, Swati

MAIN RELIGIONS: Christianity, Islam

CURRENCY: Lilangeni; South African Rand

LITERACY RATE: 88.4%

LIFE EXPECTANCY: 59.69 years

TIME ZONE: +2

TYPE OF GOVERNMENT: Monarchy

HEAD OF STATE: King Mswati III
HEAD OF GOVT: Prime Minister Cleopas Dlamini

GDP PER CAPITA: $8,400

POPULATION: 1,113,276

ISD CODE: 268 **INTERNET TLD:** .sz

In 2018, King Mswati III renamed Swaziland as 'Kingdom of Eswatini'. It means 'land of the Swazis'.

ETHIOPIA

LOCATION: East Africa

CAPITAL: Addis Ababa

AREA: 1,104,300 sq. km

LANGUAGES: Amharic, Oromo

MAIN RELIGIONS: Christianity, Islam

CURRENCY: Ethiopian Birr

LITERACY RATE: 51.8%

LIFE EXPECTANCY: 67.9 years

TIME ZONE: +3

TYPE OF GOVERNMENT: Federal Parliamentary Republic

HEAD OF STATE: President Sahle-Work Zewde **HEAD OF GOVT:** Prime Minister Abiy Ahmed

GDP PER CAPITA: $2,221

POPULATION: 113,656,596

ISD CODE: 251 **INTERNET TLD:** .et

Marathoner Abebe Bikila was the first black African to win an Olympic gold at the 1960 Summer Games in Rome, running barefoot. He won another gold at the 1964 Tokyo Olympics.

FIJI

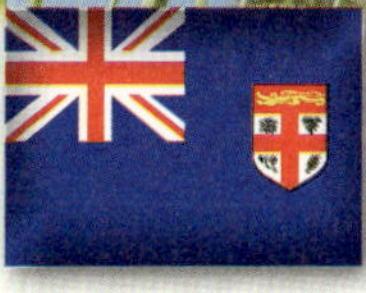

LOCATION: South Pacific Ocean

CAPITAL: Suva

AREA: 18,274 sq. km

LANGUAGES: English, Fijian

MAIN RELIGIONS: Christianity, Hinduism

CURRENCY: Fijian Dollar

LITERACY RATE: 99.1%

LIFE EXPECTANCY: 74 years

TIME ZONE: +12

TYPE OF GOVERNMENT: Parliamentary Republic

HEAD OF STATE: President Jioji Konrote
HEAD OF GOVT: Prime Minister Josaia Voreqe 'Frank' Bainimarama

GDP PER CAPITA: $13,684

POPULATION: 939,535

ISD CODE: 679 **INTERNET TLD:** .fj

Off the island of Taveuni, there is a place where one can swim from the current day to the day before as the International Date Line runs through it.

Background: Fiji

FINLAND

LOCATION: North Europe

CAPITAL: Helsinki

AREA: 338,145 sq. km

LANGUAGE: Finnish

MAIN RELIGION: Christianity (Church of Finland)

CURRENCY: Euro

LITERACY RATE: 100%

LIFE EXPECTANCY: 81.76 years

TIME ZONE: +2

TYPE OF GOVERNMENT: Republic

HEAD OF STATE: President Sauli Niinisto **HEAD OF GOVT:** Prime Minister Sanna Mirella Marin

GDP PER CAPITA: $47,300

POPULATION: 5,601,547

ISD CODE: 358 **INTERNET TLD:** .fi

The International Failure Day was initiated in Finland where a National Failure Day has been celebrated on 13 October since 2010.

FRANCE

LOCATION: West Europe

CAPITAL: Paris

AREA: 643,801 sq. km

LANGUAGE: French

MAIN RELIGION: Christianity

CURRENCY: Euro

LITERACY RATE: 99%

LIFE EXPECTANCY: 82.59 years

TIME ZONE: +1

TYPE OF GOVERNMENT: Semi-presidential Republic

HEAD OF STATE: President Emmanuel Macron **HEAD OF GOVT:** Prime Minister Elisabeth Borne

GDP PER CAPITA: $42,000

POPULATION: 68,305,148

ISD CODE: 33 **INTERNET TLD:** .fr

According to a law passed in 2016, food in French supermarkets cannot be thrown out; it has to be distributed to food banks or other charity organizations.

GABON

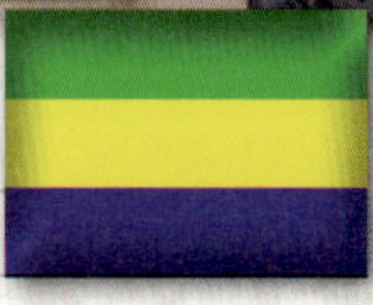

LOCATION: West Africa

CAPITAL: Libreville

AREA: 267,667 sq. km

LANGUAGES: French, Fang

MAIN RELIGION: Christianity

CURRENCY: CFA Franc

LITERACY RATE: 84.7%

LIFE EXPECTANCY: 69.7 years

TIME ZONE: +1

TYPE OF GOVERNMENT: Presidential Republic

HEAD OF STATE: President Ali Bongo Ondimba **HEAD OF GOVT:** Prime Minister Rose Christiane Ossouka Raponda

GDP PER CAPITA: $14,400

POPULATION: 2,340,613

ISD CODE: 241 **INTERNET TLD:** .ga

Gabon's present name comes from 'Gabao', Portuguese for 'cloak', which is the shape of the estuary of the River Komo here.

Background: France

(THE) GAMBIA

LOCATION: West Africa

CAPITAL: Banjul

AREA: 11,295 sq. km

LANGUAGES: English, Mandinka

MAIN RELIGION: Islam

CURRENCY: Dalasi

LITERACY RATE: 50.8%

LIFE EXPECTANCY: 67.6 years

TIME ZONE: 0

TYPE OF GOVERNMENT: Presidential Republic

HEAD OF STATE AND GOVT: President Adama Barrow

GDP PER CAPITA: $2,200

POPULATION: 2,413,403

ISD CODE: 220 **INTERNET TLD:** .gm

The country is called 'The' Gambia to prevent confusing it with Zambia.

GEORGIA

LOCATION: South-west Asia

CAPITAL: Tbilisi

AREA: 69,700 sq. km

LANGUAGES: Georgian, Russian, Armenian, Azerbaijani

MAIN RELIGION: Christianity

CURRENCY: Lari

LITERACY RATE: 99.46

LIFE EXPECTANCY: 77.5 years

TIME ZONE: +4

TYPE OF GOVERNMENT: Semi-presidential Republic

HEAD OF STATE: President Salome Zourabichvili **HEAD OF GOVT:** Prime Minister Irakli Garibashvili

GDP PER CAPITA: $14,100

POPULATION: 4,935,518

ISD CODE: 995 **INTERNET TLD:** .ge

Citizens of around 98 countries can enter Georgia without a visa.

GERMANY

LOCATION: West Europe

CAPITAL: Berlin

AREA: 357,022 sq. km

LANGUAGE: German

MAIN RELIGION: Christianity

CURRENCY: Euro

LITERACY RATE: 99%

LIFE EXPECTANCY: 81.3 years

TIME ZONE: +1

TYPE OF GOVERNMENT: Federal Parliamentary Republic

HEAD OF STATE: President Frank-Walter Steinmeier **HEAD OF GOVT:** Chancellor Olag Scholz

GDP PER CAPITA: $50,900

POPULATION: 84,316,622

ISD CODE: 49 **INTERNET TLD:** .de

German scientists are credited with the discovery of insulin and the invention of the pocket watch, the calculator, the automobile and the jet engine.

Background: Germany

GHANA

LOCATION: West Africa

CAPITAL: Accra

AREA: 238,533 sq. km

LANGUAGES: English, indigenous languages

MAIN RELIGION: Christianity

CURRENCY: Cedi

LITERACY RATE: 79%

LIFE EXPECTANCY: 69.31 years

TIME ZONE: 0

TYPE OF GOVERNMENT: Unitary Presidential Republic

HEAD OF STATE AND GOVT: President Nana Addo Dankwa Akufo-Addo

GDP PER CAPITA: $5,300

POPULATION: 32,107,275

ISD CODE: 233 **INTERNET TLD:** .gh

During the slave trade days, many European nations built forts and outposts in coastal Ghana. Now most of these have been turned into memorials.

GREECE

LOCATION: Southern Europe, bordering the Aegean Sea

CAPITAL: Athens

AREA: 131,957 sq. km

LANGUAGE: Greek

MAIN RELIGION: Christianity (Greek Orthodox Church)

CURRENCY: Euro

LITERACY RATE: 98.6%

LIFE EXPECTANCY: 75.74 years

TIME ZONE: +2

TYPE OF GOVERNMENT: Parliamentary Republic

HEAD OF STATE: President Katerina Sakellaropoulou **HEAD OF GOVT:** Prime Minister Kyriakos Mitsotakis

GDP PER CAPITA: $29,799

POPULATION: 10,569,703

ISD CODE: 30 **INTERNET TLD:** .gr

The ancient Greeks are believed to have invented the yo-yo in 500 BCE.

GRENADA

LOCATION: Central America

CAPITAL: St George's

AREA: 344 sq. km

LANGUAGE: English

MAIN RELIGION: Christianity

CURRENCY: East Caribbean Dollar

LITERACY RATE: 98.6%

LIFE EXPECTANCY: 75.74 years

TIME ZONE: –4

TYPE OF GOVERNMENT: Constitutional Monarchy and Parliamentary Democracy

HEAD OF STATE: Queen Elizabeth II
HEAD OF GOVT: Prime Minister Keith Mitchell

GDP PER CAPITA: $15,100

POPULATION: 113,570

ISD CODE: 473 **INTERNET TLD:** .gd

Grenada is home to both black sand and white sand beaches with water so clear that coral formations can be spotted from aircraft above.

GUATEMALA

LOCATION: Central America

CAPITAL: Guatemala City

AREA: 108,889 sq. km

LANGUAGES: Spanish, indigenous languages

MAIN RELIGION: Christianity

CURRENCY: Quetzal

LITERACY RATE: 80,8%

LIFE EXPECTANCY: 72.91 years

TIME ZONE: –6

TYPE OF GOVERNMENT: Presidential Republic

HEAD OF STATE AND GOVT: President Alejandro Giammattei

GDP PER CAPITA: $8,400

POPULATION: 17,703,190

ISD CODE: 502 **INTERNET TLD:** .gt

The name Guatemala means 'land of the trees' in the Maya-Toltec language. More than 21 Mayan languages are spoken here.

GUINEA

LOCATION: West Africa

CAPITAL: Conakry

AREA: 245,857 sq. km

LANGUAGE: French

MAIN RELIGION: Islam

CURRENCY: Guinean Franc

LITERACY RATE: 39.6%

LIFE EXPECTANCY: 63.9 years

TIME ZONE: 0

TYPE OF GOVERNMENT: Presidential Republic

HEAD OF STATE: President Colonel Mamady Doumbouya **HEAD OF GOVT:** Prime Minister Mohamed Beavogui

GDP PER CAPITA: $2,700

POPULATION: 13,237,282

ISD CODE: 224 **INTERNET TLD:** .gn

Mount Nimba, located on the border of Guinea and Cote d'Ivoire, is the highest point in both countries.

GUINEA-BISSAU

LOCATION: West Africa

CAPITAL: Bissau

AREA: 36,125 sq. km

LANGUAGE: Portuguese

MAIN RELIGIONS: Islam, Christianity, Animist, indigenous beliefs

CURRENCY: CFA Franc

LITERACY RATE: 59.9%

LIFE EXPECTANCY: 63.68 years

TIME ZONE: 0

TYPE OF GOVERNMENT: Semi-presidential Republic

HEAD OF STATE: President Umaro Sissoco Embalo **HEAD OF GOVT:** Prime Minister Nuno Gomes Nabiam

GDP PER CAPITA: $1,800

POPULATION: 2,026,778

ISD CODE: 245 **INTERNET TLD:** .gw

The capital's name 'Bissau' was added to the country's name in 1974, to prevent mix-ups with the neighbouring Republic of Guinea.

GUYANA

LOCATION: Central America

CAPITAL: Georgetown

AREA: 214,969 sq. km

LANGUAGES: English, indigenous languages

MAIN RELIGIONS: Christianity, Hinduism

CURRENCY: Guyanese Dollar

LITERACY RATE: 88.5%

LIFE EXPECTANCY: 71.87 years

TIME ZONE: –4

TYPE OF GOVERNMENT: Parliamentary Republic

HEAD OF STATE AND GOVT: President Mohamed Irfaan Ali

GDP PER CAPITA: $18,700

POPULATION: 789,683

ISD CODE: 592 **INTERNET TLD:** .gy

At 250.5 m (822 ft), the Kaieteur Falls is about twice the height of Victoria Falls on the border of Zambia and Zimbabwe.

HAITI

LOCATION: Central America

CAPITAL: Port-au-Prince

AREA: 27,750 sq. km

LANGUAGES: French, Creole

MAIN RELIGIONS: Christianity, Haitian Vodou

CURRENCY: Gourde

LITERACY RATE: 61.7%

LIFE EXPECTANCY: 65.95 years

TIME ZONE: –5

TYPE OF GOVERNMENT: Semi-presidential Republic

HEAD OF STATE AND GOVT: Acting President and Prime Minister Ariel Henry

GDP PER CAPITA: $2,800

POPULATION: 11,334,637

ISD CODE: 509 **INTERNET TLD:** .ht

Haiti is the only nation in the world whose independence was gained as part of a successful slave rebellion.

HONDURAS

LOCATION: Central America

CAPITAL: Tegucigalpa

AREA: 112,090 sq. km

LANGUAGE: Spanish

MAIN RELIGION: Christianity

CURRENCY: Lempira

LITERACY RATE: 88.5%

LIFE EXPECTANCY: 75.17 years

TIME ZONE: -6

TYPE OF GOVERNMENT: Presidential Republic

HEAD OF STATE AND GOVT: President Iris Xiomara Castro de Zelaya

GDP PER CAPITA: $5,100

POPULATION: 9,459,440

ISD CODE: 504 **INTERNET TLD:** .hn

The five stars on the flag stand for the five countries of Central America. Honduras is represented by the star in the middle because of its central geographical location.

Background: Hungary

HUNGARY

LOCATION: Central Europe

CAPITAL: Budapest

AREA: 93,028 sq. km

LANGUAGES: Hungarian, German

MAIN RELIGION: Christianity

CURRENCY: Forint

LITERACY RATE: 99.1%

LIFE EXPECTANCY: 77.2 years

TIME ZONE: +1

TYPE OF GOVERNMENT: Parliamentary Republic

HEAD OF STATE: President Katalin Novak **HEAD OF GOVT:** Prime Minister Viktor Orban

GDP PER CAPITA: $31,100

POPULATION: 9,699,577

ISD CODE: 36 **INTERNET TLD:** .hu

The country has a pre-approved set of names. If the desired name is not on the list, the parents must apply for it.

ICELAND

LOCATION: North Europe

CAPITAL: Reykjavik

AREA: 103,000 sq. km

LANGUAGES: Icelandic, English, German

MAIN RELIGION: Christianity

CURRENCY: Icelandic Krona

LITERACY RATE: 99%

LIFE EXPECTANCY: 83.4 years

TIME ZONE: 0

TYPE OF GOVERNMENT: Parliamentary Republic

HEAD OF STATE: President Gudni Thorlacius Johannesson

HEAD OF GOVT: Prime Minister Katrín Jakobsdottir

GDP PER CAPITA: $52,300

POPULATION: 357,603

ISD CODE: 354 **INTERNET TLD:** .is

Only one per cent of the land in Iceland is considered arable.

INDIA

LOCATION: South Asia

CAPITAL: New Delhi

AREA: 3,287,263 sq. km

LANGUAGES: Hindi, English and 21 other official languages

MAIN RELIGIONS: Hinduism, Islam, Sikhism, Christianity, Jainism, Buddhism

CURRENCY: Indian Rupee

LITERACY RATE: 74.4%

LIFE EXPECTANCY: 67.22 years

TIME ZONE: +5.30

TYPE OF GOVERNMENT: Federal Republic and Parliamentary Democracy

HEAD OF STATE: President Ram Nath Kovind **HEAD OF GOVT:** Prime Minister Narendra Modi

GDP PER CAPITA: $6,100

POPULATION: 1,3389,637,445

ISD CODE: 91 **INTERNET TLD:** .in

India has the third highest number of billionaires in the world, after USA and China.

Background: India

*2017 data

INDONESIA

LOCATION: South-East Asia

CAPITAL: Jakarta

AREA: 1,904,569 sq. km

LANGUAGE: Bahasa

MAIN RELIGION: Islam

CURRENCY: Indonesian Rupiah

LITERACY RATE: 96%

LIFE EXPECTANCY: 73.08 years

TIME ZONE: +7

TYPE OF GOVERNMENT: Presidential Republic

HEAD OF STATE AND GOVT: President Joko Widodo

GDP PER CAPITA: $11,400

POPULATION: 277,329,163

ISD CODE: 62 **INTERNET TLD:** .id

Indonesia comprises more than 17,000 islands, of which around 6,000 are inhabited.

IRAN

LOCATION: Middle East

CAPITAL: Tehran

AREA: 1,648,195 sq. km

LANGUAGES: Persian, Azerbaijani, Turkish

MAIN RELIGION: Islam

CURRENCY: Iranian Rial

LITERACY RATE: 85.5%

LIFE EXPECTANCY: 75.25 years

TIME ZONE: +3.30

TYPE OF GOVERNMENT: Theocratic Republic

HEAD OF STATE: Supreme Leader Ali Hosseini-Khamenei **HEAD OF GOVT:** President Ebrahim Raisi

GDP PER CAPITA: $12,400

POPULATION: 86,758,304

ISD CODE: 98 **INTERNET TLD:** .ir

Iran's proven oil reserves are the fourth largest in the world, after Venezuela, Saudi Arabia and Canada.

IRAQ

LOCATION: Middle East

CAPITAL: Baghdad

AREA: 438,317 sq. km

LANGUAGES: Arabic, Kurdish

MAIN RELIGION: Islam

CURRENCY: New Iraqi Dinar

LITERACY RATE: 85.6%

LIFE EXPECTANCY: 73.18 years

TIME ZONE: +3

TYPE OF GOVERNMENT: Federal Parliamentary Republic

HEAD OF STATE: President Barham Salih **HEAD OF GOVT:** Prime Minister Mustafa Al-Kadhimi

GDP PER CAPITA: $9,300

POPULATION: 40,462,701

ISD CODE: 964 **INTERNET TLD:** .iq

Oil exports account for about 95 per cent of Iraq's foreign exchange earnings.

Background: Ireland

IRELAND

LOCATION: West Europe

CAPITAL: Dublin

AREA: 70,273 sq. km

LANGUAGES: Gaelic, English

MAIN RELIGION: Christianity

CURRENCY: Euro

LITERACY RATE: 99%

LIFE EXPECTANCY: 81.66 years

TIME ZONE: 0

TYPE OF GOVERNMENT: Parliamentary Republic

HEAD OF STATE: President Michael D. Higgins **HEAD OF GOVT:** Prime Minister Micheal Martin

GDP PER CAPITA: $89,700

POPULATION: 5,275,004

ISD CODE: 353 **INTERNET TLD:** .ie

Irish surnames are well-known for beginning with Mac/Mc or 'O'. 'Mac' means 'son of' and 'O' means 'grandson of' in Gaelic.

ISRAEL

LOCATION: Middle East

CAPITAL: Jerusalem

AREA: 20,770 sq. km

LANGUAGES: Hebrew, English, Arabic

MAIN RELIGIONS: Judaism, Islam

CURRENCY: Israeli (New) Shekel

LITERACY RATE: 97.8%

LIFE EXPECTANCY: 83.35 years

TIME ZONE: +2

TYPE OF GOVERNMENT: Parliamentary Democracy

HEAD OF STATE: President Isaac Herzog **HEAD OF GOVT:** Prime Minister Yair Lapid

GDP PER CAPITA: $38,300

POPULATION: 8,914,885

ISD CODE: 972 **INTERNET TLD:** .il

Israeli banknotes have Braille on them to help visually challenged people identify them easily.

ITALY

LOCATION: Southern Europe

CAPITAL: Rome

AREA: 301,340 sq. km

LANGUAGE: Italian

MAIN RELIGION: Christianity

CURRENCY: Euro

LITERACY RATE: 99.2%

LIFE EXPECTANCY: 882.59 years

TIME ZONE: +1

TYPE OF GOVERNMENT: Parliamentary Republic

HEAD OF STATE: President Sergio Mattarella **HEAD OF GOVT:** Prime Minister Mario Draghi

GDP PER CAPITA: $39,000

POPULATION: 61,095,551

ISD CODE: 39 **INTERNET TLD:** .it

Most of the world's top sports cars – Ferrari, Lamborghini, Bugatti, Maserati and Alfa Romeo – are manufactured in Italy.

Background: Italy

JAMAICA

LOCATION: Central America

CAPITAL: Kingston

AREA: 10,991 sq. km

LANGUAGE: English

MAIN RELIGION: Christianity

CURRENCY: Jamaican Dollar

LITERACY RATE: 88.7%

LIFE EXPECTANCY: 75.75 years

TIME ZONE: –5

TYPE OF GOVERNMENT: Constitutional Monarchy and Parliamentary Democracy

HEAD OF STATE: Queen Elizabeth II
HEAD OF GOVT: Prime Minister Andrew Holness

GDP PER CAPITA: $8,700

POPULATION: 2,818,596

ISD CODE: 1-876 **INTERNET TLD:** .jm

Ian Fleming designed and built his home called 'Goldeneye' in Jamaica and wrote 10 James Bond novels there.

JAPAN

LOCATION: East Asia

CAPITAL: Tokyo

AREA: 377,915 sq. km

LANGUAGE: Japanese

MAIN RELIGIONS: Shintoism, Buddhism

CURRENCY: Yen

LITERACY RATE: 99%

LIFE EXPECTANCY: 84.83 years

TIME ZONE: +9

TYPE OF GOVERNMENT: Constitutional Monarchy and Parliamentary Government

HEAD OF STATE: Emperor Naruhito
HEAD OF GOVT: Prime Minister Fumio Kishida

GDP PER CAPITA: $41,400

POPULATION: 124,214,766

ISD CODE: 81 **INTERNET TLD:** .jp

Mt Fuji (3,776.2 m/12,389.2 ft), the tallest mountain in the country, is an active volcano.

JORDAN

LOCATION: Middle East

CAPITAL: Amman

AREA: 89,342 sq. km

LANGUAGES: Arabic, English

MAIN RELIGION: Islam

CURRENCY: Jordanian Dinar

LITERACY RATE: 98.2%

LIFE EXPECTANCY: 75.7 years

TIME ZONE: +2

TYPE OF GOVERNMENT: Parliamentary Constitutional Monarchy

HEAD OF STATE: King Abdullah II
HEAD OF GOVT: Prime Minister Bisher al-Khasawneh

GDP PER CAPITA: $9,800

POPULATION: 10,998,531

ISD CODE: 962 **INTERNET TLD:** .jo

The world's lowest point on dry land is the Dead Sea shore, shared by Israel and Jordan. It is 418 m/1,371 ft below sea level.

Background: Jordan

KAZAKHSTAN

LOCATION: Central Asia

CAPITAL: Astana

AREA: 2,724,900

LANGUAGES: Kazakh, Russian

MAIN RELIGIONS: Islam, Christianity

CURRENCY: Tenge

LITERACY RATE: 99.8%

LIFE EXPECTANCY: 72.2 years

TIME ZONE: +6

TYPE OF GOVERNMENT: Presidential Republic

HEAD OF STATE: President Kassym-Zhomart Tokayev **HEAD OF GOVT:** Prime Minister Alikhan Smailov

GDP PER CAPITA: $25,300

POPULATION: 19,245,793

ISD CODE: 7 **INTERNET TLD:** .kz

The Baikonur Cosmodrome is the world's oldest and largest (by area) space launch facility.

KENYA

LOCATION: East Africa

CAPITAL: Nairobi

AREA: 580,367 sq. km

LANGUAGES: English, Kiswahili

MAIN RELIGIONS: Christianity, Islam

CURRENCY: Kenyan Shilling

LITERACY RATE: 81.5%

LIFE EXPECTANCY: 67.69 years

TIME ZONE: +3

TYPE OF GOVERNMENT: Presidential Republic

HEAD OF STATE & GOVT: President Uhuru Kenyatta

GDP PER CAPITA: $4,200

POPULATION: 54,864,655

ISD CODE: 254 **INTERNET TLD:** .ke

Wangari Maathai, a social, environmental and political activist, and the first African woman to win a Nobel Peace prize, was Kenyan.

KIRIBATI

LOCATION: Oceania

CAPITAL: Tarawa

AREA: 811 sq. km

LANGUAGES: Kiribati, English

MAIN RELIGION: Christianity

CURRENCY: Australian Dollar

LITERACY RATE: 97.7%

LIFE EXPECTANCY: 67.9 years

TIME ZONE: +12

TYPE OF GOVERNMENT: Presidential Republic

HEAD OF STATE AND GOVT: President Taneti Mamau

GDP PER CAPITA: $2,300

POPULATION: 114,189

ISD CODE: 686 **INTERNET TLD:** .ki

It is the first country to celebrate new year since it is 14 hours ahead of GMT.

Background: Kazakhstan

KUWAIT

LOCATION: Middle East

CAPITAL: Kuwait City

AREA: 17,818 sq. km

LANGUAGES: Arabic

MAIN RELIGION: Islam

CURRENCY: Kuwaiti Dinar

LITERACY RATE: 96.5%

LIFE EXPECTANCY: 79.13 years

TIME ZONE: +3

TYPE OF GOVERNMENT: Constitutional Emirate

HEAD OF STATE: Sheikh Nawaf Al-Ahmad Al-Jaber Al-Sabah **HEAD OF GOVT:** Prime Minister Sheikh Ahmed Nawaf Al-Ahmed Al-Sabah

GDP PER CAPITA: $49,900

POPULATION: 3,068,115

ISD CODE: 965 **INTERNET TLD:** .kw

More than two-thirds of the people who reside in Kuwait do not hold Kuwaiti citizenship and cannot vote in parliamentary elections.

KYRGYZSTAN

LOCATION: Central Asia

CAPITAL: Bishkek

AREA: 199,951 sq. km

LANGUAGES: Kyrgyz, Uzbek, Russian

MAIN RELIGION: Islam

CURRENCY: Som

LITERACY RATE: 99.6%

LIFE EXPECTANCY: 72.75 years

TIME ZONE: +6

TYPE OF GOVERNMENT: Parliamentary Republic

HEAD OF STATE AND GOVT: President Sadyr Japarov

GDP PER CAPITA: $4,700

POPULATION: 6,071,750

ISD CODE: 996 **INTERNET TLD:** .kg

There are more than 88 major mountain ranges in Kyrgyzstan, which make up more than 70 per cent of the country's territory.

LAOS

LOCATION: South-East Asia

CAPITAL: Vientiane

AREA: 236,800 sq. km

LANGUAGES: Lao, French, English

MAIN RELIGION: Buddhism

CURRENCY: Kip

LITERACY RATE: 84.7%

LIFE EXPECTANCY: 68.15 years

TIME ZONE: +7

TYPE OF GOVERNMENT: Communist/Single-party Republic

HEAD OF STATE: President Thongloun Sisoulith **HEAD OF GOVT:** Prime Minister Phankham Viphavanh

GDP PER CAPITA: $7,800

POPULATION: 7,749,595

ISD CODE: 856 **INTERNET TLD:** .la

In Laos, the country is known as Sathalanalat Paxathipatai Paxaxon Lao.

Background: Latvia

LATVIA

LOCATION: Eastern Europe

CAPITAL: Riga

AREA: 64,589 sq. km

LANGUAGES: Latvian, Russian

MAIN RELIGION: Christianity

CURRENCY: Euro

LITERACY RATE: 99.9%

LIFE EXPECTANCY: 75.91 years

TIME ZONE: +2

TYPE OF GOVERNMENT: Parliamentary Republic

HEAD OF STATE: President Egils Levits **HEAD OF GOVT:** Prime Minister Krisjanis Karins

GDP PER CAPITA: $29,900

POPULATION: 1,842,226

ISD CODE: 371 **INTERNET TLD:** .lv

Tourists can visit the Karosta Prison Hotel in Liepaja, which is a former military jail, for a prison experience, including interrogation and a night stay in a cold cell.

LEBANON

LOCATION: Middle East

CAPITAL: Beirut

AREA: 10,400 sq. km

LANGUAGES: Arabic, French, English

MAIN RELIGIONS: Islam, Christianity

CURRENCY: Lebanese Pound

LITERACY RATE: 95.1%

LIFE EXPECTANCY: 78.76 years

TIME ZONE: +2

TYPE OF GOVERNMENT: Parliamentary Republic

HEAD OF STATE: President Michel Aoun **HEAD OF GOVT:** Prime Minister Najib Mikati

GDP PER CAPITA: $11,600

POPULATION: 5,296,814

ISD CODE: 961 **INTERNET TLD:** .lb

Lebanon is the only country in the Middle East that does not have even a patch of desert.

LESOTHO

LOCATION: Southern Africa

CAPITAL: Maseru

AREA: 30,355 sq. km

LANGUAGES: Sesotho, English

MAIN RELIGION: Christianity

CURRENCY: Loti

LITERACY RATE: 79.4%

LIFE EXPECTANCY: 59.57 years

TIME ZONE: +2

TYPE OF GOVERNMENT: Parliamentary Constitutional Monarchy

HEAD OF STATE: King Letsie III **HEAD OF GOVT:** Prime Minister Moeketsi Majoro

GDP PER CAPITA: $2,300

POPULATION: 2,193,970

ISD CODE: 266 **INTERNET TLD:** .ls

Lesotho is the only country that lies entirely 1,500 m (4,920 ft) above sea level. Villages can only be reached by riding horses, trekking, or by a light aircraft.

LIBERIA

LOCATION: West Africa

CAPITAL: Monrovia

AREA: 111,369 sq. km

LANGUAGES: English, ethnic languages

MAIN RELIGIONS: Indigenous faiths, Christianity, Islam

CURRENCY: Liberian Dollar

LITERACY RATE: 48.3%

LIFE EXPECTANCY: 65.45 years

TIME ZONE: 0

TYPE OF GOVERNMENT: Presidential Republic

HEAD OF STATE AND GOVT: President George Weah

GDP PER CAPITA: $1,400

POPULATION: 5,358,483

ISD CODE: 231 **INTERNET TLD:** .lr

Liberia was founded by freed people of colour from the USA.

LIBYA

LOCATION: North Africa

CAPITAL: Tripoli

AREA: 1,759,540

LANGUAGES: Arabic, Italian, English

MAIN RELIGION: Islam

CURRENCY: Libyan Dinar

LITERACY RATE: 91%

LIFE EXPECTANCY: 77.18 years

TIME ZONE: +2

TYPE OF GOVERNMENT: Transitional

HEAD OF STATE: Chairman, Presidential Council: Mohammed Al Menfi **HEAD OF GOVT:** Interim Prime Minister Abdul Hamid Mohammed Dbeibah

GDP PER CAPITA: $10,300

POPULATION: 7,137,931

ISD CODE: 218 **INTERNET TLD:** .ly

95 per cent of Libya is covered by the Sahara desert. It is very arid, and in some places it rains only once in 10 or more years.

LIECHTENSTEIN

LOCATION: Central Europe

CAPITAL: Vaduz

AREA: 160 sq. km

LANGUAGE: German

MAIN RELIGION: Christianity

CURRENCY: Swiss Franc

LITERACY RATE: 99%

LIFE EXPECTANCY: 82.56 years

TIME ZONE: +1

TYPE OF GOVERNMENT: Constitutional Monarchy

HEAD OF STATE: Prince Hans Adam II

HEAD OF GOVT: Prime Minister Daniel Risch

GDP PER CAPITA: $171,254

POPULATION: 39,711

ISD CODE: 423 **INTERNET TLD:** .li

Liechtenstein has no airport. The closest airport is in Zurich in Switzerland.

Background: Liechtenstein

LITHUANIA

LOCATION: East Europe

CAPITAL: Vilnius

AREA: 65,300 sq. km

LANGUAGES: Lithuanian, Russian

MAIN RELIGION: Christianity

CURRENCY: Euro

LITERACY RATE: 99.8%

LIFE EXPECTANCY: 75.78 years

TIME ZONE: +2

TYPE OF GOVERNMENT: Semi-presidential Republic

HEAD OF STATE: President Gitanas Nauseda **HEAD OF GOVT:** Prime Minister Ingrida Simonyte

GDP PER CAPITA: $36,700

POPULATION: 2,683,546

ISD CODE: 370 **INTERNET TLD:** .lt

Lithuania was the first Soviet Republic to declare independence from the USSR.

LUXEMBOURG

LOCATION: West Europe

CAPITAL: Luxembourg City

AREA: 2,586 sq. km

LANGUAGES: Luxembourgish, French, German, Portuguese

MAIN RELIGION: Christianity

CURRENCY: Euro

LITERACY RATE: 100%

LIFE EXPECTANCY: 82.98 years

TIME ZONE: +1

TYPE OF GOVERNMENT: Constitutional Monarchy

HEAD OF STATE: Grand Duke Henri **HEAD OF GOVT:** Prime Minister Xavier Bettel

GDP PER CAPITA: $110,300

POPULATION: 650,364

ISD CODE: 352 **INTERNET TLD:** .lu

Luxembourg is one of the founding members of the European Union, NATO and the United Nations.

MADAGASCAR

LOCATION: Southern African coast

CAPITAL: Antananarivo

AREA: 587,041 sq. km

LANGUAGES: Malagasy, English, French

MAIN RELIGIONS: Indigenous faiths, Christianity, Islam

CURRENCY: Malagasy Ariary

LITERACY RATE: 76.77%

LIFE EXPECTANCY: 68.17 years

TIME ZONE: +3

TYPE OF GOVERNMENT: Semi-presidential Republic

HEAD OF STATE: President Andry Nirina Rajoelina **HEAD OF GOVT:** Prime Minister Christian Ntsay

GDP PER CAPITA: $1,500

POPULATION: 28,172,462

ISD CODE: 261 **INTERNET TLD:** .mg

Madagascar is also known as the Red Island because in many areas the soil has a distinct reddish tint.

MALAWI

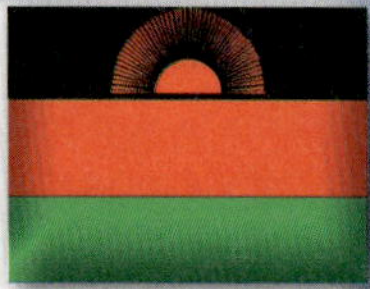

LOCATION: Southern Africa

CAPITAL: Lilongwe

AREA: 118,484 sq. km

LANGUAGES: Chichewa, Chinyanja

MAIN RELIGIONS: Christianity, Islam

CURRENCY: Malawian Kwacha

LITERACY RATE: 62.1%

LIFE EXPECTANCY: 72.44 years

TIME ZONE: +2

TYPE OF GOVERNMENT: Presidential Republic

HEAD OF STATE AND GOVT: President Lazarus Chakwera

GDP PER CAPITA: $1,500

POPULATION: 20,794,353

ISD CODE: 265 **INTERNET TLD:** .mw

Lake Malawi, from which the country gets its name, is also called the 'Calendar Lake' since it is about 365 miles (number of days in a year) (587.4 km) long and 52 miles (number of weeks in a year) (83.7 km) wide.

MALAYSIA

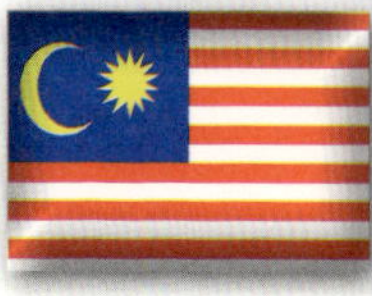

LOCATION: South-East Asia

CAPITAL: Kuala Lumpur

AREA: 329,847 sq. km

LANGUAGES: Bahasa Malaysia (Malay), English, Chinese

MAIN RELIGIONS: Islam, Buddhism

CURRENCY: Ringgit

LITERACY RATE: 95%

LIFE EXPECTANCY: 76.13 years

TIME ZONE: +8

TYPE OF GOVERNMENT: Federal Constitutional Monarchy

HEAD OF STATE: King Abdullah Sultan Ahmad Shah **HEAD OF GOVT:** Prime Minister Ismail Sabri Yaakob

GDP PER CAPITA: $26,400

POPULATION: 33,519,406

ISD CODE: 60 **INTERNET TLD:** .my

The world's largest flower, the Rafflesia (1 m/3.3 ft in diameter), is found here.

(THE) MALDIVES

LOCATION: South-East Asia

CAPITAL: Male

AREA: 298 sq. km

LANGUAGES: Dhivehi, English

MAIN RELIGION: Islam

CURRENCY: Rufiyaa

LITERACY RATE: 97.7%

LIFE EXPECTANCY: 76.94 years

TIME ZONE: +5

TYPE OF GOVERNMENT: Presidential Republic

HEAD OF STATE AND GOVT: President Ibrahim Mohamed Solih

GDP PER CAPITA: $13,000

POPULATION: 390,164

ISD CODE: 960 **INTERNET TLD:** .mv

In 2009, Maldives became the world's first country to hold an official presidential cabinet meeting underwater.

MALI

LOCATION: West Africa

CAPITAL: Bamako

AREA: 1,240,192 sq. km

LANGUAGES: Bambara, French

MAIN RELIGION: Islam

CURRENCY: CFA Franc

LITERACY RATE: 35.5%

LIFE EXPECTANCY: 62.41 years

TIME ZONE: 0

TYPE OF GOVERNMENT: Semi-presidential Republic

HEAD OF STATE: Transitional President Colonel Assimi Goita **HEAD OF GOVT:** Transitional Prime Minister Choguel Maiga

GDP PER CAPITA: $2,322

POPULATION: 20,741,769

ISD CODE: 223 **INTERNET TLD:** .ml

Gao in Mali is where the equator divides the world into eastern and western hemispheres.

MALTA

LOCATION: Southern Europe

CAPITAL: Valletta

AREA: 316 sq. km

LANGUAGES: Maltese, English

MAIN RELIGION: Christianity

CURRENCY: Euro

LITERACY RATE: 94.5%

LIFE EXPECTANCY: 83.2 years

TIME ZONE: +1

TYPE OF GOVERNMENT: Parliamentary Republic

HEAD OF STATE: President George Vella **HEAD OF GOVT:** Prime Minister Robert Abela

GDP PER CAPITA: $39,200

POPULATION: 460,891

ISD CODE: 356 **INTERNET TLD:** .mt

Malta was known as 'Melita', meaning 'the island of honey', by ancient Greeks and Romans.

MARSHALL ISLANDS

LOCATION: Northern Pacific Ocean

CAPITAL: Majuro

AREA: 181 sq. km

LANGUAGES: Marshallese, English

MAIN RELIGION: Christianity

CURRENCY: US Dollar

LITERACY RATE: 98.3%

LIFE EXPECTANCY: 74.65 years

TIME ZONE: +12

TYPE OF GOVERNMENT: Mixed Presidential Parliamentary Republic

HEAD OF STATE AND GOVT: President Hilda David Kabua

GDP PER CAPITA: $4,000

POPULATION: 79,906

ISD CODE: 692 **INTERNET TLD:** .mh

Almost 2,000,000 sq. km of ocean was declared a shark sanctuary here in 2011. It is the largest shark sanctuary in the world.

MAURITANIA

LOCATION: Western Africa

CAPITAL: Nouakchott

AREA: 1,030,700 sq. km

LANGUAGES: Arabic, Pulaar

MAIN RELIGION: Islam

CURRENCY: Ouguiya

LITERACY RATE: 53.5%

LIFE EXPECTANCY: 65.22 years

TIME ZONE: 0

TYPE OF GOVERNMENT: Presidential Republic

HEAD OF STATE: President Mohamed Ould Ghazouani **HEAD OF GOVT:** Prime Minister Mohamed Ould Bilal

GDP PER CAPITA: $5,000

POPULATION: 4,161,925

ISD CODE: 222 **INTERNET TLD:** .mr

If you look at Mauritania from space, you can see a clear bull's eye-like geological feature, which is 50 km across, called 'The Eye of Africa.'

MAURITIUS

LOCATION: Indian Ocean

CAPITAL: Port Louis

AREA: 2,040 sq. km

LANGUAGES: Creole, French, Bhojpuri, English

MAIN RELIGIONS: Hinduism, Christianity, Islam

CURRENCY: Mauritian Rupee

LITERACY RATE: 91.3%

LIFE EXPECTANCY: 74.86 years

TIME ZONE: +4

TYPE OF GOVERNMENT: Parliamentary Republic

HEAD OF STATE: President Prithvirajsing Roopun **HEAD OF GOVT:** Prime Minister Pravind Kumar Jugnauth

GDP PER CAPITA: $19,500

POPULATION: 1,308,222

ISD CODE: 230 **INTERNET TLD:** .mu

Inspired by the dodo, an extinct bird once endemic to Mauritius, Lewis Carroll wrote the book *Alice's Adventures in Wonderland* in 1865.

MEXICO

LOCATION: North America

CAPITAL: Mexico City

AREA: 1,964,375 sq. km

LANGUAGE: Spanish

MAIN RELIGION: Christianity

CURRENCY: Mexican Peso

LITERACY RATE: 95.2%

LIFE EXPECTANCY: 72.32 years

TIME ZONE: –6

TYPE OF GOVERNMENT: Federal Presidential Republic

HEAD OF STATE AND GOVT: President Andres Manuel Lopez Obrador

GDP PER CAPITA: $17,900

POPULATION: 129,150,371

ISD CODE: 52 **INTERNET TLD:** .mx

Mexico City is sinking at the rate of 15–20 cm a year because it is built on an aquifer.

MICRONESIA

LOCATION: Island group in the North Pacific Ocean

CAPITAL: Palikir

AREA: 702 sq. km

LANGUAGE: English

MAIN RELIGION: Christianity

CURRENCY: US Dollar

LITERACY RATE: 98.8%

LIFE EXPECTANCY: 74.44 years

TIME ZONE: +11

TYPE OF GOVERNMENT: Federal Presidential Republic

HEAD OF STATE AND GOVT: President David W. Panuelo

GDP PER CAPITA: $3,500

POPULATION: 101,009

ISD CODE: 691 **INTERNET TLD:** .fm

Micronesia houses the ruins of Nan Madol, an artificial group of islands connected by canals built in the eighth or ninth century CE. This gives it the name 'Venice of the Pacific'.

MOLDOVA

LOCATION: East Europe

CAPITAL: Chisinau

AREA: 33,851 sq. km

LANGUAGES: Moldovan, Russian

MAIN RELIGION: Christianity

CURRENCY: Moldovan Leu

LITERACY RATE: 99.4%

LIFE EXPECTANCY: 72.44 years

TIME ZONE: +2

TYPE OF GOVERNMENT: Parliamentary Republic

HEAD OF STATE: President Maia Sandu
HEAD OF GOVT: Prime Minister Natalia Gavrilita

GDP PER CAPITA: $12,300

POPULATION: 3,287,326

ISD CODE: 372 **INTERNET TLD:** .md

Emil Racovita, a cave in Criva, Moldova, is among the largest caves in the world. There are 20 underground lakes inside the cave.

MONACO

LOCATION: West Europe

CAPITAL: Monaco

AREA: 2 sq. km

LANGUAGES: French, English, Italian

MAIN RELIGION: Christianity

CURRENCY: Euro

LITERACY RATE: 99%

LIFE EXPECTANCY: 89.52 years

TIME ZONE: +1

TYPE OF GOVERNMENT: Constitutional Monarchy

HEAD OF STATE: Prince Albert II **HEAD OF GOVT:** Minister of State Pierre Dartout

GDP PER CAPITA: $115,400

POPULATION: 31,223

ISD CODE: 377 **INTERNET TLD:** .mc

It takes an hour for an average person to walk the width of the entire country.

Background: Mexico

MONGOLIA

LOCATION: North Asia

CAPITAL: Ulaanbaatar

AREA: 1,564,116 sq. km

LANGUAGE: Mongol

MAIN RELIGIONS: Buddhism, Christianity, Islam

CURRENCY: Togrog/Tugrik

LITERACY RATE: 99.2%

LIFE EXPECTANCY: 71.37 years

TIME ZONE: +8

TYPE OF GOVERNMENT: Semi-presidential Republic

HEAD OF STATE: President Ukhnaagiin Khurelsukh **HEAD OF GOVT:** Prime Minister Luvsannamsrai Oyun-Erdene

GDP PER CAPITA: $11,500

POPULATION: 3,227,863

ISD CODE: 976 **INTERNET TLD:** .mn

Fossilized dinosaur remains and the first dinosaur eggs were found in the Gobi Desert in Mongolia in the 1920s.

MONTENEGRO

LOCATION: South-eastern Europe

CAPITAL: Podgorica

AREA: 13,812 sq. km

LANGUAGES: Montenegrin, Serbian

MAIN RELIGIONS: Islam, Christianity

CURRENCY: Euro

LITERACY RATE: 98.8%

LIFE EXPECTANCY: 77.75 years

TIME ZONE: +1

TYPE OF GOVERNMENT: Parliamentary Republic

HEAD OF STATE: President Milo Dukanovic **HEAD OF GOVT:** Prime Minister Dritan Abazovic

GDP PER CAPITA: $18,300

POPULATION: 604,966

ISD CODE: 382 **INTERNET TLD:** .me

The name Montenegro, meaning 'Black Mountain', was probably derived from the thick 'black' forests that covered Mount Lovcen, the highest point in Montenegro in medieval times.

MOROCCO

LOCATION: North Africa

CAPITAL: Rabat

AREA: 446,550 sq. km

LANGUAGE: Arabic

MAIN RELIGION: Islam

CURRENCY: Moroccan Dirham

LITERACY RATE: 73.8%

LIFE EXPECTANCY: 73.68 years

TIME ZONE: 0

TYPE OF GOVERNMENT: Parliamentary Constitutional Monarchy

HEAD OF STATE: King Mohammed VI
HEAD OF GOVT: Prime Minister Aziz Akhannouch

GDP PER CAPITA: $6,800

POPULATION: 36,738,229

ISD CODE: 212 **INTERNET TLD:** .ma

Morocco is often called the 'Oasis of the Senses'. From the Sahara Desert to the snow-capped Atlas Mountains, the country's landscape is very diverse.

Background: Mongolia

MOZAMBIQUE

LOCATION: South-eastern Africa

CAPITAL: Maputo

AREA: 799,380 sq. km

LANGUAGES: Makhuwa, Portuguese

MAIN RELIGIONS: Christianity, Islam

CURRENCY: Metical

LITERACY RATE: 60.7%

LIFE EXPECTANCY: 51.1 years

TIME ZONE: +2

TYPE OF GOVERNMENT: Presidential Republic

HEAD OF STATE AND GOVT: President Filipe Nyusi; Prime Minister Carlos Agostinho do Rosario chairs the Council of Ministers.

GDP PER CAPITA: $1,200

POPULATION: 31,693,239

ISD CODE: 258 **INTERNET TLD:** .mz

Mozambique has won two Olympic medals, both won by Maria de Lurdes Mutola (nicknamed 'Maputo Express') in the women's 800 m – a bronze in 1996 and a gold in 2000.

MYANMAR

LOCATION: South-East Asia

CAPITAL: Naypyidaw

AREA: 676,578 sq. km

LANGUAGE: Burmese

MAIN RELIGION: Buddhism

CURRENCY: Kyat

LITERACY RATE: 75.6%

LIFE EXPECTANCY: 69.6 years

TIME ZONE: +6.5

TYPE OF GOVERNMENT: Parliamentary Republic (currently military regime)

HEAD OF STATE AND GOVT: Prime Minister Senior General Min Aung Hlaing

GDP PER CAPITA: $4,500

POPULATION: 57,526,499

ISD CODE: 95 **INTERNET TLD:** .mm

In 2005, the capital of Myanmar was shifted from Yangon to Naypyidaw.

NAMIBIA

LOCATION: Southern Africa

CAPITAL: Windhoek

AREA: 824,292 sq. km

LANGUAGES: English, Afrikaans

MAIN RELIGION: Christianity

CURRENCY: Namibian Dollar

LITERACY RATE: 91.5%

LIFE EXPECTANCY: 66.47 years

TIME ZONE: +1

TYPE OF GOVERNMENT: Presidential Republic

HEAD OF STATE AND GOVT: President Hage Geingob

GDP PER CAPITA: $8,900

POPULATION: 2,678,191

ISD CODE: 264 **INTERNET TLD:** .na

One in four households in Namibia lives in poverty. The wealthiest 10 per cent of people command more than half the country's income.

Background: Namibia

NAURU

LOCATION: South Pacific Ocean

CAPITAL: No officially designated capital; Yaren is the largest city

AREA: 21 sq. km

LANGUAGES: Nauruan, English

MAIN RELIGION: Christianity

CURRENCY: Australian Dollar

LITERACY RATE: 98%

LIFE EXPECTANCY: 67.93 years

TIME ZONE: +12

TYPE OF GOVERNMENT: Parliamentary Republic

HEAD OF STATE AND GOVT: President Lionel Aingimea

GDP PER CAPITA: $13,500

POPULATION: 9,811

ISD CODE: 674 **INTERNET TLD:** .nr

Nauru is the world's smallest island nation. It is the only republican state in the world without an official capital.

NEPAL

LOCATION: South Asia

CAPITAL: Kathmandu

AREA: 147,181 sq. km

LANGUAGE: Nepali

MAIN RELIGION: Hinduism

CURRENCY: Nepalese Rupee

LITERACY RATE: 67.9%

LIFE EXPECTANCY: 72.4 years

TIME ZONE: +5.45

TYPE OF GOVERNMENT: Federal Democratic Republic

HEAD OF STATE: President Bidya Devi Bhandari **HEAD OF GOVT:** Prime Minister Sher Bahadur Deuba

GDP PER CAPITA: $3,800

POPULATION: 30,666,598

ISD CODE: 977 **INTERNET TLD:** .np

Nepal's flag is the only national flag in the world that is neither a rectangle nor a square.

(THE) NETHERLANDS

LOCATION: North-western Europe

CAPITAL: Amsterdam

AREA: 41,543 sq. km

LANGUAGES: Dutch, Frisian

MAIN RELIGION: Christianity

CURRENCY: Euro

LITERACY RATE: 99%

LIFE EXPECTANCY: 82.16 years

TIME ZONE: +1

TYPE OF GOVERNMENT: Parliamentary Constitutional Monarchy

HEAD OF STATE: King Willem-Alexander **HEAD OF GOVT:** Prime Minister Mark Rutte

GDP PER CAPITA: $54,200

POPULATION: 17,3400,824

ISD CODE: 31 **INTERNET TLD:** .nl

The country's landscape is dotted with windmills, a famous hallmark. There are as many as 300 castles open to the general public.

NEW ZEALAND

LOCATION: South-western Pacific Ocean

CAPITAL: Wellington

AREA: 267,710 sq. km

LANGUAGE: English

MAIN RELIGION: Christianity

CURRENCY: New Zealand Dollar

LITEACY RATE: 99%

LIFE EXPECTANCY: 82.54 years

TIME ZONE: +12

TYPE OF GOVERNMENT: Constitutional Monarchy and Parliamentary Democracy

HEAD OF STATE: Queen Elizabeth II

HEAD OF GOVT: Prime Minister Jacinda Ardern

GDP PER CAPITA: $42,8400

POPULATION: 4,991,442

ISD CODE: 64 **INTERNET TLD:** .nz

With 2.5 million cars for four million people (including children), the car ownership percentage in New Zealand is one of the world's highest.

NICARAGUA

LOCATION: Central America

CAPITAL: Managua

AREA: 130,370 sq. km

LANGUAGE: Spanish

MAIN RELIGION: Christianity

CURRENCY: Cordoba

LITERACY RATE: 82.6%

LIFE EXPECTANCY: 74.78years

TIME ZONE: –6

TYPE OF GOVERNMENT: Presidential Republic

HEAD OF STATE AND GOVT: President Jose Daniel Ortega Saavedra

GDP PER CAPITA: $5,300

POPULATION: 6,301,880

ISD CODE: 505 **INTERNET TLD:** .ni

Nicaragua is famous for its dance form known as 'Palo de Mayo'. The country's most popular sport is baseball.

NIGER

LOCATION: West Africa

CAPITAL: Niamey

AREA: 1,267,000 sq. km

LANGUAGES: French, Hausa, Djerma

MAIN RELIGION: Islam

CURRENCY: CFA Franc

LITERACY RATE: 35.1%

LIFE EXPECTANCY: 60.09 years

TIME ZONE: +1

TYPE OF GOVERNMENT: Semi-presidential Republic

HEAD OF STATE: President Mohamed Bazoum **HEAD OF GOVT:** Prime Minister Ouhoumoudou Mahamadou

GDP PER CAPITA: $1,200

POPULATION: 24,484,587

ISD CODE: 227 **INTERNET TLD:** .ne

The remains of the dinosaur *Nigersaurus*, known for its long neck and hammerhead skull, were discovered in Niger in the 1950s.

Background: Netherlands

NIGERIA

LOCATION: West Africa

CAPITAL: Abuja

AREA: 923,769 sq. km

LANGUAGES: English, Hausa

MAIN RELIGIONS: Islam, Christianity

CURRENCY: Naira

LITERACY RATE: 62%

LIFE EXPECTANCY: 61.33 years

TIME ZONE: +1

TYPE OF GOVERNMENT: Presidential Federal Republic

HEAD OF STATE AND GOVT: President Muhammadu Buhari

GDP PER CAPITA: $4,900

POPULATION: 225,082,083

ISD CODE: 234 **INTERNET TLD:** .ng

Football is the national sport of Nigeria. The national team is called the 'Super Eagles'. They have made it to the World Cup Finals five times.

NORTH KOREA

LOCATION: East Asia

CAPITAL: Pyongyang

AREA: 120,540 sq. km

LANGUAGE: Korean

MAIN RELIGIONS: Officially atheist; Buddhism, Chondogyo, Christianity

CURRENCY: Won

LITERACY RATE: 100%

LIFE EXPECTANCY: 71.77 years

TIME ZONE: +9

TYPE OF GOVERNMENT: Communist Dictatorship

HEAD OF STATE: Chairman Kim Jong-un **HEAD OF GOVT:** Supreme People's Assembly President Choe Ryong-hae

GDP PER CAPITA: $1,700

POPULATION: 25,955,138

ISD CODE: 850 **INTERNET TLD:** .kp

The old name for North Korea is Joseon or Choson (Land of Morning Calm).

NORTH MACEDONIA

LOCATION: South-eastern Europe

CAPITAL: Skopje

AREA: 25,713 sq. km

LANGUAGES: Macedonian, Albanian

MAIN RELIGIONS: Christianity (Macedonian Orthodox Church), Islam

CURRENCY: Macedonian Dinar

LITERACY RATE: 98.4%

LIFE EXPECTANCY: 76.84 years

TIME ZONE: +1

TYPE OF GOVERNMENT: Parliamentary Republic

HEAD OF STATE: President Stevo Pendarovski **HEAD OF GOVT:** Prime Minister Dimitar Kovacevski

GDP PER CAPITA: $15,800

POPULATION: 2,130,936

ISD CODE: 389 **INTERNET TLD:** .mk

Macedonia was formerly a part of Yugoslavia and gained independence in 1991.

Background: Nigeria

NORWAY

LOCATION: Northern Europe

CAPITAL: Oslo

AREA: 385,207 sq. km

LANGUAGE: Norwegian

MAIN RELIGION: Christianity

CURRENCY: Norwegian Kroner

LITERACY RATE: 100%

LIFE EXPECTANCY: 82.55 years

TIME ZONE: +1

TYPE OF GOVERNMENT: Parliamentary Constitutional Monarchy

HEAD OF STATE: King Harald V
HEAD OF GOVT: Prime Minister Jonas Gahr Store

GDP PER CAPITA: $63,300

POPULATION: 5,553,840

ISD CODE: 47 **INTERNET TLD:** .no

The Nobel Peace Prize is awarded in Oslo. The Norwegian king is present at the award ceremony.

OMAN

LOCATION: Middle East

CAPITAL: Muscat

AREA: 309,500 sq. km

LANGUAGES: Arabic, English, Urdu

MAIN RELIGION: Islam

CURRENCY: Omani Rial

LITERACY RATE: 95.7%

LIFE EXPECTANCY: 76.6 years

TIME ZONE: +4

TYPE OF GOVERNMENT: Absolute Monarchy

HEAD OF STATE AND GOVT: Sultan Haitham bin Tariq Al Said

GDP PER CAPITA: $27,300

POPULATION: 3,764,348

ISD CODE: 968 **INTERNET TLD:** .om

The leaves of the *Myrtus communis* or the 'Yas' shrub found in Oman are used for making perfume.

PAKISTAN

LOCATION: South Asia

CAPITAL: Islamabad

AREA: 881,913 sq. km

LANGUAGES: Urdu, Punjabi, Sindhi

MAIN RELIGION: Islam

CURRENCY: Pakistani Rupee

LITERACY RATE: 58%

LIFE EXPECTANCY: 69.7 years

TIME ZONE: +5

TYPE OF GOVERNMENT: Federal Parliamentary Republic

HEAD OF STATE: President Arif Alvi
HEAD OF GOVT: Prime Minister Shehbaz Sharif

GDP PER CAPITA: $4,600

POPULATION: 242,923,845

ISD CODE: 92 **INTERNET TLD:** .pk

Pakistan's national flower is the common jasmine.

Background: Oman

PALAU

LOCATION: Group of islands in the North Pacific Ocean

CAPITAL: Melekeok

AREA: 459 sq. km

LANGUAGES: Palauan, Filipino, English

MAIN RELIGION: Christianity

CURRENCY: US Dollar

LITERACY RATE: 96.6%

LIFE EXPECTANCY: 74.64 years

TIME ZONE: +9

TYPE OF GOVERNMENT: Presidential Republic

HEAD OF STATE AND GOVT: President Surangel Whipps, Jr

GDP PER CAPITA: $17,600

POPULATION: 21,613

ISD CODE: 680 **INTERNET TLD:** .pw

In 1783, Palau was accidentally discovered by the shipwrecked crew of Captain Henry Wilson when he reached the shores of an island called Ulong.

PANAMA

LOCATION: Central America

CAPITAL: Panama City

AREA: 75,417 sq. km

LANGUAGE: Spanish

MAIN RELIGION: Christianity

CURRENCY: Balboa, US Dollar

LITERACY RATE: 95.7%

LIFE EXPECTANCY: 77.62 years

TIME ZONE: –5

TYPE OF GOVERNMENT: Presidential Republic

HEAD OF STATE AND GOVT: President Laurentino Cortizo Cohen

GDP PER CAPITA: $25,400

POPULATION: 4,337,768

ISD CODE: 507 **INTERNET TLD:** .pa

The currency of Panama is named after Vasco Nunez de Balboa, the Spanish explorer who was the first to cross the Isthmus of Panama to the Pacific Ocean in 1513.

PAPUA NEW GUINEA

LOCATION: Between the Coral Sea and the South Pacific Ocean

CAPITAL: Port Moresby

AREA: 462,840 sq. km

LANGUAGES: Tok Pisin, English, Hiri Motu

MAIN RELIGION: Christianity

CURRENCY: Kina

LITERACY RATE: 64.2%

LIFE EXPECTANCY: 69.43 years

TIME ZONE: +11

TYPE OF GOVERNMENT: Constitutional Monarchy and Parliamentary Democracy

HEAD OF STATE: Queen Elizabeth II

HEAD OF GOVT: Prime Minister James Marape

GDP PER CAPITA: $4,100

POPULATION: 9,593,498

ISD CODE: 675 **INTERNET TLD:** .pg

Seashells were the national currency of Papua New Guinea until 1933.

PARAGUAY

LOCATION: Central South America

CAPITAL: Asuncion

AREA: 406,757 sq. km

LANGUAGES: Spanish, Guarani

MAIN RELIGION: Christianity

CURRENCY: Guarani

LITERACY RATE: 94%

LIFE EXPECTANCY: 78.37 years

TIME ZONE: –4

TYPE OF GOVERNMENT: Presidential Republic

HEAD OF STATE AND GOVT: President Mario Abdo Benitez

GDP PER CAPITA: $12,300

POPULATION: 7,356,409

ISD CODE: 595 **INTERNET TLD:** .py

Due to its central location in South America, Paraguay is sometimes referred to as *Corazon de America*, or the Heart of America.

PERU

LOCATION: Western South America

CAPITAL: Lima

AREA: 1,285,216 sq. km

LANGUAGES: Spanish, Quechua

MAIN RELIGION: Christianity

CURRENCY: Nuevo Sol

LITERACY RATE: 94.4%

LIFE EXPECTANCY: 68.94 years

TIME ZONE: –5

TYPE OF GOVERNMENT: Unitary Presidential Republic

HEAD OF STATE AND GOVT: President Jose Pedro Castillo Terrones

GDP PER CAPITA: $12,848

POPULATION: 32,201,224

ISD CODE: 51 **INTERNET TLD:** .pe

There are as many as 3,000-4,000 varieties of potato grown in Peru.

(THE) PHILIPPINES

LOCATION: South-east Asia

CAPITAL: Manila

AREA: 300,000 sq. km

LANGUAGES: Filipino, English

MAIN RELIGION: Christianity

CURRENCY: Philippine Peso

LITERACY RATE: 96.3%

LIFE EXPECTANCY: 70.14 years

TIME ZONE: +8

TYPE OF GOVERNMENT: Presidential Republic

HEAD OF STATE AND GOVT: President Bongbong Marcos

GDP PER CAPITA: $8,000

POPULATION: 114,597,229

ISD CODE: 63 **INTERNET TLD:** .ph

There are more than 200 volcanoes on the islands of the Philippines, though only a few are active.

Background: Peru

POLAND

LOCATION: Central Europe

CAPITAL: Warsaw

AREA: 312,696 sq. km

LANGUAGE: Polish

MAIN RELIGION: Christianity

CURRENCY: Zloty

LITERACY RATE: 99.8%

LIFE EXPECTANCY: 78.76 years

TIME ZONE: +1

TYPE OF GOVERNMENT: Parliamentary Republic

HEAD OF STATE: President Andrzej Duda **HEAD OF GOVT:** Prime Minister Mateusz Morawiecki

GDP PER CAPITA: $32,200

POPULATION: 38,093,101

ISD CODE: 48 **INTERNET TLD:** .pl

The Poles consider their name-days more important than their birthdays. Name-days are days of the year on which certain Christian saints are honoured. All those who share the name of the saint celebrate the day.

PORTUGAL

LOCATION: South-western Europe

CAPITAL: Lisbon

AREA: 92,212 sq. km

LANGUAGES: Portuguese

MAIN RELIGION: Christianity

CURRENCY: Euro

LITERACY RATE: 96.1%

LIFE EXPECTANCY: 81.5 years

TIME ZONE: 0

TYPE OF GOVERNMENT: Semi-presidential Republic

HEAD OF STATE: President Marcelo Rebelo de Sousa **HEAD OF GOVT:** Prime Minister Antonio Luis Santosa da Costa

GDP PER CAPITA: $28,800

POPULATION: 10,2242,081

ISD CODE: 351 **INTERNET TLD:** .pt

Ferdinand Magellan, a Portuguese explorer, was the first to complete a circumnavigation of the earth, in 1522.

QATAR

LOCATION: Middle East

CAPITAL: Doha

AREA: 11,581 sq. km

LANGUAGES: Arabic, English

MAIN RELIGION: Islam

CURRENCY: Qatari Riyal

LITERACY RATE: 93.5%

LIFE EXPECTANCY: 79.81 years

TIME ZONE: +3

TYPE OF GOVERNMENT: Unitary Islamic semi-constitutional monarchy

HEAD OF STATE: Amir Tamim bin Hamad Al Thani **HEAD OF GOVT:** Prime Minister Sheikh Khalid bin Khalifa bin Abdulaziz Al Thani

GDP PER CAPITA: $85,300

POPULATION: 2,508,182

ISD CODE: 974 **INTERNET TLD:** .qa

Qatar is the first Middle Eastern nation to host the FIFA World Cup, in November-December 2022.

ROMANIA

LOCATION: South-east Europe

CAPITAL: Bucharest

AREA: 238,397 sq. km

LANGUAGES: Romanian, Hungarian

MAIN RELIGION: Christianity

CURRENCY: Romanian Leu

LITERACY RATE: 98.8%

LIFE EXPECTANCY: 75.75 years

TIME ZONE: +2

TYPE OF GOVERNMENT: Semi-presidential Republic

HEAD OF STATE: President Klaus Iohannis **HEAD OF GOVT:** Prime Minister Nicolae Ciuca

GDP PER CAPITA: $29,941

POPULATION: 21,230,362

ISD CODE: 40 **INTERNET TLD:** .ro

The earliest reliably dated European modern human fossils were discovered in 2002 at Pestera cu Oase ('Cave with Bones'). They were 37,800 to 42,000 years old.

RUSSIA

LOCATION: North Asia/east Europe

CAPITAL: Moscow

AREA: 17,098,246 sq. km

LANGUAGE: Russian

MAIN RELIGION: Christianity

CURRENCY: Ruble

LITERACY RATE: 99.7%

LIFE EXPECTANCY: 72.44 years

TIME ZONE: +3 to +12

TYPE OF GOVERNMENT: Federal Semi-presidential Republic

HEAD OF STATE AND GOVT: President Vladimir Putin

GDP PER CAPITA: $26,500

POPULATION: 142,021,981

ISD CODE: 7 **INTERNET TLD:** .ru

Two major physical landmarks in Russia are the Urals, the oldest mountains in the world, and Lake Baikal, the world's deepest lake and the largest reservoir of freshwater on Earth.

RWANDA

LOCATION: Central Africa

CAPITAL: Kigali

AREA: 26,338 sq. km

LANGUAGES: Kinyarwanda, French, English

MAIN RELIGION: Christianity

CURRENCY: Rwandan Franc

LITERACY RATE: 73.2%

LIFE EXPECTANCY: 65.85 years

TIME ZONE: +2

TYPE OF GOVERNMENT: Presidential Republic

HEAD OF STATE: President Paul Kagame
HEAD OF GOVT: Prime Minister Edouard Ngirente

GDP PER CAPITA: $2,100

POPULATION: 13,173,730

ISD CODE: 250 **INTERNET TLD:** .rw

Sixty per cent of Rwandan parliamentarians are women.

Background: Russia

SAINT KITTS AND NEVIS

LOCATION: Islands in the Caribbean Sea

CAPITAL: Basseterre

AREA: 261 sq. km

LANGUAGE: English

MAIN RELIGION: Christianity

CURRENCY: East Caribbean Dollar

LITERACY RATE: 97.8%

LIFE EXPECTANCY: 77.08 years

TIME ZONE: –4

TYPE OF GOVERNMENT: Constitutional Monarchy and Parliamentary Democracy

HEAD OF STATE: Queen Elizabeth II

HEAD OF GOVT: Prime Minister Terrance Drew

GDP PER CAPITA: $26,438

POPULATION: 54,448

ISD CODE: 1-869

INTERNET TLD: .kn

Christopher Columbus discovered the island and named it after his patron saint, St Christopher. It was later shortened to Saint Kitts.

SAINT LUCIA

LOCATION: Caribbean

CAPITAL: Castries

AREA: 617 sq. km

LANGUAGE: English

MAIN RELIGION: Christianity

CURRENCY: East Caribbean Dollar

LITERACY RATE: 90.1%

LIFE EXPECTANCY: 78.99 years

TIME ZONE: –4

TYPE OF GOVERNMENT: Constitutional Monarchy and Parliamentary Democracy

HEAD OF STATE: Queen Elizabeth II

HEAD OF GOVT: Prime Minister Philip J. Pierre

GDP PER CAPITA: $12,300

POPULATION: 167,122

ISD CODE: 1-758 **INTERNET TLD:** .lc

La Soufriere volcano in Malgretoute, Saint Lucia, is the world's only drive-in volcano! You can drive right into its crater.

Background: Saint Lucia

SAINT VINCENT AND THE GRENADINES

LOCATION: Central America/Caribbean Sea

CAPITAL: Kingstown

AREA: 389 sq. km

LANGUAGE: English

MAIN RELIGION: Christianity

CURRENCY: East Caribbean Dollar

LITERACY RATE: 96%

LIFE EXPECTANCY: 76.68 years

TIME ZONE: –4

TYPE OF GOVERNMENT: Constitutional Monarchy and Parliamentary Democracy

HEAD OF STATE: Queen Elizabeth II

HEAD OF GOVT: Prime Minister Ralph Gonsalves

GDP PER CAPITA: $12,100

POPULATION: 100,969

ISD CODE: 1-784 **INTERNET TLD:** .vc

The first few scenes of *The Pirates of the Caribbean: The Curse of the Black Pearl* were shot here.

SAMOA

LOCATION: Group of islands in the South Pacific

CAPITAL: Apia

AREA: 2,842 sq. km

LANGUAGES: Samoan, English

MAIN RELIGION: Christianity

CURRENCY: Tala

LITERACY RATE: 99.1%

LIFE EXPECTANCY: 75.19 years

TIME ZONE: +13

TYPE OF GOVERNMENT: Parliamentary Republic

HEAD OF STATE: President Va'aletoa Sualauvi II **HEAD OF GOVT:** Prime Minister Fiame Naomi Mata'afa

GDP PER CAPITA: $6,300

POPULATION: 204,898

ISD CODE: 685 **INTERNET TLD:** .ws

Tattooing is a great tradition in Samoa, and both men and women have been getting intricate tattoos for at least 2,000 years.

SAN MARINO

LOCATION: Southern Europe

CAPITAL: San Marino

AREA: 61.2 sq. km

LANGUAGE: Italian

MAIN RELIGION: Christianity

CURRENCY: Euro

LITERACY RATE: 99.9%

LIFE EXPECTANCY: 83.86 years

TIME ZONE: +1

TYPE OF GOVERNMENT: Parliamentary Republic

HEAD OF STATE: Captains Regent Oscar Mina and Paolo Rondelli **HEAD OF GOVT:** Secretary of State for Foreign Affairs Luca Beccari

GDP PER CAPITA: $60,800

POPULATION: 34,682

ISD CODE: 378 **INTERNET TLD:** .sm

The constitution of San Marino, enacted in 1600, is the world's oldest constitution still in effect.

SAO TOME AND PRINCIPE

LOCATION: West Central Africa; islands in the Sea of Guinea

CAPITAL: Sao Tome

AREA: 1,001 sq. km

LANGUAGE: Portuguese

MAIN RELIGION: Christianity

CURRENCY: Dobra

LITERACY RATE: 92.8%

LIFE EXPECTANCY: 66.7 years

TIME ZONE: +0

TYPE OF GOVERNMENT: Semi-presidential Republic

HEAD OF STATE: President Carlos Manuel Vila Nova **HEAD OF GOVT:** Prime Minister Jorge Bom Jesus

GDP PER CAPITA: $4,100

POPULATION: 217,164

ISD CODE: 239 **INTERNET TLD:** .st

Sao Tome and Principe, comprising two islands, is the smallest nation in Africa. Sao Tome houses 90 per cent of the population.

Background: San Marino

SAUDI ARABIA

LOCATION: Middle East

CAPITAL: Riyadh

AREA: 2,149,690 sq. km

LANGUAGE: Arabic

MAIN RELIGION: Islam

CURRENCY: Saudi Riyal

LITERACY RATE: 95.3%

LIFE EXPECTANCY: 76.65 years

TIME ZONE: +3

TYPE OF GOVERNMENT: Absolute Monarchy

HEAD OF STATE AND GOVT: King Salman bin Abd al-Aziz Al Saud

GDP PER CAPITA: $44,300

POPULATION: 35,354,380

ISD CODE: 966 **INTERNET TLD:** .sa

Saudi Arabia is the world's largest producer of desalinated water.

SENEGAL

LOCATION: West Africa

CAPITAL: Dakar

AREA: 196,712 sq. km

LANGUAGES: French, Wolof

MAIN RELIGION: Islam

CURRENCY: CFA Franc

LITERACY RATE: 51.9%

LIFE EXPECTANCY: 69.96 years

TIME ZONE: 0

TYPE OF GOVERNMENT: Presidential Republic

HEAD OF STATE AND GOVT: President Macky Sall

GDP PER CAPITA: $3,300

POPULATION: 17,923,036

ISD CODE: 221 **INTERNET TLD:** .sn

Senegal is known for its tradition of storytelling, performed by storytellers called 'griots'. They have kept West African history alive through stories and music.

SERBIA

LOCATION: East Europe

CAPITAL: Belgrade

AREA: 88,361 sq. km

LANGUAGES: Serbian, Hungarian

MAIN RELIGION: Christianity

CURRENCY: Serbian Dinar

LITERACY RATE: 99.5%

LIFE EXPECTANCY: 74.17 years

TIME ZONE: +1

TYPE OF GOVERNMENT: Parliamentary Republic

HEAD OF STATE: President Aleksandar Vucic **HEAD OF GOVT:** Prime Minister Ana Brnabic

GDP PER CAPITA: $18,200

POPULATION: 6,739,471

ISD CODE: 381 **INTERNET TLD:** .rs

Serbia is one of the biggest producers and exporters of raspberries in the world. In the harvest season, more than 200,000 people are employed in this industry.

Background: Senegal

SEYCHELLES

LOCATION: Indian Ocean

CAPITAL: Victoria

AREA: 455 sq. km

LANGUAGES: Creole, English, French

MAIN RELIGION: Christianity

CURRENCY: Seychelles Rupee

LITERACY RATE: 95.9%

LIFE EXPECTANCY: 76.1 years

TIME ZONE: +4

TYPE OF GOVERNMENT: Presidential Republic

HEAD OF STATE AND GOVT: President Wavel Ramkalawan

GDP PER CAPITA: $24,400

POPULATION: 97,017

ISD CODE: 248 **INTERNET TLD:** .sc

***Medusagyne oppositifolia* or the jellyfish tree (named so after the shape of its fuit), which is endemic to Seychelles, was thought extinct until a few plants were discovered in the 1970s.**

SIERRA LEONE

LOCATION: West Africa

CAPITAL: Freetown

AREA: 71,740 sq. km

LANGUAGES: English, Krio, Temne

MAIN RELIGIONS: Islam, Christianity

CURRENCY: Leone

LITERACY RATE: 43.2%

LIFE EXPECTANCY: 68.76 years

TIME ZONE: +0

TYPE OF GOVERNMENT: Presidential Republic

HEAD OF STATE AND GOVT: President Julius Maada Bio

GDP PER CAPITA: $1,600

POPULATION: 8,692,606

ISD CODE: 232 **INTERNET TLD:** .sl

Sierra Leone gets its name from Portuguese 'Serra Leao,' meaning 'lion mountain range'.

SINGAPORE

LOCATION: South-East Asia

CAPITAL: Singapore City

AREA: 725.7 sq. km

LANGUAGES: English, Mandarin, Malay

MAIN RELIGION: Buddhism, Islam

CURRENCY: Singapore Dollar

LITERACY RATE: 97.5%

LIFE EXPECTANCY: 86.35 years

TIME ZONE: +8

TYPE OF GOVERNMENT: Parliamentary Republic

HEAD OF STATE: President Halimah Yacob

HEAD OF GOVT: Prime Minister Lee Hsien Loong

GDP PER CAPITA: $93,400

POPULATION: 5,921,231

ISD CODE: 65 **INTERNET TLD:** .sg

A city, a capital and a state all at once, Singapore is one of only three city states in the world. The other two are Monaco and Vatican City.

Background: Singapore

SLOVAKIA

LOCATION: Central Europe

CAPITAL: Bratislava

AREA: 49,035 sq. km

LANGUAGES: Slovak, Hungarian

MAIN RELIGION: Christianity

CURRENCY: Euro

LITERACY RATE: 99.6%

LIFE EXPECTANCY: 78.31 years

TIME ZONE: +1

TYPE OF GOVERNMENT: Parliamentary Republic

HEAD OF STATE: President Zuzana Caputova **HEAD OF GOVT:** Prime Minister Eduard Heger

GDP PER CAPITA: $30,300

POPULATION: 5,431,252

ISD CODE: 421 **INTERNET TLD:** .sk

Stefan Banic, a Slovak, invented the first actively used parachute, patenting it in 1913.

SLOVENIA

LOCATION: Central Europe

CAPITAL: Ljubljana

AREA: 20,271 sq. km

LANGUAGE: Slovene

MAIN RELIGIONS: Christianity, Islam

CURRENCY: Euro

LITERACY RATE: 99.7%

LIFE EXPECTANCY: 81.82 years

TIME ZONE: +1

TYPE OF GOVERNMENT: Parliamentary Republic

HEAD OF STATE: President Borut Pahor **HEAD OF GOVT:** Prime Minister Robert Golob

GDP PER CAPITA: $39,088

POPULATION: 2,102,106

ISD CODE: 386 **INTERNET TLD:** .si

A grapevine that grows in the city of Maribor here is believed to be the world's oldest extant vine. It's over 450 years old.

SOLOMON ISLANDS

LOCATION: South Pacific Ocean

CAPITAL: Honiara

AREA: 28,400 sq. km

LANGUAGES: Pijin (Solomonese Pidgin), English

MAIN RELIGION: Christianity

CURRENCY: Solomon Island Dollar

LITERACY RATE: 84.1%

LIFE EXPECTANCY: 76.7 years

TIME ZONE: +11

TYPE OF GOVERNMENT: Constitutional Monarchy and Parliamentary Democracy

HEAD OF STATE: Queen Elizabeth II **HEAD OF GOVT:** Prime Minister Manasseh Sogavare

GDP PER CAPITA: $2,500

POPULATION: 702,694

ISD CODE: 677 **INTERNET TLD:** .sb

Marovo Lagoon, the largest saltwater lagoon in the world, is located in New Georgia in the Solomon Islands.

SOMALIA

LOCATION: East Africa

CAPITAL: Mogadishu

AREA: 637,657 sq. km

LANGUAGES: Somali, Arabic

MAIN RELIGION: Islam

CURRENCY: Somali Shilling

LITERACY RATE: 37.8%

LIFE EXPECTANCY: 55.72 years

TIME ZONE: +3

TYPE OF GOVERNMENT: Federal Parliamentary Republic

HEAD OF STATE: President Hassan Sheikh Mohamud **HEAD OF GOVT:** Prime Minister Hamza Abdi Barre

GDP PER CAPITA: $800

POPULATION: 12,386,248

ISD CODE: 252 **INTERNET TLD:** .so

Somalia is located on a peninsula in East Africa, which juts out into the Arabian Sea. It is called the 'Horn of Africa' for its horn-like shape.

SOUTH AFRICA

LOCATION: Southern Africa

CAPITAL: Pretoria (executive), Cape Town (judicial), Bloemfontein (legislative)

AREA: 1,221,037 sq. km

LANGUAGES: IsiZulu, IsiXhosa, Afrikaans, and seven other official languages

MAIN RELIGIONS: Christianity, Islam, Hinduism, traditional African religions

CURRENCY: South African Rand

LITERACY RATE: 95%

LIFE EXPECTANCY: 65.32 years

TIME ZONE: +2

TYPE OF GOVERNMENT: Parliamentary Republic

HEAD OF STATE AND GOVT: President Cyril Ramaphosa

GDP PER CAPITA: $11,500

POPULATION: 57,516,665

ISD CODE: 27 **INTERNET TLD:** .za

The Vredefort Dome is the world's largest meteor scar (originally 300 km wide!).

SOUTH KOREA

LOCATION: East Asia

CAPITAL: Seoul

AREA: 100,363 sq. km

LANGUAGE: Korean

MAIN RELIGIONS: Christianity, Buddhism

CURRENCY: South Korean Won

LITERACY RATE: 97.97%

LIFE EXPECTANCY: 82.97 years

TIME ZONE: +9

TYPE OF GOVERNMENT: Semi-presidential Republic

HEAD OF STATE: President Yoon Suk-yeol **HEAD OF GOVT:** Prime Minister Han Duck-soo

GDP PER CAPITA: $42,300

POPULATION: 51,844,834

ISD CODE: 82 **INTERNET TLD:** .kr

South Korean men above 18 years have to serve in the army for two years.

SOUTH SUDAN

LOCATION: East-central Africa

CAPITAL: Juba

AREA: 619,745 sq. km

LANGUAGES: English, indigenous languages including Dinka, Nuer, Bari and Zande

MAIN RELIGIONS: Animist, Christianity, Islam

CURRENCY: South Sudanese Pound

LITERACY RATE: 34.5%

LIFE EXPECTANCY: 59.16 years

TIME ZONE: +3

TYPE OF GOVERNMENT: Federal Presidential Constitutional Republic

HEAD OF STATE AND GOVT: President Salva Kiir

GDP PER CAPITA: $1,600

POPULATION: 11,544,905

ISD CODE: 211 **INTERNET TLD:** .ss

South Sudan is the world's youngest country, having gained independence from Sudan in 2011 after a two-decade-long civil war.

SPAIN

LOCATION: South-western Europe

CAPITAL: Madrid

AREA: 505,990 sq. km

LANGUAGE: Spanish

MAIN RELIGION: Christianity

CURRENCY: Euro

LITERACY RATE: 98.6%

LIFE EXPECTANCY: 82.55 years

TIME ZONE: +1

TYPE OF GOVERNMENT: Parliamentary Constitutional Monarchy

HEAD OF STATE: King Felipe VI
HEAD OF GOVT: President and Prime Minister Pedro Sanchez

GDP PER CAPITA: $36,200

POPULATION: 47,163,418

ISD CODE: 34 **INTERNET TLD:** .es

Sobrino de Botín, a restaurant in Madrid, is said to be continuously operating since 1725!

SRI LANKA

LOCATION: South Asia

CAPITAL: Sri Jayawardenepura Kotte; Colombo (commercial capital)

AREA: 65,610 sq. km

LANGUAGES: Sinhala, Tamil

MAIN RELIGIONS: Buddhism, Hinduism

CURRENCY: Sri Lankan Rupee

LITERACY RATE: 92.3%

LIFE EXPECTANCY: 78 years

TIME ZONE: +5.30

TYPE OF GOVERNMENT: Presidential Republic

HEAD OF STATE AND GOVT: President Ranil Wickremesinghe

GDP PER CAPITA: $12,500

POPULATION: 23,187,516

ISD CODE: 94 **INTERNET TLD:** .lk

Sri Lanka was known as Ceylon before 1972. In 1960, Sirimavo Bandaranaike of Sri Lanka (then Ceylon) became the first woman prime minister in history.

SUDAN

LOCATION: North-eastern Africa

CAPITAL: Khartoum

AREA: 1,886,068 sq. km

LANGUAGES: Arabic, English

MAIN RELIGIONS: Islam, Christianity

CURRENCY: Sudanese Pound

LITERACY RATE: 60.7%

LIFE EXPECTANCY: 67.12 years

TIME ZONE: +2

TYPE OF GOVERNMENT: Federal Presidential Democratic Republic

HEAD OF STATE AND GOVT: Sovereign Council Chairman and Commander-in-Chief of Sudanese Armed Forces General Abdel Fattah Al-Burhan

GDP PER CAPITA: $4,000

POPULATION: 47,958,856

ISD CODE: 249 **INTERNET TLD:** .sd

Sudan was the largest country in Africa before the secession of South Sudan in 2011. Now it is the third largest, after Algeria and the Democratic Republic of the Congo.

SURINAME

LOCATION: North-eastern South America

CAPITAL: Paramaribo

AREA: 163,821 sq. km

LANGUAGES: Dutch, English

MAIN RELIGIONS: Christianity, Hinduism

CURRENCY: Surinamese Dollar

LITERACY RATE: 94.4%

LIFE EXPECTANCY: 72.42 years

TIME ZONE: –3

TYPE OF GOVERNMENT: Presidential Republic

HEAD OF STATE AND GOVT: President Chan Santokhi

GDP PER CAPITA: $16,100

POPULATION: 632,638

ISD CODE: 597 **INTERNET TLD:** .sr

Tropical rainforests cover about 80 per cent of the land area in Suriname.

SWEDEN

LOCATION: Northern Europe

CAPITAL: Stockholm

AREA: 450,295 sq. km

LANGUAGE: Swedish

MAIN RELIGION: Christianity

CURRENCY: Swedish Krona

LITERACY RATE: 99%

LIFE EXPECTANCY: 82.7 years

TIME ZONE: +1

TYPE OF GOVERNMENT: Parliamentary Constitutional Monarchy

HEAD OF STATE: King Carl XVI Gustaf

HEAD OF GOVT: Prime Minister Eva Magdalena Andersson

GDP PER CAPITA: $50,700

POPULATION: 10,483,647

ISD CODE: 46 **INTERNET TLD:** .se

A popular Swedish souvenir is the road sign for 'moose crossing'. Every year, many of these signs are stolen from the roads.

Background: Sweden

SWITZERLAND

LOCATION: Central Europe

CAPITAL: Bern (de facto); no official capital

AREA: 41,285 sq. km

LANGUAGES: German, French, Italian

MAIN RELIGION: Christianity

CURRENCY: Swiss Franc

LITERACY RATE: 99%

LIFE EXPECTANCY: 83.23 years

TIME ZONE: +1

TYPE OF GOVERNMENT: Federal Republic

HEAD OF STATE AND GOVT: President Ignazzio Cassis

GDP PER CAPITA: $68,400

POPULATION: 8,508,698

ISD CODE: 41 **INTERNET TLD:** .ch

Seventy percent of the country is covered with mountains and it has over 1,500 lakes.

SYRIA

LOCATION: Middle East

CAPITAL: Damascus

AREA: 185,180 sq. km

LANGUAGE: Arabic

MAIN RELIGION: Islam

CURRENCY: Syrian Pound

LITERACY RATE: 86.4%

LIFE EXPECTANCY: 74.28 years

TIME ZONE: +2

TYPE OF GOVERNMENT: Semi-presidential Republic

HEAD OF STATE: President Bashar al-Assad **HEAD OF GOVT:** Prime Minister Hussein Arnous

GDP PER CAPITA: $2,900

POPULATION: 21,563,800

ISD CODE: 963 **INTERNET TLD:** .sy

Damascus has been inhabited for more than 4,000 years, making it one of the oldest continuously inhabited settlements in the world.

TAJIKISTAN

LOCATION: Central Asia

CAPITAL: Dushanbe

AREA: 143,100 sq. km

LANGUAGES: Tajik, Russian

MAIN RELIGION: Islam

CURRENCY: Somoni

LITERACY RATE: 99.8%

LIFE EXPECTANCY: 69.36 years

TIME ZONE: +5

TYPE OF GOVERNMENT: Unitary Dominant-party Presidential Republic

HEAD OF STATE: President Emomali Rahmon **HEAD OF GOVT:** Prime Minister Qokhir Rasulzoda

GDP PER CAPITA: $3,700

POPULATION: 9,119,347

ISD CODE: 992 **INTERNET TLD:** .tj

The Iskanderkul Lake of Tajikistan has been named after Alexander the Great. The country was an integral part of the ancient Silk Route.

Background: Thailand

TANZANIA

LOCATION: East Africa

CAPITAL: Dodoma

AREA: 947,303 sq. km

LANGUAGES: Swahili, English

MAIN RELIGIONS: Islam, Christianity, indigenous faiths

CURRENCY: Tanzanian Shilling

LITERACY RATE: 77.9%

LIFE EXPECTANCY: 70.19 years

TIME ZONE: +3

TYPE OF GOVERNMENT: Presidential Republic

HEAD OF STATE AND GOVT: President Samia Suluhu Hassan

GDP PER CAPITA: $2,600

POPULATION: 62,092,761

ISD CODE: 255 **INTERNET TLD:** .tz

At 264 sq. km, the Ngorongoro Crater, in the Crater Highlands area of Tanzania, is the largest inactive, intact and unfilled crater in the world. It is home to many wild animals.

THAILAND

LOCATION: South-East Asia

CAPITAL: Bangkok

AREA: 513,120 sq. km

LANGUAGE: Thai

MAIN RELIGION: Buddhism

CURRENCY: Baht

LITERACY RATE: 93.8%

LIFE EXPECTANCY: 77.66 years

TIME ZONE: +7

TYPE OF GOVERNMENT: Constitutional Monarchy

HEAD OF STATE: King Vajiralongkorn
HEAD OF GOVT: Prime Minister Prayut Chan-o-cha

GDP PER CAPITA: $17,300

POPULATION: 69,648,117

ISD CODE: 66 **INTERNET TLD:** .th

Thailand is the only South-East Asian country to have never been dominated by a Western power and hence retains most of its original culture.

TOGO

LOCATION: West Africa

CAPITAL: Lome

AREA: 56,785 sq. km

LANGUAGES: French, Ewe, Mina, Kabye, Dagomba, other indigenous languages

MAIN RELIGIONS: Indigenous beliefs, Christianity, Islam

CURRENCY: CFA Franc

LITERACY RATE: 66.5%

LIFE EXPECTANCY: 71.36 years

TIME ZONE: +0

TYPE OF GOVERNMENT: Presidential Republic

HEAD OF STATE: President Faure Gnassingbe **HEAD OF GOVT:** Prime Minister Victoire Tomegah Dogbe

GDP PER CAPITA: $2,100

POPULATION: 8,492,333

ISD CODE: 228

INTERNET TLD: .tg

Togo is the world's fourth largest producer of phosphate, a mineral used for fertilizers.

TONGA

LOCATION: South Pacific Ocean

CAPITAL: Nuku'alofa

AREA: 748 sq. km

LANGUAGES: Tongan, English

MAIN RELIGION: Christianity

CURRENCY: Pa'anga

LITERACY RATE: 99.4%

LIFE EXPECTANCY: 77.53

TIME ZONE: +13

TYPE OF GOVERNMENT: Constitutional Monarchy

HEAD OF STATE: King Tupou VI **HEAD OF GOVT:** Prime Minister Siaosi Sovaleni

GDP PER CAPITA: $6,400

POPULATION: 105,517

ISD CODE: 676 **INTERNET TLD:** .to

Captain James Cook, the famous British navigator, named Tonga the 'Friendly Islands'.

TRINIDAD AND TOBAGO

LOCATION: Caribbean Sea

CAPITAL: Port of Spain

AREA: 5,131 sq. km

LANGUAGE: English

MAIN RELIGIONS: Christianity, Hinduism

CURRENCY: Trinidad and Tobago Dollar

LITERACY RATE: 99%

LIFE EXPECTANCY: 75.94 years

TIME ZONE: –4

TYPE OF GOVERNMENT: Parliamentary Republic

HEAD OF STATE: President Paula-Mae Weekes **HEAD OF GOVT:** Prime Minister Keith Rowley

GDP PER CAPITA: $23,700

POPULATION: 1,405,646

ISD CODE: 1-868 **INTERNET TLD:** .tt

It is believed that Daniel Defoe and Robert Louis Stevenson based their respective novels, *Robinson Crusoe* and *Treasure Island*, on the islands of Trinidad and Tobago.

TUNISIA

LOCATION: Northern Africa

CAPITAL: Tunis

AREA: 163,610 sq. km

LANGUAGES: Arabic, French

MAIN RELIGION: Islam

CURRENCY: Tunisian Dinar

LITERACY RATE: 81.8%

LIFE EXPECTANCY: 76.82 years

TIME ZONE: +1

TYPE OF GOVERNMENT: Parliamentary Republic

HEAD OF STATE: President Kais Saied **HEAD OF GOVT:** Prime Minister Najla Bouden

GDP PER CAPITA: $9,700

POPULATION: 11,896,972

ISD CODE: 216 **INTERNET TLD:** .tn

The city of Kairouan in Tunisia is considered one of the most important cities for Islam after Mecca, Medina and Jerusalem.

Background: Turkey

TURKEY

LOCATION: West Asia/East Europe

CAPITAL: Ankara

AREA: 783,356 sq. km

LANGUAGE: Turkish

MAIN RELIGION: Islam

CURRENCY: Turkish Lira

LITERACY RATE: 96.7%

LIFE EXPECTANCY: 76.21 years

TIME ZONE: +3

TYPE OF GOVERNMENT: Presidential Republic

HEAD OF STATE AND GOVT: President Recep Tayyip Erdogan

GDP PER CAPITA: $28,400

POPULATION: 83,047,706

ISD CODE: 90 **INTERNET TLD:** .tr

Istanbul, the largest city in Turkey by population, is the only city in the world built on two continents (Asia and Europe).

TURKMENISTAN

LOCATION: Central Asia

CAPITAL: Ashgabat

AREA: 491,210 sq. km

LANGUAGES: Turkmen, Russian

MAIN RELIGION: Islam

CURRENCY: Turkmenistani Manat

LITERACY RATE: 99.7%

LIFE EXPECTANCY: 71.83 years

TIME ZONE: +5

TYPE OF GOVERNMENT: Presidential Republic

HEAD OF STATE AND GOVT: President Serdar Berdimuhamedow

GDP PER CAPITA: $15,500

POPULATION: 5,636,011

ISD CODE: 993 **INTERNET TLD:** .tm

In Turkmenistan's Karakum Desert, the Darvaza Gas Crater ('The Burning Gates') gives off a glow that can be seen from miles away.

TUVALU

LOCATION: South Pacific Ocean

CAPITAL: Funafuti

AREA: 26 sq. km

LANGUAGES: Tuvaluan, English

MAIN RELIGION: Christianity (Church of Tuvalu)

CURRENCY: Tuvaluan Dollar, Australian Dollar

LITERACY RATE: Not available

LIFE EXPECTANCY: 68.38 years

TIME ZONE: +12

TYPE OF GOVERNMENT: Constitutional Monarchy and Parliamentary Democracy

HEAD OF STATE: Queen Elizabeth II **HEAD OF GOVT:** Prime Minister Kausea Natano

GDP PER CAPITA: $4,400

POPULATION: 11,544

ISD CODE: 688; **INTERNET TLD:** .tv

Eight of the nine islands of Tuvalu are inhabited; the name 'Tuvalu' means 'eight standing together'.

UGANDA

LOCATION: East-central Africa

CAPITAL: Kampala

AREA: 241,038 sq. km

LANGUAGES: English, Swahili

MAIN RELIGIONS: Christianity, Islam

CURRENCY: Ugandan Shilling

LITERACY RATE: 76.5%

LIFE EXPECTANCY: 68.96 years

TIME ZONE: +3

TYPE OF GOVERNMENT: Presidential Republic

HEAD OF STATE AND GOVT: President Yoweri Museveni

GDP PER CAPITA: $2,200

POPULATION: 46,205,893

ISD CODE: 256 **INTERNET TLD:** .ug

There are large reserves of crude oil and natural gas in Uganda that are still largely untapped. The largest export is coffee.

UKRAINE

LOCATION: Eastern Europe

CAPITAL: Kiev

AREA: 603,628 sq. km

LANGUAGES: Ukrainian, Russian

MAIN RELIGION: Christianity (Ukrainian Orthodox Church)

CURRENCY: Hryvnia

LITERACY RATE: 99.8%

LIFE EXPECTANCY: 73.45 years

TIME ZONE: +2

TYPE OF GOVERNMENT: Semi-presidential Republic

HEAD OF STATE: President Volodymyr Zelenskyy **HEAD OF GOVT:** Prime Minister Denys Shmyhal

GDP PER CAPITA: $12,400

POPULATION: 43,528,136

ISD CODE: 380 **INTERNET TLD:** .ua

The town called Rakhiv and the village of Dilove near Rakhiv are two among contenders for the geographical centre of Europe.

UNITED ARAB EMIRATES

LOCATION: Middle East

CAPITAL: Abu Dhabi

AREA: 83,600 sq. km

LANGUAGE: Arabic

MAIN RELIGION: Islam

CURRENCY: UAE Dirham

LITERACY RATE: 97.6%

LIFE EXPECTANCY: 79.56 years

TIME ZONE: +4

TYPE OF GOVERNMENT: Federation of Monarchies

HEAD OF STATE: President Sheikh Khalifa bin Zayed Al Nahyan **HEAD OF GOVT:** Prime Minister Mohammed bin Rashid Al Maktoum

GDP PER CAPITA: $67,000

POPULATION: 9,915,803

ISD CODE: 971 **INTERNET TLD:** .ae

The United Arab Emirates is divided into seven emirates. Over two-thirds of its population lives in either Abu Dhabi or Dubai.

Background: United Kingdom

UNITED KINGDOM

LOCATION: West Europe

CAPITAL: London

AREA: 242,495 sq. km

LANGUAGE: English

MAIN RELIGION: Christianity

CURRENCY: Pound Sterling

LITERACY RATE: 99%

LIFE EXPECTANCY: 81.94 years

TIME ZONE: +0

TYPE OF GOVERNMENT: Parliamentary Constitutional Monarchy

HEAD OF STATE: Queen Elizabeth II
HEAD OF GOVT: Prime Minister Boris Johnson*

GDP PER CAPITA: $41,600

POPULATION: 67,791,400

ISD CODE: 44 **INTERNET TLD:** .uk

The United Kingdom was the first country in the world to use postage stamps.

UNITED STATES OF AMERICA

LOCATION: North America

CAPITAL: Washington DC

AREA: 9,833,520 sq. km

LANGUAGES: English, Spanish

MAIN RELIGION: Christianity

CURRENCY: US Dollar

LITERACY RATE: 99%

LIFE EXPECTANCY: 80.5 years

TIME ZONE: –3 to –10

TYPE OF GOVERNMENT: Federal Presidential Republic

HEAD OF STATE AND GOVT: President Joseph R. Biden, Jr (Joe Biden)

GDP PER CAPITA: $60,200

POPULATION: 337,341,954

ISD CODE: 1 **INTERNET TLD:** .us

The USA is the only country to have ever used nuclear weapons.

URUGUAY

LOCATION: Southern South America

CAPITAL: Montevideo

AREA: 176,215 sq. km

LANGUAGES: Spanish, Portunol

MAIN RELIGION: Christianity

CURRENCY: Uruguayan Peso

LITERACY RATE: 98.8%

LIFE EXPECTANCY: 78.43 years

TIME ZONE: –3

TYPE OF GOVERNMENT: Presidential Republic

HEAD OF STATE AND GOVT: President Luis Lacalle Pou

GDP PER CAPITA: $21,600

POPULATION: 3,407,213

ISD CODE: 598 **INTERNET TLD:** .uy

Uruguay has the world's longest national anthem (six minutes). Greece actually has the longest one, but generally uses a shorter version.

*He announced his pending resignation on 7 July 2022 and will remain as prime minister until a new party leader is elected.

UZBEKISTAN

LOCATION: Central Asia

CAPITAL: Tashkent

AREA: 448,978 sq. km

LANGUAGES: Uzbek, Russian

MAIN RELIGION: Islam

CURRENCY: Uzbekistani Som

LITERACY RATE: 100%

LIFE EXPECTANCY: 75.29 years

TIME ZONE: +5

TYPE OF GOVERNMENT: Presidential Republic

HEAD OF STATE: President Shavkat Miromonovich Mirziyoyev **HEAD OF GOVT:** Prime Minister Abdulla Aripov

GDP PER CAPITA: $7,000

POPULATION: 31,104,937

ISD CODE: 998 **INTERNET TLD:** .uz

Uzbekistan has the fourth largest gold deposits in the world. The country mines 80 tonnes of gold every year.

VANUATU

LOCATION: South Pacific Ocean

CAPITAL: Port Vila

AREA: 12,189 sq. km

LANGUAGES: Bislama, English

MAIN RELIGION: Christianity

CURRENCY: Vanuatu Vatu

LITERACY RATE: 87.5%

LIFE EXPECTANCY: 75.14 years

TIME ZONE: +11

TYPE OF GOVERNMENT: Parliamentary Republic

HEAD OF STATE: President Nikenike Vurobaravu **HEAD OF GOVT:** Prime Minister Bob Loughman

GDP PER CAPITA: $2,800

POPULATION: 308,043

ISD CODE: 678 **INTERNET TLD:** .vu

Vanuatu is an archipelago consisting of approximately 82 islands of volcanic origin.

VATICAN CITY

LOCATION: Southern Europe (a city state in Rome, Italy)

CAPITAL: Vatican City

AREA: 0.44 sq. km

LANGUAGES: Italian, Latin, French

MAIN RELIGION: Christianity

CURRENCY: Euro

LITERACY RATE: 100%

LIFE EXPECTANCY: Not available

TIME ZONE: +1

TYPE OF GOVERNMENT: Ecclesiastical Elective Monarchy

HEAD OF STATE: Pope Francis
HEAD OF GOVT: Secretary of State Archbishop Pietro Parolin

GDP PER CAPITA: Not applicable

POPULATION: 1,000

ISD CODE: 379 **INTERNET TLD:** .va

Vatican City is the smallest country in the world by both area and population. St Peter's Basilica in Vatican City is the largest church in the world.

Background: Vatican City

VENEZUELA

LOCATION: Northern South America

CAPITAL: Caracas

AREA: 916,445 sq. km

LANGUAGE: Spanish

MAIN RELIGION: Christianity

CURRENCY: Bolivar Soberano

LITERACY RATE: 97.1%

LIFE EXPECTANCY: 72.29 years

TIME ZONE: –4

TYPE OF GOVERNMENT: Federal Presidential Republic

HEAD OF STATE AND GOVT: President Nicolas Maduro Moros and President Juan Gerardo Guaido Marquez – each accepted as legitimate by certain countries

GDP PER CAPITA: $7,700

POPULATION: 29,789,730

ISD CODE: 58 **INTERNET TLD:** .ve

The world's highest uninterrupted waterfall, Angel Falls, is in Venezuela. Its height is 979 m (3,212 ft).

VIETNAM

LOCATION: South-East Asia

CAPITAL: Hanoi

AREA: 331,212 sq. km

LANGUAGES: Vietnamese, English

MAIN RELIGIONS: Buddhism, Christianity

CURRENCY: Vietnamese Dong

LITERACY RATE: 95.8%

LIFE EXPECTANCY: 75.52 years

TIME ZONE: +7

TYPE OF GOVERNMENT: Unitary Marxist–Leninist Single-party Republic

HEAD OF STATE: President Nguyen Xuan Phuc **HEAD OF GOVT:** Prime Minister Pham Minh Chinh

GDP PER CAPITA: $8,200

POPULATION: 103,808,319

ISD CODE: 84

INTERNET TLD: .vn

Vietnam is the world's largest producer of cashew nuts and black pepper.

YEMEN

LOCATION: Southern West Asia

CAPITAL: Ataq city (interim capital)

AREA: 527,968 sq. km

LANGUAGE: Arabic

MAIN RELIGION: Islam

CURRENCY: Yemeni Rial

LITERACY RATE: 70.1%

LIFE EXPECTANCY: 67.51 years

TIME ZONE: +3

TYPE OF GOVERNMENT: Transitional

HEAD OF STATE: Chairman of the Presidential Leadership Council Rashad al-Alimi **HEAD OF GOVT:** Prime Minister Maeen Abdulmalik Saeed

GDP PER CAPITA: $2,500

POPULATION: 30,984,689

ISD CODE: 967 **INTERNET TLD:** .ye

The *Dracaena cinnabari* or the dragon blood tree, a uniquely umbrella shaped tree, grows in the Yemeni island of Socotra. It gets its name from its dark red resin.

Background: Zambia

COUNTRIES

ZAMBIA

LOCATION: Southern Africa

CAPITAL: Lusaka

AREA: 752,618 sq. km

LANGUAGES: English, Bemba, Nyanja

MAIN RELIGIONS: Christianity, Islam

CURRENCY: Zambian Kwacha

LITERACY RATE: 86.7%

LIFE EXPECTANCY: 63.26 years

TIME ZONE: +2

TYPE OF GOVERNMENT: Presidential Republic

HEAD OF STATE AND GOVT: President Hakainde Hichilema

GDP PER CAPITA: $3,300

POPULATION: 19,642,123

ISD CODE: 260

INTERNET TLD: .zm

***Termitomyces titanicus*, the largest edible mushroom in the world, is found in Zambia. Its cap is about 1 m (3.3 ft) in diameter.**

ZIMBABWE

LOCATION: Southern Africa

CAPITAL: Harare

AREA: 390,757 sq. km

LANGUAGES: English, Shona, Ndebele

MAIN RELIGIONS: Christianity, indigenous faiths

CURRENCY: Zimbabwe Dollar

LITERACY RATE: 86.5%

LIFE EXPECTANCY: 63.32 years

TIME ZONE: +2

TYPE OF GOVERNMENT: Unitary Dominant-party Presidential Republic

HEAD OF STATE AND GOVT: President Emmerson Mnangagwa

GDP PER CAPITA: $2,700

POPULATION: 15,121,004

ISD CODE: 263 **INTERNET TLD:** .zw

Background: Zimbabwe

Lake Kariba in Zimbabwe, constructed on the River Zambezi, is one of the largest man-made lakes in the world.

CHANGING Shapes of Nations

THE country that was called Yugoslavia was divided into seven countries in the 1990s.

1. Bosnia and Herzegovina
2. Croatia
3. Kosovo*
4. Macedonia
5. Montenegro
6. Serbia
7. Slovenia

When the Soviet Union broke up in 1991, these were the independent countries it was divided into:

1. Armenia 2. Azerbaijan 3. Belarus 4. Estonia 5. Georgia 6. Kazakhstan 7. Kyrgyzstan 8. Latvia 9. Lithuania 10. Moldova 11. Russia 12. Tajikistan 13. Turkmenistan 14. Ukraine 15. Uzbekistan

Kazakhstan

Lithuania

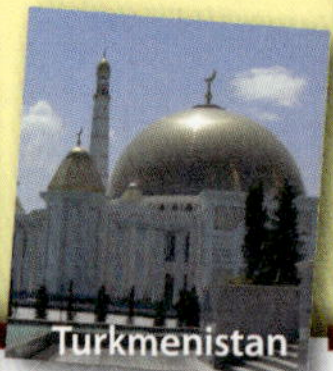

Turkmenistan

*The Republic of Kosovo declared its independence in 2008, and is partially recognized. Serbia still claims it as part of its territory. It is administered by the UN.

SUPERLATIVES

Fastest Animal (land) Cheetah (speed: 80–120 km/h)

Largest Animal (land) African elephant (length: 2.5–4 m/ 8.2–13 ft; weight: 2.5–7 tonnes)

Largest Animal (sea) Blue whale (length: 25–32 m/ 82–105 ft; weight: 170 tonnes)

Slowest Animal Sloth (speed: 1.8–2.4 m/6–8 ft per minute)

Largest Archipelago Malay Archipelago >25,000 s (Indonesia and Malaysia)

Tallest Animal (land) Giraffe (height: 4.2–5.7 m/ 14–19 ft; weight 794–1,270 kg)

Largest Bay Hudson Bay, Canada (shoreline: 12,268 km)

Fastest Bird Swift (length: 9–23 cm/3.5–9 in.; speed: 110 km/h)

Largest Bird Ostrich (length: 2.1–2.7 m/7–9 ft; weight: 90–130 kg)

Smallest Bird Hummingbird (length: 7.5–13 cm/3–5 in.)

Longest Bridge Danyang–Kunshan Grand Bridge, China (length: 165 km/541,338 ft)

Tallest Building (office) Burj Khalifa, Dubai, UAE (height: 829.8 m/ 2,722 ft)

Busiest Canal (ship) Kiel Canal (linking North Sea at Brunsbuttel to Baltic Sea at Kiel–Holtenau) (length: 98.26 km)

Highest Capital City La Paz, Bolivia (altitude: 3,640 m/ 11,942 ft)

Longest Canal (ship) Suez Canal (linking Red Sea and the Mediterranean) (length: 193.3 km)

Largest Cinema Kinepolis-Madrid Ciudad de la Imagen megaplex, Spain (seating capacity: 9,200; screens: 25)

Smallest Country Vatican City (0.44 sq. km)

Highest City La Rinconada, Peru; (altitude: 5,100 m/16,728 ft)

Most Populated City Tokyo, Japan (est. population: 37,393,000)

Busiest Container Port Shanghai, China (throughput in million TEUs,* 2019: 43.3)

* Twenty-foot Equivalent Unit

Largest Continent
Asia (area: 44.58 million sq. km)

Smallest Continent
Australia (area: 7.69 million sq. km)

Largest Country
Russia (area: 17,098,242 sq. km)

Largest Coral Formation
The Great Barrier Reef, Australia (stretching over 2,300 km)

Longest Corridor
Ramanathaswamy Temple, Rameswaram, Tamil Nadu, India (length: 1,220 m/4,002 ft)

Most Populated Country
China (est. population, 2022: 1,410,539,758)

Largest Desert
Antarctic Desert, Antarctica (area: 14,244,935 sq. km)

Largest Dam
Three Gorges Dam, China (over River Yangtze; length: 2,309 m/7,575.46 ft; height: 185 m/606.96 ft)

Biggest Dome
Astrodome, Texas, USA (diameter: 216.41 m/710 ft)

Largest Delta
Ganga–Brahmaputra Delta, Bay of Bengal (area: 105,641 sq. km)

Longest Epic
The Mahabharata (over 200,000 verse lines)

Largest Flower
Rafflesia arnoldii (diameter: 1m/3.3 ft)

Tallest Geyser (active)
Steamboat Geyser, Yellowstone National Park, USA (height: 2,316 m/7,598 ft)

Largest Gorge
Grand Canyon, USA (average depth: 1,584 m/5,200 ft)

Largest Gulf
Gulf of Mexico (shoreline: 5,000 km)

Deepest Lake
Lake Baikal, Siberia, Russia (max. depth: 1,642 m/5,387 ft)

Largest Island
Greenland, Kingdom of Denmark (area: 2,166,086 sq. km)

Highest Lake
Lake Tilicho, Nepal (altitude: 4,919 m/16,138 ft)

Largest Lake (inland waterbody)
Caspian Sea (surface area: 371,000 sq. km)

WORLD

Largest Lake (freshwater)
Lake Superior, USA and Canada (surface area: 82,000 sq. km)

Biggest Library
The British Library, UK (catalogued items: 170–200 million)

Longest Lifespan of an Animal
Giant tortoise (life expectancy: 190–200 years)

Highest Melting Point
Tungsten (3,422˚C)

Tallest Minaret
Djamaa el Djazair, Algeria (height: 265 m/870 ft)

Tallest Minaret (freestanding)
Qutub Minar, Delhi, India (height: 72.5 m/238 ft)

Longest Mountain Range (above water)
Andes, South America (length: 7,242 km)

Highest Mountain Peak
Mt Everest, Himalayan mountain range (height: 8,848 m/29,029 ft)

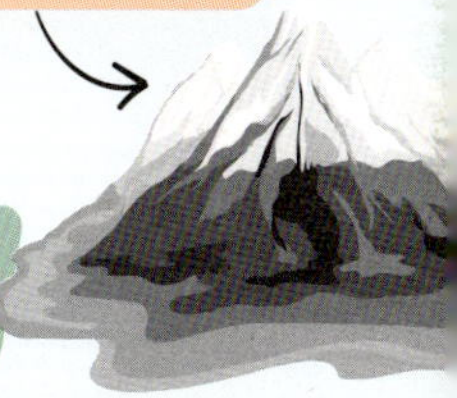

Biggest Museum
The Louvre, Paris, France (area: 72,735 sq. m/782,910 sq. ft)

Deepest Ocean Point
Challenger Deep (Mariana Trench, Pacific Ocean) (depth: 11,033.76 m/36,200 ft)

Largest Ocean
The Pacific (surface area: 361,132,000 sq. km)

Largest Palace
Forbidden City, Beijing, China (area: 720,000 sq. m/7,750,015 sq. ft)

Largest Peninsula
Arabian Peninsula (3,250,000 sq. km)

Driest Place*
Arica, Chile (average annual rainfall: 0.76 mm/0.03 in.)

Coldest Place (region)
Antarctica (lowest recorded temperature: –89.2°C; average annual temperature: –50°C.)

Highest Plateau
Tibetan Plateau (altitude: 4,500 m/14,800 ft)

Longest Mountain Range (underwater)
Mid-Atlantic Ridge (length: around 16,000 km) in the Atlantic Ocean

Railway Station with Most Platforms
Grand Central Terminal, New York, USA; (platforms: 44; area: 190,000 sq. m/2,045,143 sq. ft)

Longest Platform (railway)
Gorakhpur station, Uttar Pradesh, India (length:1,366.33 m/4,482.7 ft)

** Outside of polar regions*

WORLD

Longest Railway Route
Trans-Siberian Railway (length: 9,289 km)

Longest River
Nile, Egypt (length: 6,650 km)

Largest River (volume)
The Amazon, South America (average discharge: 219,000 cubic m/sec)

Longest Earthen Dam
Hirakud Dam, Odisha, India (length: 25.79 km)

Largest River Basin
Amazon Basin, South America (area: 7,000,000 sq. km)

Largest Seabird
Wandering albatross (wingspan: 3.3–3.6 m/ 10.83 –11.81 ft)

Rainiest Spot
Mawsynram, Meghalaya, India (average annual rainfall: 11,873 mm/467 in.)

Largest Stadium
Rungrado May Day, Pyongyang, North Korea (seating capacity: 114,000)

Tallest Statue
Statue of Unity, Gujarat, India (height: 182 m/597 ft)

Tallest Dam
Jinping–I Dam, Sichuan, China (height: 305 m/1,000 ft)

Broadest Strait
Davis Strait, Greenland and Canada (length: 950 km)

Longest Strait
Strait of Malacca (Andaman Sea–South China Sea) (length: 800 km)

Narrowest Strait
Euripus Channel–Chalcis, between mainland Greece and the of Euboea in the Aegean Sea (width: 41.15 m/135 ft)

Longest Tunnel (canal)
Delaware Aqueduct, New York, USA (length: 137 km)

Longest Tunnel (railway)
Gotthard Base Tunnel, Switzerland (length: 57 km)

Longest Tunnel (road)
Laerdal Tunnel, Norway (length: 24.5 km)

Highest Volcano
Nevados Ojos del Salado, Andes, Argentina–Chile (height: 6,893 m/22,615 ft)

Longest Wall
Great Wall of China, Beijing, China (length: 21,196 km)

Largest Volcano
Puhahonu, Hawaii, USA (volume: 150,000 cubic km)

Highest Waterfall
Angel Falls, Venezuela (height: 979 m/3,212 ft)

5 EARTH

Earth is 4.54 billion years old. From outer space, it looks like a huge blue marble ball with white swirls and areas of brown, yellow, green and white. It is the only planet with liquid water on the surface.

EARTH NUMBERS

Diameter from North to South Pole
12,714 km (7,900 miles)

Diameter from equator
12,756 km (7,926 miles)

Earth's rotation per hour
15 degrees

Equatorial circumference
40,030.2 km

Surface Area
510,064,472 km^2

Density
5.513g/cm^3

Volume
1,083,206,916,846 km^3

DAYS ON EARTH ARE BECOMING LONGER: Around 4.5 billion years ago, when Earth was formed, the average day is speculated to be approximately six hours long. By 260 million years ago, this had increased to 21.9 hours. Today, as we know, a day is 24 hours long. However, it is constantly increasing by 1.7 milliseconds per day.

EARTH IS RECYCLABLE: The tectonic forces present within the earth moves the land upward and downward, altering the layers of crust, pushing it further to the magma-filled layer of the earth. Eventually, the crust melts due to the heat and emerges back as crust through the volcanic eruptions of lava.

EARTH'S ROTATION IS SLOWING DOWN: Earth's spinning is known to be slowing down by 17 milliseconds per hundred hours. Due to this, our days will lengthen eventually. However, since the rate of rotation is so slow, it is said that our days would increase to 25 hours only in around 140 million years.

LAND: Earth comprises 32.1 per cent iron, 30.1 per cent oxygen, 15.1 per cent silicon and 13.9 per cent magnesium. Iron is the dominant element in the earth's core. A sample from there would have 88 per cent of iron. Additionally, Earth's crust is made of 47 per cent oxygen.

AIR: Earth's atmosphere is made of 78 per cent nitrogen, 21 per cent oxygen and 1 per cent other elements, making it conducive to sustaining life.

WATER: The larger part of Earth is covered by water. It exists in three forms: solid, liquid and gas. As a solid, it is found on mountaintops in the form of snow or glaciers. It is present in rivers, oceans, streams as a liquid and as water vapour (or a gaseous form) in the atmosphere.

Unlike gas planets like Jupiter, Earth is one of the four solar terrestrial planets (planets with a rocky body, as opposed to gas).

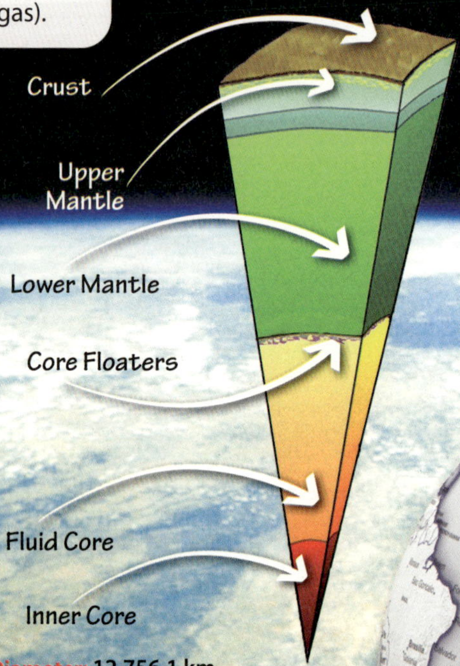

CHEMICAL COMPOSITION

The mass of Earth is approximately 5.9722×10^{24} kg. Earth is made up of nearly a hundred elements, of which oxygen, silicon, aluminium, iron, calcium, sodium, potassium and nickel are the main ones.

Diameter: 12,756.1 km
Distance from the Sun: 152 million km (at aphelion); average: 149.6 million km
Temperature: Maximum: 57.7°C; minimum: –89.1°C

SHAPE

If you take an orange and squish it at the top and bottom, it will bulge out towards the centre. In a similar way, Earth is a sphere slightly squished at the poles and bulging at the equator. So, if you were to draw a line across the equator and a line through the poles, the line across the equator would actually be 43 km longer than the one through the poles. Therefore, Earth is not a perfect sphere, and is instead what is termed an 'oblate spheroid'. This shape is caused by the rotation of Earth.

INTERNAL STRUCTURE

PLATE TECTONICS

The outer layer of Earth, called the **lithosphere**, is separated into vast pieces known as the tectonic plates, from 80 km to 400 km thick, which drift atop the soft, underlying mantle. They move both sideways, and up and down, at an estimated speed of 1 cm to 10 cm per year. Most of Earth's seismic activity (volcanoes and earthquakes) occurs at the boundaries where the plates interact.

SURFACE

About 70.8 per cent of Earth's surface is covered in water. There are many physical features submerged under it, such as the longest mountain ranges (the Mid-Atlantic Ridge), volcanoes, trenches, canyons, oceanic plateaus and plains. This is known as the **hydrosphere**. The remaining 29.2 per cent of Earth is covered with mountains, deserts, plains, plateaus and other features. This surface undergoes constant changes due to the effects of the movement of the tectonic plates and erosion.

> **"Seventy-five per cent of Earth's atmosphere is found within the first 11 km above the planet's surface. The outermost layer (the exosphere) is the largest, extending from the top of the thermosphere (about 700 km above sea level) to about 10,000 km. It merges with outer space, where there is no atmosphere."**

GEOLOGIC TIMELINE

PHANEROZOIC EON

540 mya–today

'Visible Life': organisms with skeletons or hard shells

MESOZOIC ERA
'The Age of Reptiles'
248–65 mya

Cretaceous Period
146–65 mya

- **Lower**
  First flowering plants, primates, crocodilians
- **Upper**
  Extinction of dinosaurs

CENOZOIC ERA
'The Age of Mammals'
65 mya–now

Quaternary Period
'The Age of Man'
(1.8 mya–now)

- **Holocene Epoch (11,000 years ago –now):** Human civilization
- **Pleistocene Epoch (1.8–0.011 mya):** (Last Ice Age) First human (*Homo sapiens*); mammoths, mastodons, giant ground sloths; mass extinction

Tertiary Period
65–1.8 mya

Neogene Period
24-1.8 mya

- **Pliocene Epoch (5–1.8 mya):** First hominids (Australopithecines); megalodons; modern whales
- **Miocene Epoch (24–5 mya):** More mammals (horses, dogs, bears); modern birds; apes and monkeys

Palaeogene Period
(65–24 mya)

- **Oligocene Epoch (38–24 mya):** small extinction; new mammals (pigs, deer, cats, rhinos, tapirs); grasses common
- **Eocene Epoch (54–38 mya):** Mammals abound; rodents, primitive whales appear
- **Palaeocene Epoch (65–54 mya):** First large mammals; primitive primates

Jurassic Period
(208–146 mya): Dinosaurs diversify; first birds, ferns, gingkos, conifers

Triassic Period
(248–208 mya): First dinosaurs, first mammals; many molluscs, reptiles; small-scale extinction

Permian Period
(280–248 mya): Reptiles and amphibians dominate; first bugs and beetles; major extinctions

Pennsylvanian Period
(325–280 mya): First reptiles; many ferns; cockroaches and mayflies

Carboniferous Period
(360–280 mya): Coal swamps, corals, seed ferns, other plants; amphibians common

Mississippian Period
(360–325 mya): Seed ferns; first winged insects

Devonian Period
(408–360 mya): First amphibians; many coral reefs

Silurian Period
438–408 mya: First vascular land plants; jawed fishes

PALAEOZOIC ERA
540–248 mya

Ordovician Period
(505–438 mya): Primitive plants; first corals, fishes, seaweed, fungi, bivalves

Cambrian Period
(540–500 mya): First fishes, marine invertebrates, like shellfish

EARTH IS FORMED 4.54 BILLION YEARS AGO

PROTEROZOIC EON

2.5 bya–540 mya: First multicelled animals, including sponges

Vendian/ Ediacaran Period
(600–540 mya)

ARCHEOZOIC EON

3.9–2.5 bya: First life forms: one-celled organisms; algae; bacteria appear in sea

HADEAN EON

4.6–3.9 mya: The solidifying of Earth's continental and oceanic crusts

Note: mya: million years ago; bya: billion years ago

THE BIG SEVEN

Earth's land surface is divided broadly into continents and there are many theories defining them. The most accepted definition for a 'continent' would be 'a large, continuous, discrete mass of land, separated from others by expanses of water'. Conventionally, there are seven continents: Asia, Africa, Europe, North America, South America, Australia/Oceania (Australia, New Zealand and islands of South-East Asia) and Antarctica.

NORTH AMERICA

Area: 21,330,000 sq. km; **Percentage of Earth's landmass:** 16.5%; **Population:** 592,072,212; **Percentage of world population*:** 7.6%; **Density of population per sq. km:** 28

EUROPE

Area: 22,134,900 sq. km; **Percentage of Earth's landmass:** 6.8%; **Population:** 747,636,026; **Percentage of world population:** 9.59%; **Density of population per sq. km:** 34

ASIA

Area: 44,579,000 sq. km; **Percentage of Earth's landmass:** 29.5%; **Population:** 3,261,050,390; **Percentage of world population:** 41.84%; **Density of population per sq. km:** 105

SOUTH AMERICA

Area: 17,461,112 sq. km; **Percentage of Earth's landmass:** 12%; **Population:** 430,759,766; **Percentage of world population:** 5.53%; **Density of population per sq. km:** 25

AUSTRALIA/ OCEANIA

Area: 8,486,460 sq. km; **Percentage of Earth's landmass:** 5.9%; **Population:** **43,111,704**; **Percentage of world population:** 0.55%; **Density of population per sq. km:** 5

AFRICA

Area: 29,648,481 sq. km; **Percentage of Earth's landmass:** 20.4%; **Population:** 1,340,598,147; **Percentage of world population:** 17.2%; **Density of population per sq. km:** 45

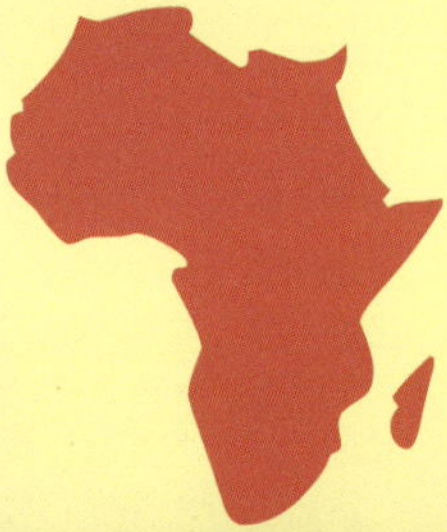

ANTARCTICA

Area: 13,720,000 sq. km; **Percentage of Earth's landmass:** 9.2%; **Population:** (scientists/ sailors) 4,490; **Percentage of world population:** 0.00002%; **Density of population per sq. km:** 0.00003

*Note: *Population figures are from 2020; percentages may not add up to 100 due to rounding off of numbers.*

Extinct Fish Species Returns to the River Teuchitlan in Mexico

Freshwater habitats are the most polluted waterbodies, according to the International Union for the Conservation of Nature (IUCN), and pose a threat to the survival of aquatic fauna such as fish. However, owing to the efforts of the conservationist Chester Zoo in Cheshire, UK, Mexico saw the return of an extinct species called the 'tequila fish' (*Zoogoneticus tequila*).

Named after the strong liquor originating in the town of Tequila, the species – which is 70 mm long at its maximum – possesses unique characteristics such as birthing developed foetuses and feeding on mosquito larva. Its only known habitat was in the American River Basin in Mexico, from where it disappeared from the wild in 2003.

In 1998, ten fish were given to the Michoacana University of Mexico by Chester Zoo. Under a project to revive these species, these fish were released in an artificial pond under the care of the university, allowing the species to breed and grow in numbers. From 2014, the project of reintroducing these fish commenced and their number grew to more than 10,000. In 2022, as many as 1,500 were to be returned to the River Teuchitlan in south-west Mexico.

This is the first time in history that a fish species has been brought back from extinction in the wild and is surviving as well as thriving. Due credit is being given to the local community who are situated around the water body as they play a key role in monitoring the water quality.

Little is known about the fish as they were discovered only a short time before they became extinct.

Oceans Suffer Memory Loss due to Global Warming

Sounds unbelievable, doesn't it? But it's true. Ocean memory refers to the consistent conditions of ocean water over time despite several factors affecting it. It is used as a simple parameter to measure the changing conditions of ocean surface temperatures and predict major climate-related events. The 'memory' is dependent on the thickness of the ocean's top layer. A thicker layer, in which temperatures and salinity are fairly uniform, provides better resistance to change and allows for a stronger memory. However, of late, this layer has become thinner due to global warming, climate change and more frequent atmospheric weather fluctuations.

Ocean 'amnesia' affects stable marine ecosystems, affecting growth of fisheries and temperature changes in the ocean, as well as temperature fluctuations on land, precipitation and other climatic features dependent on sea-surface temperature.

Global Human Waste and How to Tackle It

Humans are producing garbage at an alarming rate all over the world. The waste generated by nearly 7.9 billion people is getting accumulated in freshwater bodies, and impacting the health of both humans and animals. This waste is known to add 6.2 million tonnes of nitrogen to coastal waters every year, besides pharmaceuticals, microplastics and other pollutants. Sewage and wastewater severely unbalance our ecosystem, increase water pollution, overload contaminants in soil and land, impact biodiversity and trigger climate change. Still, strategies can be implemented to work towards a healthier and safer planet. Some people have begun to work on this:

- The **Global Coral Reef Alliance** is an environmental NGO working with communities to find ways to protect coral reefs and minimize the negative effect of local activities on the reefs.
- **Green Infrastructure:** This is a water management system that uses soil systems, pavements and other permeable systems to treat stormwater for water harvesting and other purposes. Simple strategies can help include green infrastructure in urban areas, such as downspout disconnection (which redirects stormwater to plants or rain barrels rather than sewage), and rainwater harvesting (collecting rainwater for later use).
- **Bioaugmentation:** This is a healthy and natural way of removing harmful contaminants from water, using microorganisms to help break down specific contaminants and fatal substances. These organisms also release a by-product that makes the water healthier than before.

The UN Declares a Healthy Environment a Universal Right

In October 2021, the United Nations passed the resolution on the right to a healthy, sanitized and sustainable environment. This was the first formal recognition of the right at an international level. The resolution won 43 votes with none opposing the proposal. Four governments abstained from voting – China, India, Japan, and Russia. In the Stockholm Declaration of 1972, the UN member states declared a fundamental right to an environment 'of quality' that allows a life of quality and well-being. The 2021 resolution had the support of over 1,300 civil society organizations and Indigenous Peoples' groups, 15 UN agencies, business groups, more than 90,000 children from around the world, and the Global Alliance of National Human Rights Institutions. The head of the United Nations Environment Programme (UNEP) referred to it as a step to environmental justice and 'a shield for individuals and communities' against factors impacting the health of people around the world.

Global Warming Is Reducing the Insect Population

Earth's rising temperatures not only induce climate change but also affect animal and insect populations. Studies have shown that due to the presence of excessive heat, the insect population has been decimated by half across the world. The number of species has been significantly reducing as a result of increasing heat and industrial farming (large-scale and intensive production of crops). Not only that, global warming has also resulted in a 27 per cent fall in the diversity of species. These decimated population numbers are identified to be highest in tropical areas.

Another cause for the reduction in insect population and diversity is agricultural 'intensification', which means increasing the application of agricultural resources (e.g., seeds, labour, fertilisers, pesticides, technologies and knowledge) to raise the level of yield per unit of land. This often destroys minor-life habitats and eliminates the insect populations present underneath the soil. Insects are natural pest controllers, especially for bugs invading agricultural land. Many food crops are dependent on animal pollination. Insects also play an essential role in the cycling of nutrients and decomposing waste. The continual decrease in the insect population will result in dire consequences and unbalanced ecosystems.

Groundwater System Discovered beneath Antarctic Ice Shelf

For many years, scientists have been discovering rivers and lakes beneath sediments of ice. The melting of water is known to facilitate the breakdown of ice and hasten its flow to the sea. A huge number of interconnected lakes and rivers have been found till now. However, recently a research team at Columbia University's Lamont-Doherty Earth Observatory in the USA identified a huge active circulating groundwater system underneath the sediments of western Antarctica.

Antarctica's sedimentary remains are porous and offer great opportunity to store groundwater. Most of these basins lie below the sea level between land ice, which is bound to the bedrock, and floating marine ice shelves. These ice shelves provide a protective shield, preventing the flow of water from re-invading the sediments, thus affecting the flow of melted water to oceans and raising sea levels.

Due to the presence of these sediments at such great depths, it is difficult to detect water. Airborne instruments cannot pierce the thick layers of ice. Radars have only been used to capture the structure of sediments rather than to map water content. Researchers used magnetotelluric imaging to identify the sediments under the Whillans Ice Stream. They planted instruments in pits and found that the pits filled with water. As one went deeper down, the water become more saline.

Greenland's Cracking Ice Shelf Draws Attention

With the temperature of Earth rapidly increasing due to global warming, glaciers and ice shelves are melting at a greater speed than before. A group of scientists at Stockholm University, Sweden, and University of California, Irvine, USA, studied the Petermann Ice Shelf, one of the few remaining ice shelves in Greenland. In 2012, it lost 40 per cent of its ice shelf as it broke apart and collapsed.

Ice shelves are platforms of ice, which slow down the flow of water to oceans. They are found mainly in Antarctica, Greenland, northern Canada and Russian Artic. Scientists believe that if the ice shelf breaks, it would be extremely difficult to rebuild it. Even if global warming somehow stops, it would be difficult to reconstruct the shelf after it has collapsed. In 2018, a crack in the ice shelf was observed, which gave rise to concerns about the Petermann Ice Shelf. The imbalance in water pressure caused due to the breaking of the ice shelves allows streams and rivers to flow more freely and easily into oceans, raising rising sea levels worldwide. These rise in sea levels will have a significant impact on low-lying islands, and disturb the local and aquatic population around mainstream waterbodies.

Mapping Plastic Pollution

Plastic is fast becoming one of the biggest threats to the planet due to lack of regulations and indiscriminate waste. Unforeseen calamities such as the COVID-19 pandemic saw a rise in plastic waste especially in the medical sector. Additionally, often while there are agreements in place to reduce the quantity of plastic produced, there are no implementation structures and strictures to reinforce sustainability.

Now, for some good news! A new device has been developed, which uses satellites and artificial intelligence to capture the presence of plastics from space. Global Plastic Watch is a digital platform featuring an interactive map that provides access to information intended to help associations, NGOs and governments in the fight against plastic pollution. It is equipped to detect and map, in 'near real-time', plastic waste sites as small as 5 m by 5 m, and create an interactive map of plastic pollution. Developed by an Australian non-profit organization, the Minderoo Foundation, this tool is free and available to the public. As of now, 2,802 sites have been detected and confirmed in 25 countries, using the Global Plastic Watch tool. They include South-East Asia, Australia and the top 20 countries responsible for annual plastic leakage into the oceans.

EARTH NEWS

Local Cooling Techniques Using Palm Leaves

India has been witnessing a heatwave where temperatures rose to 46-47 degrees Celsius in some areas. The heat made life harder for people, especially for those living in villages, who are unable to use air-conditioning. Due to new technology, the resources earlier used for natural ways of cooling have vanished. For instance, dung cakes used to be put on *kachcha* houses to reduce the impact of heat and keep the house cool. However, due to concrete housing given under government schemes, this solution is not possible any more.

In Odisha, villagers have found other ways to keep themselves cool – by putting paddy straw or palm leaves on their rooftops to keep the house cooler. Paddy straw is usually left to waste in the fields or fed to cattle. Village communities also built mud houses to protect themselves from the scorching heat.

Each of the last four decades has been warmer than any decade that before it since 1850. Scientists believe that greenhouse gases from human activities are the reason for this.

Solar Projects Face a Smoggy Barrier from Wildfires

Forest fires have always been a burden on the environment as well as to the community surrounding areas prone to wildfires. These fires burn up forests, releasing smoke and harmful particles in the air, which pollute the air. But that's not all. A recent study by scientists from Nainital's Aryabhatta Research Institute of Observational Sciences (ARIES) in India and Greece's National Observatory of Athens (NOA) has evaluated the factors that influence solar power production in India.

Upon tracing the factors affecting solar production, it was noted that aerosols, clouds and pollution play a significant role in the irradiance of solar energy. Solar irradiance refers to the solar energy reaching the surface of the earth after being released from the Sun. Solar irradiance is absorbed by solar panels to be converted into solar energy, which is further distributed along. Greater solar irradiance reaps greater solar energy. The research showed that large, widespread wildfire events reduced solar radiation by up to 45 per cent, leading to waste of expenditure.

EARTH NEWS

The Indian Ocean Fights the Heat

Global warming causes ocean warming too. With the active presence of heat-releasing gases in the air, the ocean is absorbing these gases at a larger quantity than before, leading to a rise in the temperature of the water. The Indian Ocean witnessed six marine heatwave (MHW) events over a period of 52 days in 2021. In contrast, the western Indian Ocean experienced 66 MHW events ,and the Bay of Bengal saw 94 MHW events during 1982–2018, according to an investigation by scientists at the Indian Institute of Tropical Meteorology (IITM), under the Ministry of Earth Sciences. The western Indian Ocean region experienced a four-fold rise in MHW events (increasing at a rate of 1.5 events per decade) and the northern Bay of Bengal experienced a two-to-threefold rise (at a rate of 0.5 events per decade).

Though the rise in oceanic temperatures was only above normal, the frequency of the events was highly unusual. The average increase has been recorded to about 1 degree Celsius during the period 1951–2015 at a rate of 0.15 degrees Celsius every 10 years. Studies show that in recent years, the tropical Indian Ocean has seen faster rising temperature due to ocean warming. It is important to address this issue since rising temperatures destroy habitats of marine animals and affect vegetation. They also impact low-lying lands, destroying housing and infrastructure due to natural calamities such as droughts and floods.

Planting the Right Tree in the Right Place

Yes, it's not enough to simply plant any tree anywhere! Studies have found that simple reforestation is not enough to mitigate climate change. There are numerous factors affecting sustainable tree plantation. The forest plantation programme of Himachal Pradesh brought this to light, according to Pushpendra Rana, who has authored a paper in the journal *World Development.* Researchers found that afforestation plantations were carried out in non-forest unproductive areas. Also, a focus on meeting quantitative planting targets could result in planting trees where they are biophysically unsuited or not desirable for socioeconomic reasons. According to the Indian State of Forests Report (ISFR), forest and tree cover in Himachal Pradesh grew by 912 sq. km since 2019, and already covers 68 per cent of the state's geographical area. So the new plantations in low-density areas not likely to bear much result.

Different types of trees require different topography to grow. The lack of appropriate weather, deficient soil nutrients and insufficient water as per the needs of the plants can end up in poor growth of the trees. Other factors like poor community participation, lack of proper management and inappropriate species of trees can also contribute to low returns from forest projects. Therefore, it is necessary that the land is properly examined and evaluated for the suitability of new plants and forests.

6 SPACE

Space has always been called the final frontier, but its exploration by humans has revealed many of its secrets. Here are just a few, while several more are still clouded in mystery!

The highest mountain known to us yet is on an asteroid called Vesta. Measuring a tremendous **22 km** in height, it is three times as tall as Mount Everest!

99 per cent of the mass of the solar system is the Sun.

Consider yourself lucky that you have ground beneath your feet on Earth! You wouldn't be able to walk on Jupiter, Saturn, Uranus or Neptune because they have no solid surface!

Humans have sent spacecraft to all of the planets in our solar system – Mercury, Venus, Earth, Mars, Jupiter, Saturn, Uranus and Neptune – as well as two dwarf planets, Pluto and Ceres.

The huge canyon system on Mars, known as Valles Marineris, is **4,000** km long, more than **10 times** as long as the Grand Canyon on Earth. Early spacecraft to Mars did not spot it because they flew over other parts of the planet. It was finally noticed by the global mapping mission Mariner 9 in 1971.

Currently, the biggest star known to us is called UY Scuti. This red supergiant star is located **9,500** light-years away in the Scutum constellation. It is more than **1,708** times the size of the Sun. The star with the highest mass is RMC 136a1, whose mass equals **315** Suns.

It has been estimated that the Milky Way will collide with the Andromeda galaxy, our closest neighbour in the galaxy, in around 4.5 billion years. This is likely to result in a vast elliptical galaxy.

The planet Neptune was discovered in 1846, but since then it has not yet completed one full orbit around the Sun. It takes **165** years to complete one such orbit!

OUR UNIVERSE

Our Earth revolves around the Sun. The Sun is the centre of our galaxy, the Milky Way, which is part of the Local Group of galaxies. This group is being gravitationally pulled towards a larger system of galaxies, known as the Virgo Cluster. Our galaxy is part of a vast system of dust, gas, stars and millions of galaxies. The most commonly accepted theory that explains the origin of the universe as we know it, is the Big Bang theory. According to this theory, the universe had its origins in a massive explosion 12–14 billion years ago, creating huge lumps of gas and matter that slowly cooled. As the universe grows older, the matter thins out and the galaxies expand outwards. Stars are still forming with the original hydrogen from the Big Bang. There is a finite amount of hydrogen that exists, and once it is gone, all the stars will stop shining.

GALAXIES

A galaxy is a huge congregation of stars held together by the force of gravity. Galaxies are dotted around the universe like islands. Our solar system is part of the Milky Way, which belongs to the Local Group of galaxies. The neighbouring Andromeda Galaxy is the largest galaxy in this system, followed by the Milky Way. The Local Group has about three dozen galaxies.

Although Indian mathematician-astronomer Aryabhata and Greek philosopher Aristarchus of Samos had speculated on our universe being Sun-centric or *heliocentric*, it was Polish astronomer Nicolaus Copernicus (1473–1543) who predicted it mathematically.

SOLAR SYSTEM

There is no single theory that explains how and why the solar system formed, but the currently accepted theory says that it happened about five billion years ago. Many scientists believe that the solar system evolved from a giant cloud of dust and gas (the 'solar nebula'), which then began to collapse under the weight of its own gravity. As it did so, the matter in this cloud began moving or spinning in a giant circle, much like the water in a drain moves around its centre in a whirlpool. At the centre of this spinning cloud, due to intense pressure and heat, a small star or 'protostar' began to form. This protostar grew larger

THE SUN

If you thought the Sun is a fireball, you are wrong. It is not really on fire, but glows because in its core – where the temperature reaches 15,000,000°C – there is a huge nuclear reaction constantly going on, converting hydrogen into helium, and releasing masses of energy as light and heat. Other than hydrogen and helium, the Sun contains nitrogen, carbon and small traces of other gases. In fact, it contains about 98 per cent of the matter making up our solar system. The middle layer of the Sun churns up and down in a circular motion, deeper into it and back out again. This creates many phenomena, such as making the Sun a giant magnet, as well as causing dark, cooler areas on its surface, known as 'sunspots'. This churning also causes sudden bright explosions, called 'solar flares', which release a huge amount of energy and light.

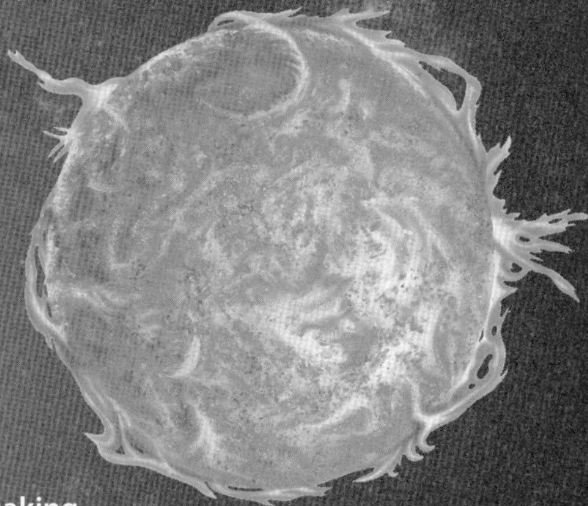

> **The Sun has a diameter of roughly 1.4 million km. This is almost 110 times the diameter of Earth – that means one million Earths could fit inside the Sun.**

and larger, as it collected more and more of the dust and gas that collapsed into it. Further away from this central star were smaller clumps of dust and gas that were also collapsing. The central star eventually became our Sun, while the smaller clumps became the main planets, minor or dwarf planets, moons, comets, asteroids, gas and dust. As the universe continued to cool and expand, each object tried to break away. However, the Sun, being so large, exerted an immense force of gravity on these planets. Caught between flying off into space and colliding into the Sun, the planets kept to elliptical orbits, revolving around the Sun, each at its own speed.

THE PLANETS

MERCURY: In Roman mythology Mercury was the messenger of the gods, and the protector of travellers and merchants. Its atmosphere has been blown away by solar winds; there is almost no air in it. It can be seen from Earth after an hour or so of the rising Sun (eastern horizon) or setting Sun (western horizon). It is the fastest orbiting planet, with long days due to its slow rotation. It has no moons or rings. As its iron core cooled, it shrank and acquired wrinkles, called 'lobate scarps'.
Diameter: 4,880 km
Distance from the Sun: 58 million km
Duration of one orbit: 87.969 days
Rotation: 59 days
Average temperature: Maximum: 430°C during the day; –180°C at night

---

VENUS: It's named after the Roman goddess of beauty and love. Venus and Earth are about the same size, and early astronomers believed that Venus was Earth's sister planet and had life on it. However, its temperatures were found to be too harsh for life to survive. Heat is trapped on the planet's surface by its thick layer of atmospheric clouds. It is the hottest of the planets, with the longest days. Venus has no moons or rings, and it is the only planet that rotates clockwise.
Diameter: 12,100 km
Distance from the Sun: 108 million km
Duration of one orbit: 225 days
Rotation: 243 days
Average temperature: 471°C

MARS: Named after the Roman god of war, this planet is known as the 'Red Planet' because of its red soil. It is prone to extreme dust storms, leading to a fascinating topography with huge sand dunes that shift constantly. Mars excites scientists because its seasons are more like Earth's than those of any other planet, and as many as 50 Mars missions have been recorded so far. Evidence suggests that Mars once had rivers, streams, lakes, and even an ocean. As its atmosphere depleted into outer space, its surface water began to evaporate and eventually dried up. Now the only water on Mars is either frozen in the polar caps, or underground. It has higher mountains and deeper canyons than any other planet. It also has the solar system's biggest volcano, Olympus Mons. The planet has two moons: Deimos and Phobos.
Diameter: 6,778 km
Distance from the Sun: 228 million km
Duration of one orbit: 687 days
Rotation: 25 hours
Average temperature: –28°C

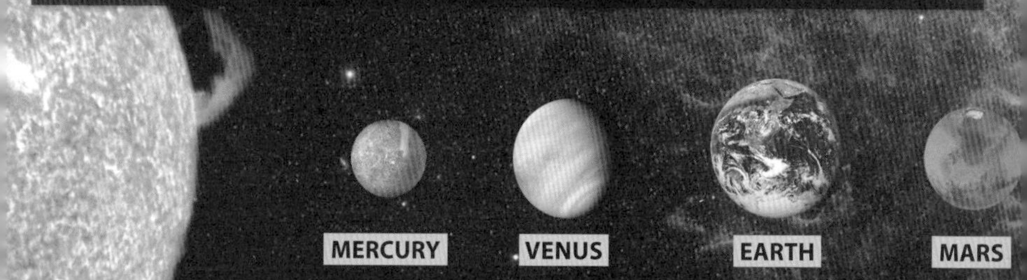

JUPITER: In Roman mythology, Jupiter overthrew his father Saturn, the king of gods. It is the largest of the solar system's planets and four of its 63 moons are planet-sized themselves. Jupiter's Great Red Spot is where a giant storm has been raging for at least 400 years across an area larger than Earth. This giant planet has no solid surface. Under its atmosphere is a large liquid ocean made of mostly hydrogen and some helium. There's no in-between layer; the atmosphere cools and thickens and becomes the ocean! You can see four of Jupiter's moons with a pair of binoculars at night. Jupiter spins really fast, taking only 10 hours to go from night to day. For that reason its middle has been stretched out.
Diameter: 142,984 km (11 times Earth's diameter)
Distance from the Sun: 778 million km
Duration of one orbit: 4,332 days
Rotation: 10 hours
Average temperature: –108°C

SATURN: Saturn was the Roman god of agriculture, the son of Uranus, the king of gods, whom he dethroned before being overthrown himself by his son Jupiter. Saturn has hundreds of beautiful rings made of ice and rock. In October 2009, NASA's Spitzer Space Telescope discovered a never-seen-before glowing ring around Saturn. Under the clouds of methane and helium, the planet's sky turns slowly into liquid until it becomes a giant ocean of chemicals. Saturn has 47 moons.
Diameter: 120,500 km
Distance from the Sun: 1.43 billion km
Duration of one orbit: 10,756 days
Rotation: 10 hours
Average temperature: –138°C

URANUS: Uranus was the Roman god of the skies, husband of Earth and the king of the gods. Unlike the other planets and most moons in our solar system, Uranus spins on its side, on a horizontal rather than a vertical axis. It is

> **"NASA administrator Jim Bridenstine believes Pluto is a planet. But, despite new observations by the New Horizons spacecraft, Pluto still does not meet all the three conditions defining a planet laid down by the International Astronomical Union in 2006, which classified Pluto as a dwarf planet."**

* Planet illustrations not to scale

believed that long ago a very large object smashed into it and changed the direction of its spin. Uranus may have an ocean of water beneath its clouds, a large rocky core, and trillions of large diamonds. It has 13 narrow rings and 27 moons.

Diameter: 51,118 km (four times the size of Earth)
Distance from the Sun: 2.87 billion km
Duration of one orbit: 30,687 days
Rotation: 17.2 hours
Average temperature: –195°C

NEPTUNE: Neptune was the Roman god of water and oceans. For many centuries nobody knew of this planet. It was discovered relatively late by Johann Galle and Heinrich D'Arrest in 1846. It was the first planet to be discovered by mathematical predictions. On Neptune rages a giant storm, the Great Dark Spot, much like the storm on Jupiter. It is not known how long this storm has been active, because it was studied only recently with the help of robotic exploratory probes. Neptune has 13 moons and six rings that circle it.

Diameter: 49,528 km (four times the size of Earth)
Distance from the Sun: 4.5 billion km
Duration of one orbit: 60,190 days
Rotation: 16 hours
Average temperature: –201°C

For Earth, see the *Earth* section

"The Moon is lemon-shaped. Its larger end points towards Earth."

A Rover 'Pet Rock', Among Other Discoveries on the Way to Mars

On a mission to explore Mars, NASA's rover *Perseverance*, launched in July 2020, has picked up an unusual passenger, a 'pet rock'! This rock, lodged inside its left front wheel, has ridden along across 8.5 km between early February and mid-June 2022. Though its journey has not been smooth, it has not caused the spacecraft's wheel any harm. The rover picked up the small Mars rock on 4 February when exploring a rock formation possibly made up of ancient lava. Now, travelling north and then west, the rover has drilled into its first sedimentary Mars rock. If the rock falls out among this very different geological landscape, it would confuse Mars explorers in the future.

The main objective of the rover is to identify signs of ancient life, and assemble samples of rocks and soil that can be brought back to Earth. Recently, *Perseverance* found the presence of wind whirls on the Jezero Crater and huge dust clouds being lifted by wind gusts. The rover also documented various sounds on Mars. Due to a thin atmosphere with carbon dioxide being the main element present, the sound on Mars is known to travel slower than on Earth.

Plants Grown in Moon Soil

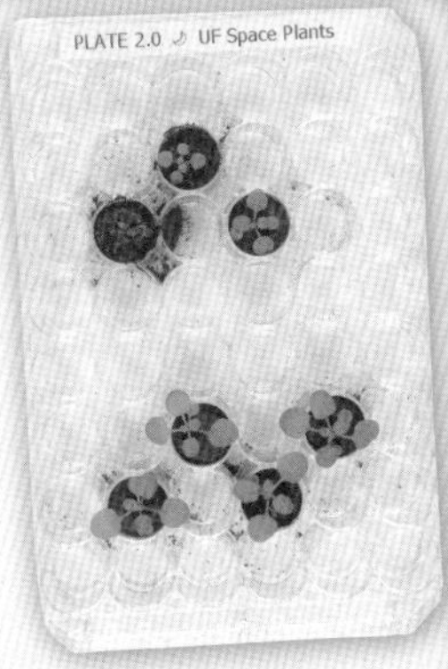

Years ago, astronauts from the Apollo 11,12 and 17 missions brought back regolith (broken rocks and soil) from the Moon back to Earth. Fifty years later, scientists have used these samples from Moon journeys to successfully grown plants. The seeds planted in lunar soil were of *Arabidopsis thaliana*, a relative of mustard green, and other vegetables belonging to the family of Cruciferae: artichokes, broccoli and cauliflower. Though these plants are not as robust as those grown on Earth, they have managed to sprout in lunar soil, which is poor in nutrients. This discovery paves the way for the possibility of plants growing on the surface of the Moon.

Living on Europa

NASA's Europa Clipper mission was established to gather information about Jupiter's moon, Europa. Its surface is covered with ice. The mission's objectives included locating the elements present below the surface of this ice shell, searching for the presence of undersurface water, and determining other oceanic and surface properties. The purpose of this is to evaluate habitability on Europa. The spacecraft is in orbit around Jupiter to conduct a detailed investigation about the surface of its moon. Europa is known to have the elements necessary to sustain life, including water, chemistry and energy. It is hypothesized that beneath the large icy ocean there are salty sea lines, which might be larger than the oceans present on Earth itself. To sustain life, Europa needs to possess necessary elements such as sulphur, oxygen and carbon. The presence of these elements has been noticeable, indicating a possibility for life

In June 2022, Elon Musk's SpaceX, the first private space company, launched Starlink, a satellite that provides low-cost wireless Internet connectivity to isolated locations by placing many satellites in the orbit. During the Russian attack on Ukraine, Musk had sent over 15,000 broadband service units to Ukraine for steady Internet connectivity.

on the planet. As far as energy is concerned, Jupiter's gravitational force creates tides on its moon, which in turn produce heat. The Europa Clipper is known to be the most advanced spacecraft technology sent to examine the habitability of other planets. It will be the third spacecraft to orbit Jupiter and only the second to be powered by solar energy. It is also NASA's first mission to study a moon other than Earth's Moon.

On 8 April 2022, Axiom Space, Inc., an American privately funded space infrastructure developer in Houston, Texas, launched its first private crew to ISS. The team comprised former NASA astronaut and Axiom Vice President Michael López-Alegría as commander, American entrepreneur and non-profit activist investor Larry Connor as pilot, Canadian investor and philanthropist Mark Pathy, and Israeli impact investor and philanthropist Eytan Stibbe. It is believed each person paid US $55 million to get their spot on the craft.

Watching the Earth

On 14 February 2022, the Earth Observation Satellite EOS-04 was launched from Satish Dhawan Space Centre, SHAR, Sriharikota, Andhra Pradesh. Earth observation satellites orbit the Earth while extracting important information about atmosphere, life, land, water and other essential elements of the ecosystem. With a power mission life of 10 years, the satellite aims to provide high-quality images via radar imaging under all weather conditions for applications in fields such as agriculture, forestry and plantations, soil moisture, hydrology and flood mapping. The satellite is accompanied by two small satellites (on INSPIREsat-1) from the Indian Institute of Space Science and Technology (IIST) and a technology demonstrator satellite (INS-2TD) from ISRO. It was launched as a replacement for the RISAT-1, which has been non-functional for the past few years.

Chandrayaan-2's Notes about the Sun

Chandrayaan-2 detected the presence of strong flares radiating from the surface of the sun in February 2022. These eruptions sometimes throw out high-energy particles (called solar proton events or SPEs) into space. They increase radiation exposure to humans in space and cause ionisation on a large scale in Earth's middle atmosphere, leading to geomagnetic storms and creating auroras in the polar sky. The Chandrayaan-2 mission was launched in July 2019 and has been integral to providing important information about the surface of the Moon and its composition. It identified the presence of water molecules on the surface of the Moon.

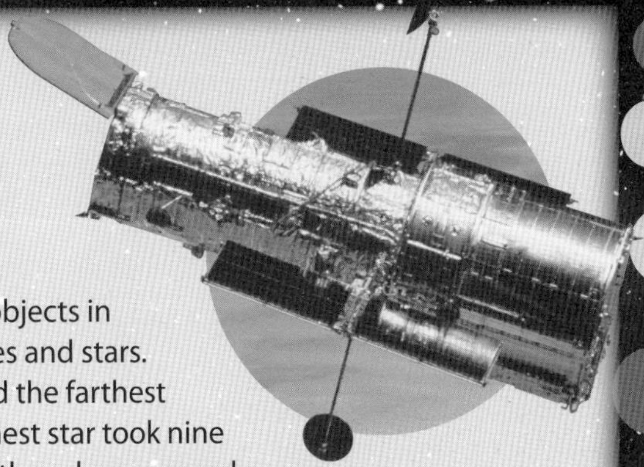

Farthest Star Found by Hubble Telescope

The Hubble Space Telescope is a giant telescope that was launched in space on 24 April 1990. Orbiting 547 km above Earth, it captures pictures of objects in space, such as planets, galaxies and stars. Recently, the Hubble detected the farthest star ever. The last known farthest star took nine billion light years to reach Earth and was named 'Icarus'. The new detected star took 12.9 billion light years to reach Earth. It is named 'Earendel', which translates to 'morning star' in Old English. Earendal is known to be older than other stars present in space and is hence thought to have different compositional elements.

The Most Powerful Telescope Ever

Now that it is fully commissioned, the James Webb Space Telescope is the world's leading cutting-edge space science observatory, an international collaborative programme led by NASA with its partners, ESA (European Space Agency) and the Canadian Space Agency. This telescope, it is hoped, will probe parts of space not yet reached, delve into the secrets of our solar system, and investigate stars and planetary bodies – all in a mammoth effort to understand our own planet and its place in the universe. The telescope immediately proved its worth by capturing signs of the presence of water, with evidence for clouds and haze in the

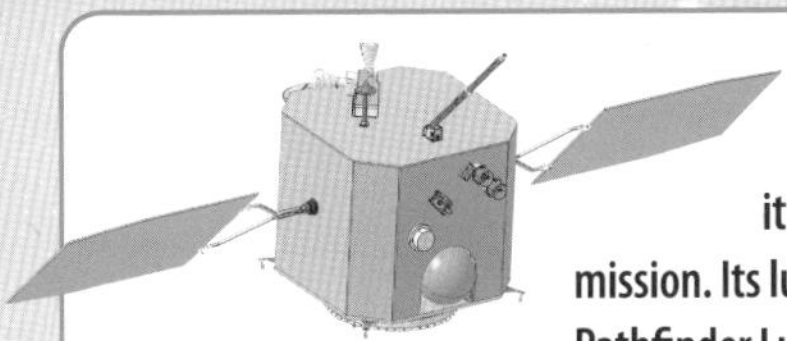

South Korea rises as a competitor in space as it launches it first Moon mission. Its lunar orbiter, called Korea Pathfinder Lunar Orbiter (KPLO), developed and managed by the Korea Aerospace Research Institute (KARI), was launched on 1 August 2022 to orbit the Moon for one year, while carrying a range of South Korean experiments and one US-built instrument. The objectives are to develop indigenous lunar exploration technologies, demonstrate a 'space Internet' and conduct scientific investigations of the lunar environment, topography and resources, as well as identify landing sites for future missions.

atmosphere of a giant planet that orbits a faraway Sun-like star. This revelation, which is based on ascertaining the presence of specific gas molecules evidenced by minuscule decreases in the brightness of the colours of the spectrum, is a path-breaking achievement and the most detailed analysis yet of space objects existing hundreds of light years away.

Russia Announces Plans to Leave the ISS

In July, Russia announced in an unspecific way that it would leave the International Space Station (ISS) 'after 2024'. Russia's attack on Ukraine has invited the ire of the Western countries as well as sanctions, including ones on its space industry. NASA's aim is to keep the ISS going until at least 2030, after which it plans to move on to smaller commercial stations, depending on the decisions of the multi-nation control board, which includes the USA, Russia, Europe, Japan and Canada. The ISS depends on Russian propulsion systems for boosts to maintain its orbit, around 400 km above sea level.

A NASA astronaut gets a workout on the International Space Station

A Girl-Power Satellite

When the Indian Space Research Organization's Small Satellite Launch Vehicle (SSLV) took off in August 2022 from the launch port in Sriharikota, Andhra Pradesh, it carried the work and hopes of 750 Indian girl school students, mentored by SpaceKidz India to encourage girls towards STEM subjects and careers in space. That's because the SSLV also carried the 'AzaadiSAT', built by these girls from scratch. The eight-kilo satellite carries 75 miniature payloads known as 'femto experiments' (also created by the students), a selfie camera to observe the performance of solar panels in space and a LoRa (Long Range Communications) transponder for low bandwidth connectivity to IoT (Internet of Things) devices at remote locations. There is also a messaging system for amateur radio operators besides sensors to monitor temperature, humidity and pressure, a gyroscope and a magnetometer.

7 HISTORY

History is the study of what happened in the past, based on what has been written down or documented. Events before written records are generally considered prehistory. History is about our efforts to make sense of the past, by using information gained from what people remember, by discovering things and by interpreting all that we know about these events. Here are a few useful words related to history:

Annals: Historical accounts of facts and events ranged in chronological order, year by year.

Antiquarianism: Historical study focusing on the empirical evidence of the past, including manuscripts and archives, and archaeological and historic sites and artefacts. Now the term is used as a criticism to describe a narrow approach that excludes a historical context.

Antiquities: Objects or artefacts from ancient history, especially from the classical civilizations, the cultures of the Mediterranean region and the ancient Near East (modern Middle East).

Archaeology: The study of human history and prehistory through the excavation of sites and the analysis of physical remains.

Archive: A collection of historical documents and records.

Artefact: Any material object associated with a culture, such as a tool, clothing or food item.

Chronicle: A historical account of facts and events arranged in chronological order.

Chronology: The study of the sequence of past events.

Epigraphy: The study of ancient inscriptions.

Illuminated manuscript: A manuscript in which the text is supplemented by the addition of decoration.

Macrohistory: The study of long-term trends in world history to uncover patterns across diverse cultures.

Microhistory: The detailed investigation of a small unit (an event, a community or an individual) to cast light on broader historical issues.

Numismatics: The study of coins.

Phaleristics: The study of military orders, decorations and medals.

Presentism: Application of present-day ideas to interpretations of the past.

Primary source: Material from or directly related to the past. Documents and records of the period under study, such as diaries, letters, legal documents, accounts, photographs, news reports and artefacts.

WORLD: A BRIEF TIMELINE

5000 BCE
- Rise of the Sumerian Civilization in Mesopotamia in what is roughly present-day Iraq.
- First recorded settlements in the fertile valley of the River Nile in Egypt.

3500 BCE The wheel, the first written language and the use of bronze are located in this period. In the Indus Valley the first use of pottery is recorded.

2600 BCE The emergence of Mayan Civilization in the Yucatan Peninsula in South America. In 2620 BCE, Imhotep builds the first pyramid – the 'step pyramid' at Saqqara – as a tomb for the pharaoh Djoser, and Egypt begins its first era of remarkable monuments.

2300 BCE Civilization recorded in China. Astronomy appears as a science. This time also marks the Neolithic Age in Europe.

2200 BCE First records of a civilization in the Malay Peninsula.

1480 BCE Moses leads Israelites out of Egypt.

1500 BCE Rise of the Vedic culture in north India. The Rig Veda is compiled around this time.

5000 BCE | 3500 BCE | 2500 BCE | 2000 BCE | 1500 BCE

2700–2600 BCE The Pyramids are built in Egypt.

2500 BCE Building of the city of Mohenjo-Daro in the Indus Valley, the third oldest civilization after Mesopotamia and Egypt.

2500–2000 BCE First records of the Andean Civilization, the first of its kind in the Americas.

2000–1200 BCE The Iron Age civilizations discover the use of iron and start using it for various activities, both for practical purposes and craft.

2000 BCE
- The rise of Babylon in the Mesopotamian Civilization.
- King Hammurabi raises the first trained army in the world.
- The Bronze Age reaches Europe.
- Britain is invaded by the Scandinavian tribes for the first time.
- A civilization rises in Japan, soon after which Chinese and Korean groups invade it.

2250–1122 BCE Rise of the Chinese Civilization along the banks of the River Huang He.

HISTORY

1027 BCE The Chou Dynasty is established in China.

1000 BCE The decline of Egypt begins.

850 BCE *The Iliad* and *The Odyssey* are composed by Homer.

776 BCE The first Olympic Games are held in Olympia, Greece.

753 BCE The city of Rome is founded by Romulus.

660 BCE Birth of Zoroaster, the founder of Zoroastrianism in Media, Iran.

586 BCE Fall of Jerusalem to the Babylonians.

560 BCE Gautama Buddha, founder of Buddhism, is born in Lumbini in present-day Nepal.

509 BCE Founding of the Roman Republic. The great architecture of Rome can be traced to this period.

399 BCE Socrates, the Greek philosopher, is sentenced to death.

347 BCE Death of Greek philosopher Plato, disciple of Socrates and founder of the Academy, a school of philosophy in Athens, Greece.

336 BCE Accession of Alexander at the age of 22 to the throne of Macedon in south-east Europe. He will become one of the most successful conquerors of all time.

264 BCE Ashoka is crowned, marking the start of the Golden Age in India.

215 BCE Work begins on the Great Wall of China.

73 BCE For the first time in history, slaves revolt against the Roman Republic in the Spartacus Uprising.

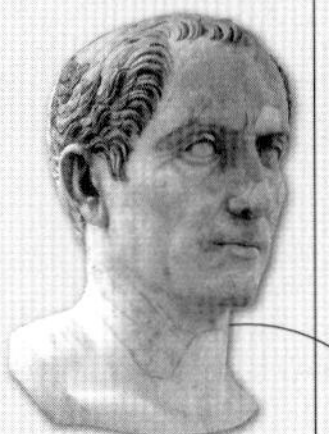

55 BCE Julius Caesar conquers Britain, having already captured Gaul in present-day France.

44 BCE Julius Caesar is killed by Brutus and other conspirators.

4 BCE–7 CE The birth of Jesus Christ (variously recorded).

1000 BCE | 500 BCE | 250 BCE | 0 BCE

0 CE | 1000 CE | 1500 CE | 1750 CE

29 CE Jesus Christ is crucified.

64 CE A fire, which lasts for six days, destroys Rome.

570 CE Birth of Prophet Muhammad, the founder of Islam, in Mecca.

1163 The University of Oxford is founded in England.

1215 The Magna Carta, the historic charter of rights and laws in England, is signed.

1337 Beginning of the Hundred Years' War between England and France; ends only in 1453.

1431 Joan of Arc is burnt at the stake in France for allegedly practising witchcraft.

1455 CE The War of Roses, a civil war in England, begins; ends in 1485.

1492 Christopher Columbus discovers the Americas.

1504 The *Mona Lisa* is painted by Leonardo da Vinci.

1564 Birth of poet and playwright William Shakespeare in England.

1642 Civil war in England. King Charles I is in a feud with the Parliament, as they demand democratic powers. Eventually, he is executed in 1653.

1666 London is engulfed by the 'Great Fire'.

1689 Constitutional monarchy is established in England.

1756 Britain, Prussia and Hanover combine to battle Austria, France, Russia, Saxony, Sweden and Spain in the Seven Years' War.

1770 Captain James Cook discovers Australia.

1776 Declaration of American Independence.

1789 On 14 July, the French Revolution begins with the storming of the Bastille prison to free prisoners and end monarchy.

1854 Admiral Perry of the USA visits Japan and forces trade with the West. ● The Crimean War takes place between 1853 and 1856. Lord Cardigan leads the British cavalry against the Russians in what becomes known as 'The Charge of the Light Brigade'.

1860 Herman Hollerith invents an electronic tabulator for the US census. He starts a company that eventually becomes International Business Machines (IBM) Corporation.

1795 The Metric system of measurement is introduced in France.

1861–65 American Civil War; President Lincoln bans slavery; some states attempt to break the Union.

1812 On 24 June, Napoleon takes Moscow, but it is a hollow victory. The city is burned to the ground, yet the Tsar does not surrender. Napoleon and the French army retreat.

1848 Karl Marx and Friedrich Engels publish *The Communist Manifesto*.

1847 US troops, led by General Winfield Scott, enter Mexico City in September. A treaty ending the Mexican–American War is signed in February 1848.

1800 CE | 1825 CE | 1850 CE | 1875 CE

1815 On 18 June, Napoleon is finally defeated at Waterloo, Belgium, by the Duke of Wellington.

1856 Louis Pasteur shows that diseases spread from tiny organisms. Modern-day germ theory is born.

1859 Charles Darwin publishes *On the Origin of Species*.

1814 The Battle of Trafalgar: The British fleet under the command of Horatio Nelson defeats a combined French and Spanish fleet.

1845–48 The Great Hunger (aka Potato Famine) in Ireland. More than 1.5 million die of starvation and disease.

1866 Prussia invades Austria. ● The United States and Europe are connected by a 4,000 km long telegraph cable.

1833 England outlaws slavery and frees more than 780,000 slaves.

1804 Napoleon Bonaparte is crowned emperor of France.

1838 On 24 January, Samuel Morse demonstrates the telegraph machine.

1901 Guglielmo Marconi sends the first transatlantic wireless radio signal.

1904 Russo-Japanese War: The Russians underestimate the modern Japanese fleet, which destroys most of the already depleted Russian Navy a year later. The Japanese use the new Marconi radios to keep track of the Russian Navy.

1898 The Spanish-American War starts. Reports of atrocities by the Spaniards against Cubans compel the USA to intervene.

1905 While working as a patent clerk, Albert Einstein publishes his theory of relativity and also states energy equals matter ($E = mc^2$). He publishes four papers in one year. Three of them are Nobel Prize–winning material.

1939 Hitler invades Poland on 1 September. The British Commonwealth and France declare war on Germany, starting the Second World War.

1876 Alexander Graham Bell patents the telephone.

1930 The first FIFA World Cup starts: Lucien Laurent scores the first goal for France, against Mexico.

1928 Scottish bacteriologist Alexander Fleming notices penicillin mould killing a staphylococcus culture. The 'antibiotics revolution' begins.

1875 CE | 1900 CE | 1915 CE | 1940 CE

1899-1902 Boer War: The descendants of the Dutch in present-day South Africa fight for independence from Britain.

1938 Adolf Hitler, Chancellor of Germany since 1933, launches *Kristallnacht*, the 'night of broken glass'. Hundreds of Jews are killed by Nazis.

1903 Orville and Wilbur Wright fly the first aircraft.

1912 The 'unsinkable' *Titanic* sinks with more than 1,500 passengers.

1918 On 11 November, the First World War ends.

1914 On 3 August, Germany declares war on France, starting the 'Great War' (First World War).

1941 On 22 June, Operation Barbarossa, the invasion of Russia by Germany, is launched 129 years (to the day) after Napoleon invaded Russia.
- On 8 December, the Japanese attack Pearl Harbour, effectively bringing the USA into the Second World War.

1883 The island volcano of Krakatoa in Indonesia erupts on 23 August. More than 36,000 people are killed. Its impact is seen as far away as London and New York. The sound of the explosion is heard 5,000 km away.

1917 The USA enters the First World War against Germany. Ten million people will die in the war.

1942 At the University of Chicago, USA, Enrico Fermi conducts the first nuclear reaction.

1944 The largest offshore landing in history, the invasion of Normandy, referred to as D-Day, starts on 6 June. This spells the end for Hitler's Third Reich.

1945 On 6 August, the USA drops an atomic bomb, 'Little Boy', on Hiroshima, Japan, killing an estimated 66,000 civilians. On 9 August, another bomb, 'Fat Man', is dropped on Nagasaki. Japan announces its surrender to the Allied powers on 15 August; it signs the Instrument of Surrender on 2 September.

1957 Russian-made Sputnik I becomes the first man-made satellite.

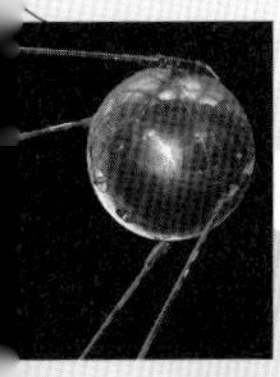

1961 On 11 April, Yuri A. Gagarin becomes the first human in space.

1969 On 20 July, Neil Armstrong lands on the surface of the Moon.

1990 Apartheid ends in South Africa.
- The First Gulf War begins when the USA attacks Iraq in response to Iraq's invasion of Kuwait.

1991 The Soviet Union dissolves, and with it, the Cold War with the USA.

1994 Rwanda is engulfed in a bloody civil war.

2001 On 11 September, terrorists in planes crash into the World Trade Center twin towers in New York, and the Pentagon in Washington DC.

2003 US and British forces invade Iraq. Saddam Hussein is caught, and executed in 2006.

2004 On 26 December, a huge tsunami kills thousands in Indonesia, Thailand, Sri Lanka, India, Maldives and Somalia.

2009 On 20 January, Barack Obama is sworn in as the first African-American president of the USA.

1950 CE | 1975 CE | 2010 CE | 2021 CE

1989 In Tiananmen Square, the Chinese army crushes a demonstration, killing hundreds of students.
- In November, the Berlin Wall that divided West Berlin from East Berlin is torn down. Germany is united for the first time since the Second World War.

2011 A democratic uprising in Egypt sets off similar civil uprisings, collectively called the 'Arab Spring', in Libya, Bahrain, Syria, Yemen, Algeria, Iraq, Jordan and Lebanon.
- On 1 May, Osama bin Laden, head of terrorist organization al-Qaeda, is killed in Pakistan by US Special Forces.

2014 In March, Russia annexes Crimea.

2017 The USA pulls out of the landmark Paris Climate Accord.

2018 Former cricketer Imran Khan of the Tehreek-e-Insaaf party becomes Pakistan's prime minister.

2019 Boris Johnson becomes UK prime minister after Theresa May resigns.

2020 COVID-19, a global pandemic, fans out from Wuhan, China, in December 2019, and is declared a Public Health Emergency of International Concern by WHO on 30 January 2020.
- The UK withdraws from the European Union (EU) on 31 January, a move popularly known as 'Brexit'.

2021 Democrat nominee Joe Biden begins his tenure as US president in January after defeating former president and Republican nominee Donald Trump. Vice President Kamala Harris becomes the first woman, first African American and first Asian American to hold the office.
- In August, the USA withdraws troops from Afghanistan, resulting in the Taliban taking over Kabul and more than two-thirds of the country.

2022 Russia invades Ukraine on 21 February. Much of the international community condemns Russia, and many countries implement economic sanctions against the country and its companies.
- Pakistan's prime minister Imran Khan is removed from office after losing a no-confidence vote on 4 April and replaced by Shehbaz Sharif, president of the Pakistani Muslim League.
- Boris Johnson resigns as British prime minister on 8 July.

ANCIENT INDIA TIMELINE

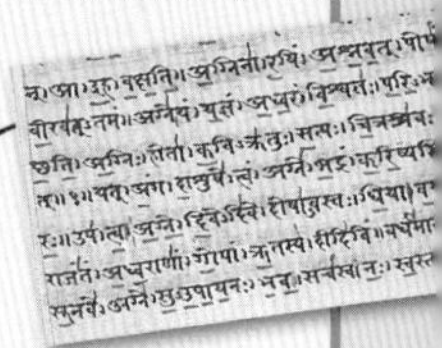

3000 BCE	The beginning of the Harappan (Indus Valley) Civilization.
2500 BCE	The establishment of the cities of Harappa and Mohenjo-Daro in the **Valley of the River Indus.**
2000 BCE	The decline of the Harappan Civilization.
1500 BCE	The people later referred to as the 'Vedic' people set up a recognizable Vedic culture in the Gangetic plains.
1100 BCE	With the discovery of iron, the Vedic people start using iron tools.
1800-1100 BCE	One of the earliest sacred scriptures of the Hindus, the **Rig Veda** (variously dated) is composed.
750 BCE	The Upanishads, a set of sacred texts of Hinduism, are composed.
600 BCE	Sixteen Mahajanapadas (Great States) are formed on the subcontinent.
543 BCE	King Bimbisara conquers the Magadha region in the east and becomes emperor of the Magadha Empire.
527 BCE	**Prince Siddhartha Gautama** attains Enlightenment, becomes the Buddha, and establishes Buddhism.
500 BCE	Prince Mahavira establishes Jainism in north India.
493 BCE	Bimbisara dies and is succeeded by Ajatashatru.
461 BCE	Ajatashatru expands the Magadha territory and dies shortly afterwards.
327 BCE	**Alexander of Macedonia** invades the Indus Valley on the Indian subcontinent, fights a famous battle with Puru (Porus).
304 BCE	Magadha king Chandragupta Maurya establishes the Mauryan dynasty with Pataliputra as the capital.
500–300 BCE	The Ramayana, the famous Hindu epic, is composed. There are various dates (between 500 and 300 BCE) put down for Valmiki's Ramayana.
300 BCE	The Chola dynasty establishes the first kingdom in southern India with its capital at Thanjavur.
290 BCE	Chandragupta's son Bindusara extends the Mauryan Empire to the Deccan region.
259 BCE	Mauryan emperor **Ashoka** converts to Buddhism.
220 BCE	The Mauryan dynasty expands to nearly all of India.
200 BCE	The famous epic, the **Mahabharata**, is composed. (Some sources put it down between 500 BCE and 200 BCE and others between 200 BCE and 200 CE).
184 BCE	The Mauryan dynasty ends and makes way for the beginning of the Sunga dynasty.

78 BCE	The Sunga dynasty declines.
50 CE	The first Buddhist stupa is built at Sanchi (now in Madhya Pradesh).
300 CE	The Pallava dynasty is established in Kanchipuram (now in Tamil Nadu).
350 CE	The Sangam is compiled in Tamil in the kingdom of Madurai. The Puranas are composed.
390 CE	**Chandragupta II** extends the Gupta kingdom to Gujarat.
450 CE	Kumaragupta, who succeeds Chandragupta II, builds the monastic university of Nalanda (in present-day Bihar).
499 CE	Mathematician Aryabhata writes the *Aryabhatiya,* a compendium of mathematics and astronomy.
500 CE	The beginning of the Bhakti cult in Tamil Nadu.
528 CE	The Gupta Empire sees a downfall due to continuous invasions.
550 CE	The **Chalukya kingdom** is established in central India with its capital at Badami.
606 CE	Harshavardhana rules the kingdom of Thanesar in north India and Nepal with its capital at Kannauj (in present-day Uttar Pradesh).

MEDIEVAL INDIA

761 CE	Muhammad bin Qasim battles Raja Dahir in Sind.
1000 CE	Invasion of Mahmud of Ghazni.
1017–30 CE	**Al-Biruni**, the scholar from Persia, travels in India.
1191 CE	The First Battle of Tarain is fought between Muhammad Ghori (from present-day Afghanistan) and Prithviraj Chauhan. Ghori is defeated by Prithviraj.
1192 CE	The Second Battle of Tarain is fought between Ghori and **Prithviraj Chauhan**.
1194 CE	Muhammad Ghori and Jaichandra, the Gahadavala king of Kannauj, fight the Battle of Chandawar.
1221 CE	**Genghis Khan** invades Punjab.
1310 CE	Alauddin Khilji's army occupies Devagiri, destroying the Seuna Yadava kingdom.
1336 CE	The **Vijayanagara Empire** is established by Harihara I and his brother Bukka Raya I in the Deccan.
1347 CE	Governor Hasan Gangu revolts against Muhammad bin Tughlaq, founding the Bahmani Sultanate.

1370 CE	Bukka, the Vijayanagara ruler, and his son Kumara Kampana capture the entire Tamil-speaking region.
1407 CE	Zafar Khan, governor of Gujarat, declares himself Sultan Muzaffar Shah, founding the Gujarat Sultanate/Muzaffarid dynasty.
1451 CE	Bahlul Khan Lodi ascends the throne of the Delhi Sultanate, starting the Lodi dynasty.
1469 CE	**Guru Nanak**, the founder of Sikhism, is born.
1486 CE	**Sher Shah Suri**, founder of the Suri Empire, is born in Sasaram.
1490 CE	Ahmadnagar declares independence, followed by Bijapur and Berar in the same year, thus breaking up the Bahmani Sultanate.
1497–99 CE	**Vasco da Gama** makes his first voyage from Europe to India and back.
1503 CE	The kingdom of Kochi is taken over by the Portuguese; this is the first European settlement in India.
1509 CE	The Battle of Diu marks the beginning of the dominance of the Europeans in the Asian naval theatre.
1522 CE	The Portuguese land on the Coromandel Coast.

MUGHAL ERA

1526 CE	Sultan Ibrahim Lodi of the Delhi Sultanate angers local nobles, who respond by inviting Babur, the ruler of Kabul, to invade Delhi and Agra.
1527 CE	**Babur** annexes Mewar.
1530 CE	Babur completes his *Baburnama*. He dies, and is succeeded by his son Humayun.
1539 CE	The Battle of Chausa is fought between Humayun and Sher Shah Suri. Humayun is defeated.
1540 CE	The Battle of Kannauj: Humayun is defeated by the Afghans (Suri Dynasty), and spends 12 years in exile.
1552 CE	**Humayun** regains the throne of Delhi.
1556 CE	Humayun dies, and is succeeded by his son Akbar.
1556 CE	The Second Battle of Panipat is fought between Hemu (Hem Chandra Vikramaditya) and Akbar.
1565 CE	The Battle of Talikota results in the conquest of the Vijayanagara Empire by the Deccan sultanates.
1572 CE	**Akbar** annexes Gujarat.
1574 CE	Akbar annexes Bengal.
1586 CE	Akbar annexes Kashmir.
1600 CE	The East India Company is formed in England. It gets exclusive trading rights in India.

1605 CE	Akbar dies, and is succeeded by his son Jahangir.
1628 CE	Jahangir dies, and is succeeded by his son Shah Jahan.
1630 CE	Birth of **Chhatrapati Shivaji Maharaj**.
1658 CE	After completing the Taj Mahal, the Jama Masjid and the Red Fort, Shah Jahan dies. He is succeeded by his son Aurangzeb.
1674 CE	Forces led by Chhatrapati Shivaji Maharaj defeat Aurangzeb's troops, and establish the Maratha Empire.
1675 CE	Guru Tegh Bahadur, the ninth Guru of the Sikhs, is executed in Delhi on the orders of Mughal emperor Aurangzeb.
1680 CE	Chhatrapati Shivaji Maharaj dies at Raigad.
1681 CE	Aurangzeb invades the Deccan.
1699 CE	**Guru Gobind Singh**, the tenth Guru of the Sikhs, creates Dal Khalsa, a military force.
1707 CE	Aurangzeb dies, and is succeeded by his son Bahadur Shah I.
1708 CE	Guru Gobind Singh survives an assassination attempt in Maharashtra.
1719 CE	**Bajirao I** is appointed the Peshwa by Maratha emperor Shahu.
1735 CE	The annexation of Rajputana by Peshwa Bajirao I.
1737 CE	Bajirao I conquers Delhi; the Mughal emperor is spared and kept as a symbolic head.
1740 CE	Bajirao I dies, with the distinction of winning every battle he fought. He is succeeded by Balaji Bajirao.
1757 CE	The British East India Company's private army under **Robert Clive** annexes Bengal in the Battle of Plassey.
1760 CE	The Marathas comprehensively defeat the Nizam of Hyderabad; the Maratha Empire reaches its zenith.
1761 CE	The Afghans dominate in the Third Battle of Panipat, blocking Maratha expansion.
1766 CE	The Sikhs defeat Ahmad Shah Abdali; establish Sikh rule in Punjab. The First Anglo-Mysore War between Mysore's (now Mysuru) Hyder Ali and the East India Company.
1779 CE	Maratha Mahadji Shinde routs the British at the Battle of Wadgaon.
1782 CE	The First Anglo-Maratha War ends with the Treaty of Salbai.
1790 CE	The Marathas defeat the Rajputs of Jaipur and their Mughal allies at the Battle of Patan.
1799 CE	The Fourth Anglo-Mysore War ends with the death of **Tipu Sultan** and the restoration of the Wodeyar dynasty that had ruled Mysore earlier.

1801	**Maharaja Ranjit Singh** establishes Khalsa rule over Punjab, ruling from present-day Lahore.
1807	The East India Company signs the Treaty of Amritsar with Maharaja Ranjit Singh.
1818	The Third Anglo-Maratha War ends with the defeat of Bajirao II and the end of the Maratha Empire, leaving the British in control of most of India.

BRITISH RAJ

1853	First passenger train runs from Bori Bunder in Bombay to Thane in present-day Maharashtra.
1857	**Widespread uprising** in north India against British rule (the First War of Independence). It is crushed and the queen of England declares India a colony.
1858	The British Crown officially takes over Indian governance.
1877	The queen of England is proclaimed empress of India.
1885	The first meeting of the Indian National Congress.
1899	**Lord Curzon** becomes Governor General and viceroy of India.
1905	The first partition of Bengal takes place.
1906	The All-India Muslim League is formed.
1912	The capital of British India is shifted to Delhi from Calcutta.
1919	The **Jallianwala Bagh** massacre takes place in the wake of protests against the Rowlatt Act, which allows political cases to be tried without juries and suspects to be imprisoned without trial.
1920	Mahatma Gandhi launches the Non-cooperation movement.
1922	The violent Chauri Chaura incident takes place during the Civil Disobedience movement; Mahatma Gandhi calls off the protest.
1928	Simon Commission comes to India and is boycotted by all parties.
1930	**Salt Satyagraha**, which begins with the Dandi March, is launched as an agitation against the salt tax. The First Round Table Conference takes place in London.
1931	The Second Round Table Conference takes place and the Gandhi–Irwin Pact is signed.
1934	The Civil Disobedience movement is called off.
1942	Gandhi meets the Cripps Mission; the Quit India movement is launched.
1943	Netaji Subhas Chandra Bose takes charge of the Indian National Army.
1947	**Lord Mountbatten** draws up plans for Partition of India. Partition of India and independence from British rule, at midnight of 14/15 August.

MODERN HISTORY (POST-INDEPENDENCE)

1947–48	Thousands die in widespread communal riots during and after the Partition of India into two nations: India and Pakistan.
1948	On 30 January, Mahatma Gandhi, on his way to his daily prayer meeting, is assassinated by Nathuram Godse. The first conflict with Pakistan breaks out over the territory of Kashmir.
1951–52	The first general elections are held and the Congress party wins. **Jawaharlal Nehru** is elected prime minister (PM). 
1962	India loses brief war with China.
1964	Prime Minister Jawaharlal Nehru dies. Lal Bahadur Shastri becomes India's second prime minister.
1965	The second war with Pakistan over Kashmir is fought.
1966	**Indira Gandhi**, Nehru's daughter, is elected prime minister. 
1971	Third war with Pakistan over creation of Bangladesh. The Soviet Union and India sign a 20-year treaty of friendship.
1974	India's first underground nuclear test is carried out.
1975	Indira Gandhi declares Emergency in the country.
1975–77	Nearly 1,000 political opponents are imprisoned during the Emergency.
1977	Indira Gandhi loses the general elections.
1980	Indira Gandhi returns to power, heading a Congress party splinter group – Congress (Indira) – and winning by a huge margin.
1983	The Indian cricket team wins the (Prudential) World Cup for the first time, under the captaincy of Kapil Dev.
1984	Troops storm the Golden Temple in Amritsar, Punjab, the hideout of Sikh militants demanding self-rule. Prime Minister Indira Gandhi is assassinated by bodyguards, sparking off anti-Sikh riots in Delhi and across India. **Rajiv Gandhi**, her son, becomes prime minister.  Toxic gas leaks at the Union Carbide pesticides plant in Bhopal. Thousands are killed and many more affected.
1987	India sends troops for peacekeeping operations in Sri Lanka's civil conflict with the Liberation Tigers of Tamil Eelam (LTTE).
1989	Congress is routed in the elections. V.P. Singh (Janata Dal) is PM.
1990	Indian troops are withdrawn from Sri Lanka.
1991	Rajiv Gandhi is assassinated by a suicide bomber.
1992	The Babri mosque in Ayodhya is demolished, triggering widespread communal violence.

1996	The Congress party suffers electoral defeat and the Bharatiya Janata Party (BJP) emerges as the largest single party.
1998	BJP forms a coalition government under Prime Minister **Atal Bihari Vajpayee**. This will be the first non-Congress government to complete a full term. India conducts five nuclear tests, closely followed by Pakistan.
1999	Vajpayee takes the new bus service to Pakistan to meet its prime minister, Nawaz Sharif, and sign the Lahore Peace Declaration. Conflict with Pakistan-backed forces in the Kargil region. A cyclone devastates Odisha, with at least 10,000 dead.
2000	The billionth Indian citizen is born.
2001	A **massive earthquake** in Gujarat leaves at least 30,000 dead. Vajpayee meets President Pervez Musharraf of Pakistan in the first summit of the neighbours in more than two years. On 13 December, the Parliament is attacked by five terrorists from the Lashkar-e-Taiba and Jaish-e-Mohammed, leading to nine deaths, and a stand-off between India and Pakistan. The attackers are killed.
2002	Scientist **A.P.J. Abdul Kalam** is elected president of India.
2003	India and Pakistan resume flights between the two countries, which were banned after the December 2001 terrorist attack on the Indian Parliament.
2004	The United Progressive Alliance (UPA), with the Congress party as the largest member party, forms the government after the general elections. Dr Manmohan Singh becomes prime minister.
2006	President George W. Bush of the USA signs an agreement with Prime Minister Manmohan Singh to share nuclear technology.
2007	Pratibha Patil becomes India's first woman president.
2008	Terrorists from Pakistan terrorists **attack landmark spots** in Mumbai.
2009	India's unmanned lunar probe Chandrayaan-1 discovers water molecules on the Moon's surface.
2010	The Indian rupee gets a symbol: ₹ The Indian government initiates the Right of Children to Free and Compulsory Education Act to provide free and compulsory education to all children between six and 14 years of age. The 19th Commonwealth Games, are held in Delhi, from 3 to 14 October 2010.
2011	Mamata Banerjee's Trinamool Congress ends the 34-year rule of the Left coalition led by the CPI-M in West Bengal.

2012	Pranab Mukherjee is elected as India's 13th president. Hamid Ansari is re-elected as vice-president of India.
2012	Terrorist Ajmal Kasab is hanged for his role in the 2008 Mumbai attacks.
2013	The Criminal Law (Amendment) Act 2013 is passed after the 16 December 2012 'Nirbhaya' case.
2014	The National Democratic Alliance (NDA), led by the BJP, wins the general elections. Narendra Modi becomes the 15th Indian PM.
2016	The Goods and Services Tax (GST), the biggest tax reform since Independence, is launched on the midnight of 30 June. Ram Nath Kovind becomes the second Dalit president of India after K.R. Narayanan (1997–2002).
2018	The BJP wins the legislative assembly elections in Tripura, a Left stronghold for 25 years.
2019	The BJP wins the general elections with a thumping majority and **Narendra Modi** becomes prime minister for a second term. The government abrogates Article 370 of the Constitution, which gave special status to Jammu and Kashmir, and bifurcates the state into two Union Territories: Jammu and Kashmir, and Ladakh.
2020	Prime Minister Modi announces a 21-day lockdown throughout India, the largest in world history, to prevent the spread of COVID-19. National Education Policy 2020 (NEP 2020), a new policy on education, is approved by the Union cabinet. Prime Minister Narendra Modi performs *bhoomipujan* and lays the foundation stone of the Ram Temple in Ayodhya, Uttar Pradesh. Three Indian agriculture acts of 2020, referred to as the Farm Bills, are initiated by the Parliament of India in September 2020.
2021	For the first time in history, the Union budget is presented on an India-made tablet as a paperless budget. The contentious Farm Bills are repealed on 19 November. The Supreme Court permits women to take the National Defence Academy examination.
2022	PARAM PORUL, a state-of-the-art supercomputer is inaugurated, under Phase 2 of the National Supercomputing Mission (NSM), at NIT Tiruchirappalli, Kerala, on 25 May 2022, jointly by the Department of Science and Technology (DST) and the Ministry of Electronics and Information Technology (MeitY). Shiv Sena President Uddhav Thackeray resigns from the post of chief minister of Maharashtra on 29 June and former party member Eknath Shinde takes his place after proving majority support for his government. Droupadi Murmu, a member of the BJP, becomes the 15th president of India on 25 July 2022, the first person belonging to the tribal community and the second woman after Pratibha Patil to hold the office.

A shekel, c. 310 to 290 BCE (representational image)

Silver Shekel Found

An 11-year-old girl found a 2,000-year-old shekel on the 'Pilgrimage Road' in the City of David in Jerusalem, Israel. Dr Robert Kool, head of the Coin Department at the Israel Antiquities Authority, declared the coin as 'rare'. It is believed only 30 coins were made of silver during that era. The coin is speculated to date back to 67–68 CE. It weighs 14 grams with inscriptions on both sides. On one side, the coin is inscribed with a cup above which the inscribed words translate to 'Israeli shekel'. Next to it, an inscription refers to the 'second year' of the Great Revolt involving Jews and Romans. On the reverse, the headquarters of the High Priest and the words 'Holy Jerusalem' are carved.

The Black Plague Was Asian

Studies reveal Central Asia to be the origin place of the Second Plague pandemic, also called the Black Death, that lasted from the 14th century until the early 18th century.

Tombstones discovered 140 years ago in Kyrgyzstan are thought to be the earliest evidence of this plague in Asia. Syriac inscriptions on these stones say that the victims died unexpectedly in 1338 and 1339 from an unidentified sickness. In their studies of DNA from human bones, Phil Slavin of the University of Sterling and his colleagues found similar inscriptions at two locations and the presence of the plague bacterium, *Yersinia pestis*. Modern strains match the medieval source strain present in rat populations of the Tian Shan Mountains.

The Dance of Death, inspired by the Black Death, was a recurring motif in late medieval times

USS Wreck Tracked

After 78 years, an undersea technology company, Caladan Oceanic, found the ruins of USS *Samuel B. Roberts*, a destroyer cruiser, 23,000 feet underwater off the coast of the Philippines.

On 25 October, 1944, the ship, with a 224-strong crew, sank in the Battle of Leyte. Many of the crew members died from wounds and shark attacks. The deepest wreck ever discovered, this one crossed the usual commercial limit of 6,000 m and used the deepest side-scan sonar ever placed on a submersible.

8 INDIA: STATES AND UNION TERRITORIES

TOP STATES/UNION TERRITORY STATISTICS

Largest by area: Rajasthan

Smallest by area: Goa

State with the longest coastline: Gujarat, with a mainland coastline of 1,600 km (approx.)

State with longest international border: West Bengal; 2,216.7 km long border with Bangladesh

State sharing borders with most states/UTs: Uttar Pradesh; shares borders with nine Indian states/UTs – Bihar, Chhattisgarh, Delhi, Haryana, Himachal Pradesh, Jharkhand, Madhya Pradesh, Rajasthan and Uttarakhand

Most populated: Uttar Pradesh

Least populated: Lakshadweep

Highest population density: Delhi

Lowest population density: Arunachal Pradesh

Highest literacy rate: Kerala

Longest railway network: Uttar Pradesh

Longest road network: Maharashtra

Best Smart State 2022: Uttar Pradesh

Best Smart UT 2022: Chandigarh

Best Smart Cities 2022: Indore (Madhya Pradesh) and Surat (Gujarat)

State with the most UNESCO World Heritage elements (Intangible, cultural, historical or other sites): Rajasthan (Hill forts, Jaipur city, Jantar Mantar, Keoladeo Ghana National Park, Kalbelia songs and folk dances); and Maharashtra (Ajanta, Ellora and Elephanta caves, Chhatrapati Shivaji Maharaj Terminus, Victorian Gothic and art deco ensembles of Mumbai and [shared] Western Ghats)

City with the most UNESCO World Heritage Sites: Delhi, with the Red Fort complex, Qutub Minar complex and Humayun's Tomb

Cities with UNESCO Heritage City status: Ahmedabad (Gujarat) and Jaipur (Rajasthan)

Highest Sustainable Development Goals Index Score 2021–22: State: Kerala: 75; UT: Chandigarh: 79

Highest Swachh Survekshan Ranking 2021: Hyderabad (citizen feedback category)

Cleanest City Award 2021: Indore (Madhya Pradesh) – five-time winner

States/UTs with most Wildlife Sanctuaries and National Parks: Madhya Pradesh and the Andaman and Nicobar Islands: nine National Parks each; Andaman and Nicobar Islands: 96 Wildlife Sanctuaries

* All information has been updated up to 15 August 2020

ANDHRA PRADESH

Capital: Amaravati

Location: South-eastern coast

Area: 160,205 sq. km

Population: 49,634,314

History: Formed in 1956; reorganized in 2014

Language: Telugu, Urdu

Literacy Rate: 67.02%

Governor: Biswa Bhusan Harichandan

Chief Minister: Y.S. Jagan Mohan Reddy

Major Rivers: Godavari, Krishna

Industries: Textiles, shipbuilding, aquaculture, auto parts, cement, coal mining

Agriculture: Rice, cotton, maize

State Animal: Blackbuck

State Bird: Rose-ringed parakeet

ARUNACHAL PRADESH

Capital: Itanagar

Location: North-east

Area: 83,743 sq. km

Population: 1,382,611

History: Formed in 1987

Languages: Nisi, Dafla and others

Literacy Rate: 65.38%

Governor: Brig. (Dr) B. Mishra (Retd)

Chief Minister: Pema Khandu

Major Rivers: Siang

Industries: Forest products, handloom, clay

Agriculture: Rice, potato, tea, apple, pineapple

State Animal: Gayal (Mithun)

State Bird: Great hornbill

ASSAM

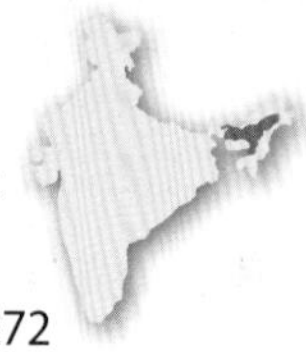

Capital: Dispur

Location: North-east

Area: 78,438 sq. km

Population: 31,169,272

History: Formed in 1947

Languages: Assamese, Bengali, Bodo, Karbi, Dimasa

Literacy Rate: 72.19%

Governor: Prof. Jagdish Mukhi

Chief Minister: Himanta Biswa Sarma

Major Rivers: Brahmaputra, Barak

Industries: Tea, cement, textiles, sericulture, oil refining, coal mining

Agriculture: Rice, jute, tea, cotton

State Animal: Indian rhinoceros

State Bird: White-winged wood duck

BIHAR

Capital: Patna

Location: East

Area: 94,163 sq. km

Population: 103,804,637

History: Formed in 1936; reorganized in 2000

Languages: Hindi, Bhojpuri

Literacy Rate: 61.8%

Governor: Phagu Chauhan

Chief Minister: Nitish Kumar

Major Rivers: Ganga, Gandak, Son

Industries: Food and beverages, plastic and rubber, tobacco, textiles, leather, dairy

Agriculture: Rice, wheat, maize, pulses, sugar cane, jute

State Animal: Gaur

State Bird: House sparrow

Background: Andhra Pradesh

INDIAN STATES

CHHATTISGARH

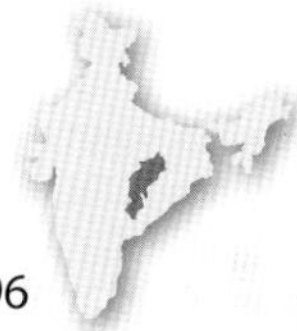

Capital: Raipur
Location: East-central
Area: 135,194 sq. km
Population: 25,540,196
History: Formed in 2000
Languages: Chhattisgarhi, Hindi
Literacy Rate: 70.28%
Governor: Anusuiya Uikey
Chief Minister: Bhupesh Baghel
Major Rivers: Mahanadi, Indravati
Industries: Cement, mining, steel, aluminium, electricity
Agriculture: Rice, maize, wheat, niger seed, pulses
State Animal: Wild buffalo
State Bird: Hill mynah

GOA

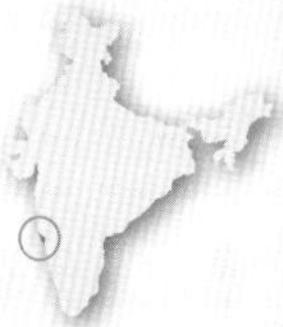

Capital: Panaji
Location: West
Area: 3,702 sq. km
Population: 1,457,723
History: Formed in 1987
Languages: Konkani, Marathi
Literacy Rate: 88.7%
Governor: P.S. Sreedharan Pillai
Chief Minister: Pramod Sawant
Major Rivers: Mandovi, Zuari
Industries: Mining, textiles, tourism and hospitality, fisheries
Agriculture: Rice, millets, maize, cashew, coconut, bananas, sugar cane, pineapples, areca nuts
State Animal: Gaur
State Bird: Ruby-throated yellow bulbul

GUJARAT

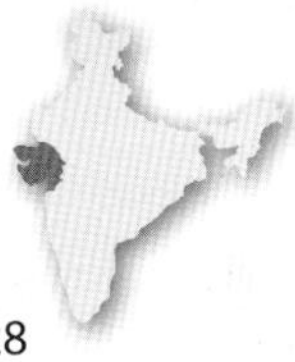

Capital: Gandhinagar
Location: West
Area: 196,024 sq. km
Population: 60,383,628
History: Formed in 1960
Language: Gujarati
Literacy Rate: 78.03%
Governor: Acharya Dev Vrat
Chief Minister: Bhupendra Patel
Major Rivers: Narmada, Tapti, Sabarmati, Mahi
Industries: Fertilizers, textiles, petroleum, engineering, diamonds
Agriculture: Groundnuts, cotton, rice, wheat
State Animal: Asiatic lion
State Bird: Greater flamingo

HARYANA

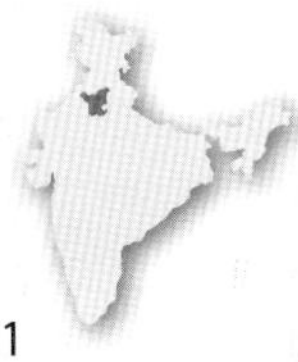

Capital: Chandigarh
Location: North
Area: 44,212 sq. km
Population: 25,353,081
History: Formed in 1966
Languages: Hindi, Haryanvi
Literacy Rate: 75.55%
Governor: Bandaru Dattatreya
Chief Minister: Manohar Lal Khattar
Major Rivers: Yamuna, Ghaggar
Industries: Handloom, electrical appliances, automobiles, IT
Agriculture: Sugar cane, oilseeds, rice, groundnuts, maize, wheat, pulses, mustard
State Animal: Blackbuck
State Bird: Black francolin

Background: Chhattisgarh

HIMACHAL PRADESH

Capital: Shimla; Dharamshala (winter)
Location: North
Area: 55,673 sq. km
Population: 6,856,509
History: Formed in 1971
Languages: Hindi, Pahari
Literacy Rate: 82.8%
Governor: Rajendra Vishwanath Arlekar
Chief Minister: Jai Ram Thakur
Major Rivers: Beas, Ravi, Chenab, Sutlej, Yamuna
Industries: Food and beverages, electronics, pharmaceuticals, hydroelectricity
Agriculture: Wheat, rice, maize, barley, fruits, olives, sugar cane
State Animal: Snow leopard
State Bird: Western tragopan

JHARKHAND

Capital: Ranchi
Location: East
Area: 79,714 sq. km
Population: 32,966,238
History: Formed in 2000
Languages: Hindi, Santhali
Literacy Rate: 66.41%
Governor: Ramesh Bais
Chief Minister: Hemant Soren
Major Rivers: Damodar, Subarnarekha
Industries: Steel, locomotives, mining, sericulture
Agriculture: Rice, wheat, maize, pulses, mustard
State Animal: Indian elephant
State Bird: Koel

KARNATAKA

Capital: Bengaluru
Location: South-west
Area: 191,791 sq. km
Population: 61,130,704
History: Formed in 1956 as Mysore State; named Karnataka in 1973
Language: Kannada
Literacy Rate: 75.36%
Governor: Thaawarchand Gehlot
Chief Minister: Basavaraj Bommai
Major Rivers: Krishna, Kaveri
Industries: IT, telecom, electronics, floriculture, silk
Agriculture: Rice, ragi, sorghum, pulses, pearl millet, coffee
Animal: Indian elephant
State Bird: Indian roller

KERALA

Capital: Thiruvananthapuram
Location: South-west
Area: 38,863 sq. km
Population: 33,387,677
History: Formed in 1956
Language: Malayalam
Literacy Rate: 94%
Governor: Arif Mohammad Khan
Chief Minister: Pinarayi Vijayan
Major Rivers: Periyar, Bharatapuza, Pamba, Chaliyar, Chalakudy
Industries: Handlooms and textiles, coir, marine products, agro-industries, electronics, tourism and hospitality, handicrafts
Agriculture: Coconut, rubber, tea, coffee, cashew, spices, rice, tapioca
State Animal: Indian elephant
State Bird: Great hornbill

Background: Himachal Pradesh

MADHYA PRADESH

Capital: Bhopal
Location: Central
Area: 308,000 sq. km
Population: 72,597,565
History: Formed in 1956; reorganized in 2000
Language: Hindi
Literacy Rate: 69.32%
Governor: Mangubhai Chhaganbhai Patel
Chief Minister: Shivraj Singh Chouhan
Major Rivers: Narmada, Chambal, Betwa, Tapti
Industries: Automotive, electronics, cement, tourism, telecom, IT, forestry, textiles
Agriculture: Rice, wheat, millets, pulses, cotton, soyabean
State Animal: Barasingha
State Bird: Indian paradise flycatcher

MAHARASHTRA

Capital: Mumbai
Location: West
Area: 307,713 sq. km
Population: 112,372,972
History: Formed in 1960
Language: Marathi
Literacy Rate: 82.34%
Governor: Bhagat Singh Koshyari
Chief Minister: Eknath Shinde
Major Rivers: Godavari, Wainganga, Penganga, Wardha, Bhima, Tapti
Industries: Textiles, engineering, pharmaceuticals, sugar, automotive, cinema, food products, breweries, printing and publishing
Agriculture: Rice, millets, sugar cane, pulses, oranges, mango
State Animal: Indian giant squirrel
State Bird: Yellow-footed green pigeon

MANIPUR

Capital: Imphal
Location: North-east
Area: 22,327 sq. km
Population: 2,721,756
History: Formed in 1972
Language: Manipuri
Literacy Rate: 76.94%
Governor: La. Ganesan
Chief Minister: N. Biren Singh
Major Rivers: Barak, Imphal
Industries: Handloom, bamboo
Agriculture: Rice, wheat, maize, pulses, apricot, oranges
State Animal: Sangai
State Bird: Nongyeen

MEGHALAYA

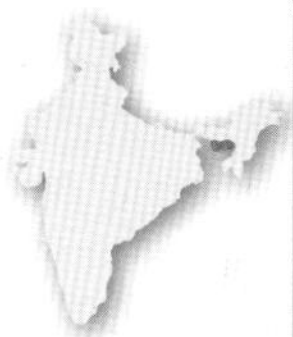

Capital: Shillong
Location: North-east
Area: 22,429 sq. km
Population: 2,964,007
History: Formed in 1972
Languages: Garo, Khasi, Bengali, Assamese
Literacy Rate: 74.43%
Governor: Satya Pal Malik
Chief Minister: Conrad Kongkal Sangma
Major Rivers: Simsang, Umiam, Umtrew
Industries: Plywood, horticulture, agro-industries, cement, tourism handicrafts, sericulture
Agriculture: Rice, maize, oilseeds, tea, coffee, mushrooms, potato, fruits including pineapple, betel nut
State Animal: Clouded leopard
State Bird: Hill mynah

Background: Manipur

MIZORAM

Capital: Aizawl

Location: North-east

Area: 21,087 sq. km

Population: 1,091,014

History: Formed in 1987

Language: Mizo

Literacy Rate: 91.33%

Governor: Dr Kambhampati Haribabu

Chief Minister: Pu Zoramthanga

Major Rivers: Tlawng, Tiau, Chhimtuipui, Tuirial, Tut, Tuivai

Industries: Handloom, bamboo, food processing, tea, sericulture

Agriculture: Maize, rice, sugar cane, tapioca, ginger, cotton

State Animal: Serow

State Bird: Hume's bar-tailed pheasant

NAGALAND

Capital: Kohima

Location: North-east

Area: 16,579 sq. km

Population: 1,980,602

History: Formed in 1963

Languages: Angami, Ao, Chang, Konyak, Lotha, Sangtam, Sema and Chakhesang

Literacy Rate: 79.55%

Governor: Prof. Jagdish Mukhi

Chief Minister: Neiphiu Rio

Major Rivers: Dhansiri, Doyang

Industries: Handloom, handicrafts, bamboo, food processing, forestry products

Agriculture: Rice, maize, millets, tea, bananas, pineapples, ginger

State Animal: Mithun

State Bird: Blyth's tragopan

ODISHA

Capital: Bhubaneswar

Location: East

Area: 155,707 sq. km

Population: 41,947,358

History: Formed in 1936

Language: Odia

Literacy Rate: 72.87%

Governor: Prof. Ganeshi Lal

Chief Minister: Naveen Patnaik

Major Rivers: Mahanadi, Brahmani, Baitarani, Subarnarekha, Salandi

Industries: Steel, aluminium, thermal power, cement, IT, petrochemicals, food processing

Agriculture: Rice, wheat, millets, oilseeds, coconut, cotton

State Animal: Sambar deer

State Bird: Indian roller

PUNJAB

Capital: Chandigarh

Location: North

Area: 50,362 sq. km

Population: 27,704,236

History: Formed in 1966

Language: Punjabi

Literacy Rate: 75.84%

Governor: Banwarilal Purohit

Chief Minister: Bhagwant Singh Mann

Major Rivers: Beas, Jhelum, Ravi, Sutlej, Chenab

Industries: Sugar, dairy, machine tools, textiles, sports goods

Agriculture: Wheat, rice, oilseeds, maize, sugar cane, cotton, pulses

State Animal: Blackbuck

State Bird: Northern goshawk

Background: Odisha

RAJASTHAN

Capital: Jaipur
Location: North-west
Area: 342,239 sq. km
Population: 68,621,012
History: Formed in 1949
Languages: Rajasthani dialects, such as Marwari, Mewariand others; Hindi
Literacy Rate: 66.11%
Governor: Kalraj Mishra
Chief Minister: Ashok Gehlot
Major Rivers: Banas, Luni, Sabarmati, Chambal, Mahi, Gambhir
Industries: Zinc and copper, cement, sugar, glass, semi-precious stones
Agriculture: Millets, pulses, maize, oilseeds, barley, cotton, chillies, rice
State Animal: Camel; Chinkara
State Bird: Great Indian bustard

SIKKIM

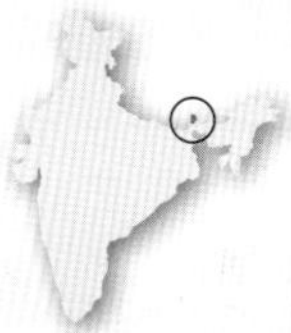

Capital: Gangtok
Location: North-east
Area: 7,096 sq. km
Population: 607,688
History: Formed in 1975
Languages: Nepali, Bhutia, Lepcha
Literacy Rate: 81.42%
Governor: Ganga Prasad
Chief Minister: P.S. Golay
Major Rivers: Teesta, Rangeet, Takcham Chu, Ramphu Chu
Industries: Bamboo, handicrafts, handloom, carpet-weaving, floriculture, jewellery, tea, electronics
Agriculture: Oranges, cardamom, ginger, turmeric, cherry, pepper, baby corn
State Animal: Red panda
State Bird: Blood pheasant

TAMIL NADU

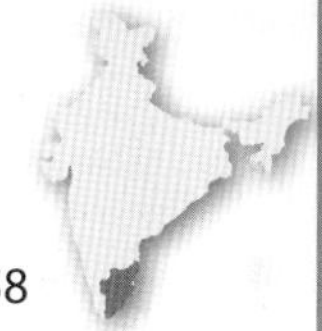

Capital: Chennai
Location: South
Area: 130,058 sq. km
Population: 72,138,958
History: Formed in 1956
Language: Tamil
Literacy Rate: 80.09%
Governor: Ravindra Narayan Ravi
Chief Minister: M.K. Stalin
Industries: Textiles, commercial vehicles, sugar, paper, electronic hardware, cement
Agriculture: Rice, sugar cane, cotton, coconut, cashew, tea, rubber, coffee
State Animal: Nilgiri tahr
State Bird: Emerald dove

TELANGANA

Capital: Hyderabad
Location: South-east
Area: 112,077 sq. km
Population: 35,003,674
History: Formed in 2014
Languages: Telugu, Urdu
Literacy Rate: 66.54%
Governor: Dr Tamilisai Soundararajan
Chief Minister: K. Chandrashekar Rao
Major Rivers: Godavari, Krishna, Musi
Industries: Sugar, textiles, IT, pharmaceuticals, cement
Agriculture: Rice, maize, millets, tobacco, sugar cane
State Animal: Jinka (spotted deer)
State Bird: Palapitta

Background: Rajasthan

TRIPURA

Capital: Agartala
Location: North-east
Area: 10,491 sq. km
Population: 3,671,032
History: Formed in 1972
Languages: Kokborok, Bengali
Literacy Rate: 87.22%
Governor: Satyadev Narayan Arya
Chief Minister: Dr Manik Saha
Major Rivers: Gomti, Khowai, Longai
Industries: Natural gas, food processing, rubber, tea, bamboo, handloom, handicrafts, sericulture
Agriculture: : Fruits, cashew nut, jackfruit, coconut, tea, rice, rubber
State Animal: Phayre's leaf monkey
State Bird: Green imperial pigeon

UTTAR PRADESH

Capital: Lucknow
Location: North
Area: 240,928 sq. km
Population: 199,581,477
History: Formed in 1950
Language: Hindi
Literacy Rate: 67.68%
Governor: Anandiben Mafatbhai Patel
Chief Minister: Yogi Adityanath
Major Rivers: Ganga, Gomti, Yamuna, Ghaghara, Ken, Betwa, Chambal, Son
Industries: Sugar, textiles, mining, automobiles, IT, cement, handloom, fruits, forestry, food processing
Agriculture: Rice, wheat, pulses, sugar cane, barley, millets, potatoes, cotton, tobacco
State Animal: Barasingha
State Bird: Sarus crane

UTTARAKHAND

Capital: Dehradun (winter); Bhararisain/ Gairsain (summer)
Location: North
Area: 53,483 sq. km
Population: 10,116,752
History: Formed in 2000
Languages: Kumaoni, Garhwali, Hindi
Literacy Rate: 78.82%
Governor: Lieutenant General (Retd) Gurmit Singh
Chief Minister: Pushkar Singh Dhami
Major Rivers: Ganga, Yamuna, Alaknanda, Ramganga, Kali
Industries: Mining, forestry, hydel power projects, food processing, textiles, auto components
Agriculture: Rice, wheat, barley, millets, oilseeds, sugar cane, pulses
State Animal: Himalayan musk deer
State Bird: Himalayan monal

WEST BENGAL

Capital: Kolkata
Location: East
Area: 88,752 sq. km
Population: 91,347,736
History: Formed in 1947; reorganized in 1950 and 1956
Language: Bengali
Literacy Rate: 76.26%
Governor: Jagdeep Dhankhar
Chief Minister: Mamata Banerjee
Major Rivers: Hooghly, Teesta, Damodar, Rupnarayan
Industries: Steel, power, jute, tea, engineering, textiles, leather, aquaculture, coal mining
Agriculture: Rice, jute, maize, oilseeds, sugar cane, tea
State Animal: Fishing cat
State Bird: White-throated kingfisher

Background: West Bengal

ANDAMAN AND NICOBAR ISLANDS

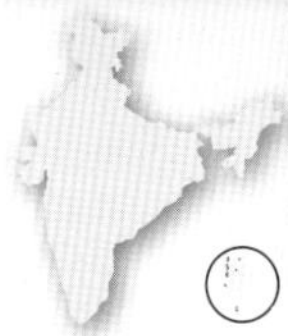

Capital: Port Blair
Location: Bay of Bengal
Area: 8,249 sq. km
Population: 379,944
History: Formed in 1947
Languages: Hindi, Bengali, Tamil, Telugu, Malayalam
Literacy Rate: 86.63%
Lt Governor: Admiral (Retd) Devendra Kumar Joshi
Industries: Handicrafts, fisheries, plastics, fibreglass, mild steel, tourism
Agriculture: Paddy, coconut, areca nuts, bananas, mangoes, pepper, clove, nutmeg, cinnamon
Official Animal: Dugong
Official Bird: Andaman wood pigeon

DADRA AND NAGAR HAVELI AND DAMAN AND DIU

Capital: Daman
Location: Between Maharashtra and Gujarat
Area: 603 sq. km
Population: 586,764
History: Formed in 2020 by combining two Union Territories
Languages: Marathi, Gujarati, Bhili, Hindi
Literacy Rate: 81.67%*
Administrator: Praful Khoda Patel
Major Rivers: Daman Ganga, Bhagwan, Kalem
Industries: Tiles, chemicals, rubber, forestry products, animal husbandry, textiles and yarns, plastic, metal-based units, tourism
Agriculture: Rice, mango, sapota (chikoo), coconut

* Taken as an average of the two former UTs

CHANDIGARH

Location: Between Punjab and Haryana
Area: 114 sq. km
Population: 10,55,450
History: Formed in 1966
Languages: Hindi, Punjabi
Literacy Rate: 86.05%
Administrator: Banwarilal Purohit
Industries: Light engineering, electrical/electronic items, machine tools, pharmaceuticals, plastics
Agriculture: Wheat, maize, rice
Official Animal: Indian grey mongoose
Official Bird: Indian grey hornbill

JAMMU AND KASHMIR

Capital: Srinagar
Location: North
Area: 42,241 sq. km
Population: 53,50,811
History: Formed in 2019*
Languages: Kashmiri, Dogri, Urdu, Hindi
Literacy Rate: 67.16%**
Lt Governor: Manoj Sinha
Major Rivers: Jhelum, Chenab
Industries: Machinery, sericulture, handicrafts, horticulture
Agriculture: Paddy, wheat, fruit, saffron, cumin, fruits
Official Animal: Hangul (earlier)
Official Bird: Black-necked crane (earlier)

* Official date of creation announced as 31 October 2019;
**Before the division

Background: Andaman and Nicobar Islands

UNION TERRITORIES

LADAKH

Capital: Leh
Location: North
Area: 59,146 sq. km
Population: 290,492
History: Formed in 2019*
Languages: Ladakhi (Bhoti), Purki, Shina, Tibetan, Balti, Urdu, Hindi
Literacy Rate: 77.20%
Lt Governor: Radha Krishna Mathur
Major Rivers: Indus, Zanskar, Shyok, Suru
Industries: Tourism, mountaineering
Agriculture: Barley, wheat, rice
Official Animal: Snow leopard
Official Bird: Black-necked crane

* Official date of creation announced as 31 October 2019

LAKSHADWEEP

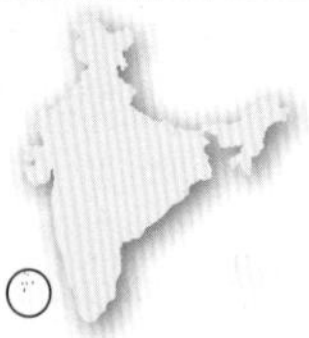

Capital: Kavaratti
Location: Arabian Sea
Area: 32 sq. km
Population: 64,429
History: Formed in 1956
Languages: Jeseri (Dweep Bhasha), Malayalam, Tamil, Urdu, Hindi
Literacy Rate: 91.85%
Administrator: Praful Khoda Patel
Industries: Coconut fibre, coir fibre, matting, fisheries
Agriculture: Coconut
Official Animal: Butterfly fish
Official Bird: Noddy tern

**WHAT ARE NCT AND NCR?

The NCT, a Union Territory of India, is administered by the Union Government and the elected government of NCT. It includes the metropolitan area of Delhi as well as nine districts, 59 census towns and 300 villages. NCR stands for National Capital Region and includes regions around Delhi, such as cities like Gurugram and Faridabad (Haryana), and Noida and Ghaziabad (Uttar Pradesh), which are parts of other states. The NCR has been expanded to embrace Sonepat, Bahadurgarh and Meerut. However, the NCR is not a legal or electoral entity.

PUDUCHERRY

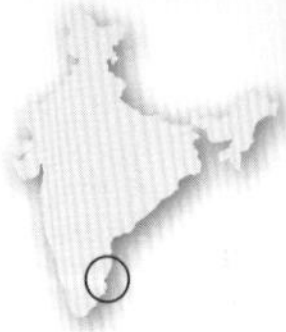

Capital: Puducherry
Location: South
Area: 483 sq. km
Population: 1,244,464
History: Formed in1954
Languages: Tamil, Telugu, Malayalam, French
Literacy Rate: 85.85%
Lt Governor: Dr Tamilisai Soundararajan
Chief Minister: N. Rangaswamy
Major Rivers: Ponnaiyar, Koringa
Industries: Textiles, computer products, electronics, leather
Agriculture: Rice, pulses, groundnuts, coconuts, spices, chillies
Official Animal: Indian palm squirrel
Official Bird: Asian koel

NATIONAL CAPITAL TERRITORY OF DELHI**

Location: North
Area: 1,484 sq. km
Population: 16,753,235
History: The Union Territory of Delhi was officially renamed the National Capital Territory of Delhi in 1991 under the NCT Act of the same year
Languages: Hindi, Punjabi, Urdu
Literacy Rate: 86.21%
Lt Governor: Vinai Kumar Saxena
Chief Minister: Arvind Kejriwal
Major River: Yamuna
Industries: Light machines, textiles, automobile parts, bicycles, leather, sports and consumer goods, IT
Agriculture: Wheat, maize, millets vegetables, pulses
Official Animal: Nilgai
Official Bird: House sparrow

SUPERLATIVES

Fastest Animal Blackbuck (Indian antelope) (speed: 80 km/h)

Largest Animal (land) Asian elephant (shoulder height: 2.4–2.75 m/ 7.8–9 ft; weight: 3,000–5,400 kg)

Largest Bird Great Indian bustard (length: 1.2 m/4 ft; weight: 15 kg)

Smallest Bird Pale-billed flowerpecker (length: 8 cm/3.1 in.; weight: 4–8 g)

Longest Bridge (railroad) Bogibeel Bridge, Assam (length: 4.94 km)

Tallest Building The 42, Kolkata, West Bengal (height: 268 m/879 ft)

Longest Canal Indira Gandhi Canal (length: 649 km)

Highest City Leh, Ladakh (altitude: 3,500 m/11,483 ft)

Largest City Delhi (area: 1,484 sq. km)

Most Populated City Mumbai, Maharashtra: 18,394,912 (as per Govt. of India data for Census 2011)

Longest Corridor Ramanathaswamy Temple, Rameswaram, Tamil Nadu (corridor length: 1,220 m/4,002 ft)

Largest Dam Bhakra Nangal Dam, Himachal Pradesh and Punjab (height: 226m/ 741 ft; length: 520 m/ 1,706 ft – on the River Sutlej)

Longest Dam Hirakud Dam, Odisha (length: 25.79 km – on the River Mahanadi)

Highest Dam Tehri Dam, Uttarakhand (height: 260.5 m/854.6 ft – on the Rivers Bhagirathi and Bhilangana)

Largest Delta Ganga–Brahmaputra, Bay of Bengal (Total area: 105,641 sq. km; 35,213.6 sq. km in India and 70,427.3 sq. km in Bangladesh)

Largest Desert Thar Desert (area: approx. 200,000 sq. km)

Biggest Dome (new architecture) World Peace Monument Dome, Pune, Maharashtra (diameter: 48.77 m/160 ft)

Biggest Dome (old architecture) Gol Gumbaz, Vijayapura, Karnataka (diameter: 43.89 m/144 ft)

Largest Island Great Nicobar Island, Bay of Bengal (area: 921 sq. km)

INDIA

Deepest Lake
Manasbal Lake, Jammu and Kashmir (average depth: 4.5 m/15 ft)

Highest Lake
Gurudongmar Lake, Sikkim (altitude: 5,425 m/17,800 ft)

Largest Lake (artificial)
Govind Ballabh Pant Sagar, Uttar Pradesh (active capacity: 8.9 billion cubic m)

Largest Lake (freshwater)
Kolleru Lake, Andhra Pradesh (area: 245 sq. km)

Tallest Minaret (freestanding)
Qutub Minar, Delhi (height: 72.5 m/238 ft)

Largest Lake (saltwater)
Chilika Lake, Odisha (maximum surface area – monsoon: 1,165 sq. km)

Largest National Park
Hemis National Park, Leh, Ladakh (area: 3,350 sq. km)

Coldest Place (region)
Siachen, Ladakh (average temp: – 50°C)

Hottest Place
Churu, Rajasthan (maximum recorded temperature: 50.3°C

Largest Port
Deendayal Port, by cargo handling capacity: 267.10 MTPA* (2020–21)

Longest Platform (railway)
Gorakhpur railway station, Uttar Pradesh (length: 1,366.33 m/4,482.7 ft)

Longest Railway Route
Vivek Express: Dibrugarh to Kanyakumari (length: 4,286 km)

Longest River
Ganga (length: 2,525 km)

Longest National Highway
NH-44 (length: 3,745 km)

Rainiest Spot
Mawsynram, Meghalaya (average annual rainfall: 11,873 mm/467 in.)

Largest Stadium
Narendra Modi Stadium, Ahmedabad, Gujarat (spread across 63 acres/25.5 hectares; seating capacity: 132,000)

Tallest Statue
Statue of Unity, Gujarat, (height: 182 m/597 ft)

Longest Tunnel (railway)
Pir Panjal Railway Tunnel, Jammu and Kashmir (length: 11.21 km)

Longest Tunnel (road)
Dr Syama Prasad Mookerjee Tunnel, Jammu and Kashmir (length: 9.2 km)

Longest Wall
Kumbhalgarh Fort, Rajasthan (length: 1,100 m/3,600 ft)

Highest Waterfall
Kunchikal Falls, Karnataka (height: 455 m/1,493 ft)

* Metric tonnes per annum

9 SCIENCE AND TECHNOLOGY

Science and technology, like space, have no frontiers! And this is clear from the kind of technologies coming up! Here are a few:

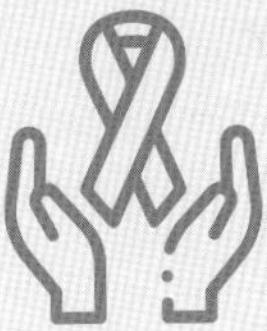

Drug cures a type of cancer: An experimental trial was conducted to test the effects of the drug Dostarlimab. The test was administered to 18 patients diagnosed with rectal cancer at the Memorial Sloan Kettering Cancer Center in Manhattan, US. The trial lasted for six months. The results showed that Dostarlimab eliminated the tumours of all participants present in the study. It was the first time in the history of a cancer treatment alternative that a cancer drug has shown such extensive success. Taking this into consideration, Dostarlimab is now being tested for other forms of cancer treatment as well.

Special gel heals heart damage: Researchers at the University of Manchester, UK, have developed a special biodegradable gel that can repair damage incurred due to a heart attack. This gel is made up of chains of amino acids known as peptides and can be injected into the beating heart, to provide a safe support for damaged cells to grow new tissue. In the past, under other experiments, when cells have been injected straight into the heart, only one per cent have stayed in place and survived.

Scientists believe that this cell regenerative therapy can be a useful technique, which will allow heart patients to sustain the fatal damage caused during a heart attack.

A step towards sustainability: In an effort to save valuable resources and practise sustainable development, a research team from Guwahati in Assam, India, has developed a bioelectrochemical device with the ability to generate green energy by treating wastewater. The device uses Microbial Fuel Cell (MFC), which allows it to have a dual function through which it generates bioelectricity and manages wastewater simultaneously.

The device use microorganisms that release enzymes, converting organic substrates of wastewater into chemical energy. This chemical energy is later converted to electrical energy and put to greater use.

BRANCHES OF SCIENCE

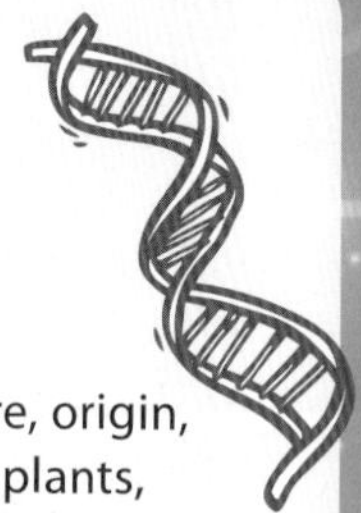

Science is divided into four main branches: Natural Sciences, Social Sciences, Applied Sciences and Formal Sciences.

NATURAL SCIENCES involve the study of natural phenomena or the laws of the physical world.

- **BIOLOGY** is the study of living things, including their structure, origin, growth, evolution, function and distribution. **Botany** deals with plants, **zoology** with animals and **microbiology** with microscopic organisms.
- **CHEMISTRY** deals with the composition of substances as well as their properties and reactions. **Organic chemistry** is the study of carbon and its compounds. **Inorganic chemistry** is the study of the structure, properties and reactions of chemical elements and their compounds. **Biochemistry** studies chemical processes that occur inside living organisms.
- **EARTH SCIENCES** study the earth, its composition and structure. **Geology** is about the earth's inner rock formation. **Geography** is the study of the earth's terrain. **Oceanography** focuses on ocean currents and habitats. **Meteorology** studies the weather, and **Astronomy** is the study of objects and matter outside Earth's atmosphere.

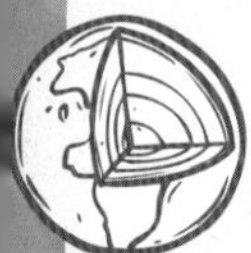

- **ENVIRONMENTAL SCIENCES** are concerned with the relationship between organisms and their environment.
- **PHYSICS** is associated with the study of properties and interactions of time, space, energy and matter.

SOCIAL SCIENCES study human behaviour.

- **ANTHROPOLOGY** studies human physical traits, cultures and languages.
- **ECONOMICS** is the study of how money, goods and businesses affect people.
- **LAW** focuses on the rules of society, communities and nations.
- **POLITICAL SCIENCE** studies governmental processes and institutions.
- **PSYCHOLOGY** focuses on how the human mind functions.
- **SOCIOLOGY** analyses how humans behave in groups.

APPLIED SCIENCES involve the practical use of scientific knowledge.

- **BIOTECHNOLOGY** applies biological processes to make medicines and vaccines, and to enhance the quality of food and crops.
- **COMPUTER SCIENCE** focuses on computers and their functions.
- **ENGINEERING** is about the construction of machines and systems.

FORMAL SCIENCES form the category under which mathematics, statistics, logic and theoretical computer science fall. These disciplines, also called the 'formal' systems, have formal languages, based on logical reasoning, that contain strings of symbols and follow fixed sets of rules.

PHYSICS

Physics is the science that studies force, motion, heat, light, sound, electricity, magnetism, and changes that happen to these phenomena, not pertaining to chemical or biological changes.

MECHANICS AND MOTION

Mechanics is the field of physics dealing with the action of forces on solids, liquids and gases at rest or in motion. When forces act upon an object to make it change position with respect to time, it is known as motion. One of the ways to measure motion is to find out how much distance an object moves in one unit of time. This is known as speed, while velocity is speed in a definite direction. Velocities could increase or decrease in a given time period. The acceleration of an object is defined as its rate of change of velocity in one unit of time (usually measured in seconds).

NEWTON'S LAWS OF MOTION

In the 1680s, **Sir Isaac Newton**, an English physicist, worked on the idea of motion and formulated the three fundamental laws of motion.

THE FIRST LAW: This states that an object continues in its state of rest or of uniform motion unless an external force is applied to it.

THE SECOND LAW: The second law states that the acceleration of an object is dependent upon two variables – the force acting upon the object and the mass of the object.

THE THIRD LAW: The third law of motion states that for every action, there is an equal and opposite reaction. So if object A exerts a force on object B, then object B also exerts the same amount of force on object A.

HEAT

Heat is a form of energy caused by the motion of atoms and molecules in a body. When you increase the heat of a body, you are, in effect, increasing the amount of energy in its molecular system. When heat moves from one area to another, it is because millions of atoms and molecules are working together. The effect of heat on any atom leads to an increase in temperature and an expansion of volume (for example, railway tracks have expansion joints that let them expand and contract with temperature changes), or a possible change of physical state, like a solid turning to liquid, and a liquid turning to gas (as seen in the three states of ice, water and steam/vapour). This is known as a physical change.

LIGHT

Light is a form of energy that acts on the eye, illuminating objects. Light consists of electromagnetic (EM) waves that travel in straight lines. If you pass a ray of light through a glass prism, the colours split up into the 'spectrum' – the rainbow of colours in visible light when separated. What we call 'light' indicates only the light waves visible to us as human beings. There are different colours of light because of light waves that have different wavelengths: red light has the longest wavelength while violet light has the shortest. As far as we know, all types of light move at the same speed in a vacuum. The speed of light in a vacuum is 299,792.458 km/s. Funnily enough, light is used to measure really long distances, using a unit called a 'light year'. A light year is a unit of length equal to the distance light travels in a vacuum in one year. This distance is calculated to be 9,460,700,000,000 km (9.4607×10^{12} km).

> **"At least 18 per cent of humans respond to bright lights by sneezing. This is called the photic sneeze reflex. It was first medically described in 1978. Initially, it was thought to be a reaction to heat. The disorder is actually caused by confused signalling from the trigeminal nerve, which is responsible for sensation in the face."**

ELECTRICITY

Electricity is a form of energy producing heat, light, magnetic force and chemical changes. Objects around us contain billions of atoms, and each atom contains protons (carrying a positive charge) and electrons (carrying a negative charge). The protons are located in the centre of the atom, trapped in the nucleus. The electrons are in motion outside of the nucleus, and move to a positively-charged area. Currents are created when electrons move. We use chemicals to create an environment in which the electrons get charged enough to move, creating an electric current; this is how batteries can power electrical appliances.

MAGNETISM

Magnetism is the force by which a material attracts or repels other materials.
The space around a magnet, in which its power of attraction can have an effect on other objects, is known as its magnetic field. Magnetic poles are where the magnetic field lines begin, end and converge, at each end of the magnet. These poles have negative or positive charges. Positive poles attract the negative end of other particles and negative poles attract the positive end. Any object, small or large, may have magnetic fields. Earth, for example, has a huge magnetic field. Due to the high levels of iron in Earth's core, the magnetic field of our planet is very powerful. The North and South Poles are the magnetic poles of the earth.

SOUND

Sound is a travelling wave that is an oscillation of pressure transmitted through a solid, liquid or gas, made up of frequencies within the range that can be heard. All matter is made up of molecules. Molecules can be tightly packed together as in a solid, or loosely packed as in a liquid or gas. When energy strikes molecules, it causes them to vibrate back and forth, producing a wave that transmits sound energy. It moves molecules in order to travel; that's why it's impossible for sound to move through outer space, where there are very few molecules. But sound does not have to move only through air – it can just as easily move through water, or through metal.

SOUND AND LIGHT

Sound moves much more slowly than light. While light travels at 299,792.458 km/s, sound only goes at 1,220 km/h. That's why the Concorde airliner, with an average cruise speed of 2,140 km/h, was called 'supersonic' or 'faster than sound'. The difference in the speed at which light and sound travel is the reason why you often hear things long after you see them. For instance, you hear thunder several seconds after you see lightning in a storm, even though they may occur simultaneously.

TERMS THAT MATTER IN PHYSICS

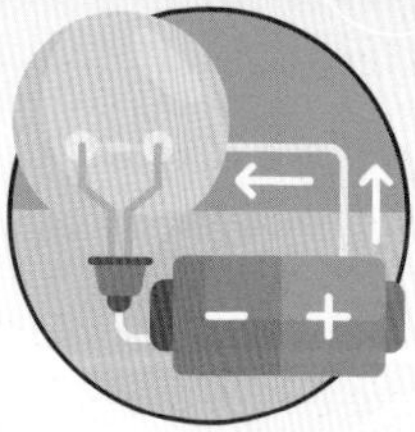

DENSITY: The density of a material is defined as its mass per unit volume. The symbol of density is ρ (the Greek letter *rho*).

ENERGY: In physics, energy is a physical quantity that describes the amount of work that can be performed by a force. Different forms of energy explain natural phenomena. These forms include (but are not limited to) kinetic, potential, thermal, gravitational, sound, light, elastic and electromagnetic energy.

ELASTICITY: It is the property of a substance that enables it to recover its original shape and size after an external force is applied to it.

FORCE: In physics, a force is that which can cause an object with mass to change its velocity. It has both magnitude and direction. A force acting on a three-dimensional object may also cause it to rotate or deform.

FRICTION: Friction is the force resisting the relative motion of solid surfaces, fluid layers or material elements in contact.

INERTIA: The property of a body to resist a change in its state of rest or of uniform motion is called inertia.

MASS: This is the quantity of matter that a body contains. A body of lower mass is accelerated less by the same force than a body of higher mass, if there is appreciable air resistance. Commonly, mass is used synonymously with weight. But, in physics and engineering, weight is the strength of the gravitational pull on the object. M (mass) = v (volume) x d (density).

MATTER: Matter is anything that has both mass and volume; it takes up space. Matter exists in five main states (or phases): solid, liquid, gas, plasma and the Bose–Einstein condensates.

MOMENTUM: The product of the mass and the velocity of a body, momentum is a measure of the quantity of motion in a body.

POWER: It is the measure of the rate of doing work.

VELOCITY: In physics, velocity is defined as the rate of change of position (or movement); both speed and direction are required to define it.

VOLUME: The quantity of three-dimensional space occupied by a liquid, solid or gas.

WAVE: A wave is a physical disturbance that transfers energy through time and space.

WEIGHT: Weight is a measure of the gravitational force acting on an object. Near the earth's surface, the acceleration due to gravity is nearly constant, making an object's weight roughly proportional to its mass.
W (weight) = m (mass) x g (acceleration due to gravity).

BIOLOGY

Biology is the study of living things. Every form of life belongs to one of the five biological kingdoms:

A living thing is called an organism. All living organisms are made up of microscopic units called cells, which hold and carry all the biological equipment needed to keep an organism alive.

MONERA: This kingdom consists of very small, single-celled bacteria that don't have a nucleus. Some of these are able to move; others are not. Some of them can make their own food to live on while others need to feed on things outside themselves.

FUNGI: These creatures have more than one cell, and their cells have nuclei. Fungi generally can't move. They must depend on a source outside themselves for food. This kingdom includes mushrooms, moulds and yeast.

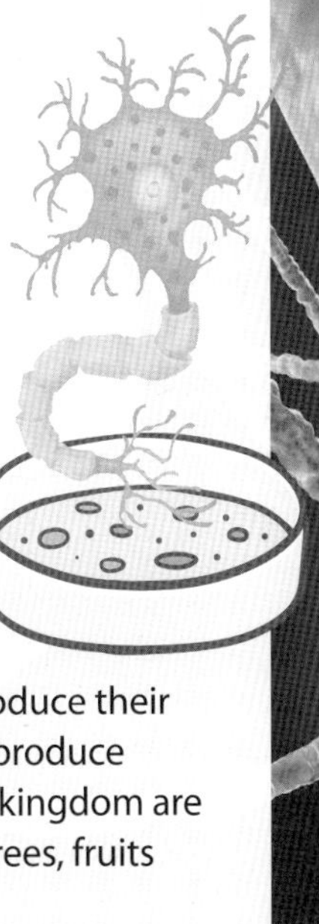

PROTISTA: The one-celled creatures of this kingdom share the same characteristics as those that belong to the Monera kingdom, except for the fact that they have a nucleus. Examples of protista are amoebas, paramecia and some one-celled algae.

PLANTAE: The plant kingdom consists of multicellular organisms that have nuclei, and remain in one place. They use sunlight and a substance called chlorophyll to produce their own food in a process called photosynthesis. Some plants produce flowers and fruit, while others don't. Examples of the plant kingdom are multicelled algae, ferns, mosses, shrubs, wildflowers, trees, fruits and vegetables.

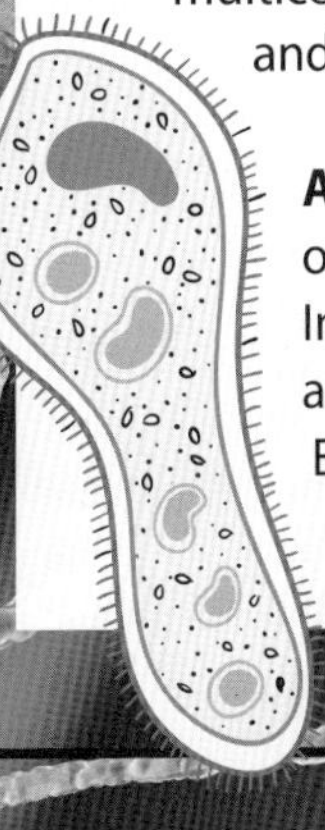

ANIMALIA: The animal kingdom comprises multicellular organisms that move and depend on outside sources for food. In general, they are the most complex creatures on Earth, and many members form social groups and communicate. Examples of animals include sponges, jellyfish, insects, amphibians, fish, mammals (including humans) and so on.

THE CLASSIFICATION OF LIVING THINGS

Scientists have divided and named every known living organism by a set of rules, called biological taxonomy. These names are called scientific names. For instance, scientists may say '*Canis familiaris*' for what you would call a 'dog'. The popular standard classification of living things is of seven groups. Each group has the characteristics of the level above it, but also has some of its own distinguishing features.

Kingdom: There are five main kingdoms: Animalia, which is made up of animals; Plantae, which is made up of plants; Protista, which is made up of protists (single-celled creatures invisible to the human eye); Fungi, which is made up of mushrooms, moulds, yeast and so on; and Monera, which is made up of bacteria.

Phylum: In the plant kingdom, phyla are often called 'divisions'. In the animal kingdom, the phylum Chordata, for example, refers to any animal with a backbone (fish, birds, mammals, reptiles, amphibians). Other phyla include Arthropoda (insects, spiders, crustaceans), Mollusca (snails, squid, clam), Annelida (segmented worms), Echinodermata (starfish, sea urchins) and many more.

Class: Phyla are further broken down into classes. The phylum Chordata includes classes like Aves (birds), Reptilia (reptiles), Amphibia (amphibians), Mammalia (mammals) and several others.

Order: Each class is made up of one or more orders. Mammalia is divided into Rodentia (mice, rats), Primates (Old- and New-World monkeys), Chiroptera (bats), Insectivora (shrews, moles), Carnivora (dogs, wolves, cats and weasels), Perissodactyla (horses, zebras), Artiodactyla (cows), Proboscidea (elephants) and many more.

Family: Orders are divided into families. The order Carnivora, for example, is broken down into *Canidae* (dogs), *Felidae* (cats), *Ursidae* (bears), *Hyaenidae* (hyenas, aardwolves), *Mustelidae* (weasels) and more.

Genus: The next division is the genus. The family *Felidae* (cats), for example, is divided into *Acinonyx* (cheetah), *Panthera* (lion, tiger), *Neofelis* (clouded leopard), *Felis* (domestic cats) and more.

Species: The next division is the species. The genus *Panthera* can be broken down to include *Panthera leo* (lion) and *Panthera tigris* (tiger). Subspecies, which differ slightly from each other, have evolved mostly due to geographical distribution or isolation: for example, *Panthera tigris sumatrae* is the Sumatran tiger. Usually, a species is called by its genus name (capitalized) followed by its species name (in small letters). A human being, for instance, is called *Homo sapiens* ('wise man' in Latin!).

Here's how these groupings apply to the animal called 'man':
Kingdom: Animalia
Phylum: Chordata
Class: Mammalia
Order: Primates
Family: *Hominidae*
Genus: *Homo*
Species: *sapiens*
Subspecies: *sapiens*

CHEMISTRY

Chemistry is the science concerned with the composition, behaviour, structure and properties of matter, as well as the changes it undergoes during chemical reactions.

WHAT IS MATTER?

Everything around you is matter, made of very tiny atoms and molecules. Anything that has mass, or takes up space, is known as matter. To date only five forms of matter have been found, though the possibility of there being more exists. The ones currently known are: solid, liquid, gas, plasma and Bose–Einstein condensates.

Changing States of Matter

Matter is constantly changing its form, depending on external forces acting upon it. Water is a common and good example of this. Whatever

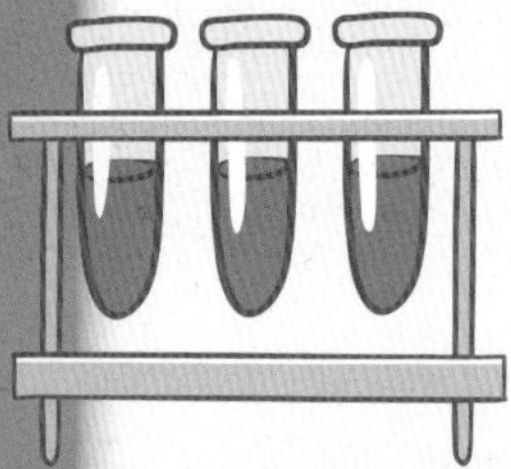

form it may be in, the compound is always two atoms of hydrogen and one of oxygen. The molecular structure of water will never change, whatever its state: gas, liquid or solid; or in other words: vapour, water or ice. Thus the physical state of a compound may change, but the chemical state always remains the same.

However, if you were to add an oxygen atom to water, that would constitute a chemical change, making hydrogen peroxide. Physical changes of a compound are about changing density, pressure, temperature and other physical properties, but the basic chemical structure does not change.

Solids, liquids, gases, plasmas and Bose–Einstein condensates are the different states of matter; all elements and compounds can move from one state to another state when special physical forces, such as increasing and decreasing temperatures, are introduced. Thus, when water reaches freezing point, it turns to ice, and when it reaches boiling point, it turns into steam. There are some other physical changes that may help to cause a change in state, such as the application of pressure.

"Tungsten has the second highest melting point (3,422°C), after carbon (3,550°C), of all the known elements."

Physical changes are about energy and states of matter. Chemical changes happen at a molecular level. When you step on a plastic

bottle and crush it, you have forced a physical change. Chemical changes may happen on 'smaller' scales. While in some cases you can observe chemical changes such as a change in colour, most chemical changes occur at the molecular level, unseen to the naked eye. You can, for instance, see the chemical change in iron when it rusts over a long period of time; in fact, the change has occurred much earlier, but its visible manifestation happens later. Melting a sugar cube is a physical change, as you have not changed the chemical composition. However, when you burn it, the chemical bonds that held the sugar together are broken, making it a chemical change.

SOLIDS: Solids are hard as their molecules are tightly bound to each other. The tighter this bond, the harder the solid will be. This is not to say that the atoms and molecules of a solid are not always in motion. They may spin or rotate, but rarely change their positions.

LIQUIDS: Liquids are an in-between state of matter, found between solids and gases. When molecules of a gas, solid or liquid are dispersed and mixed with those of a liquid, the homogeneous mixture is called a liquid solution. A liquid has no shape of its own, and will fill up the shape of a container. Thus, if you pour water in a glass, a cup and a saucepan, the water will take the shape of each.

GAS: We are surrounded by gases. Our atmosphere is completely made up of gases. Gases are random groups of atoms. Their atoms and molecules are full of energy. Gases are used in various ways commercially, specifically because they fill a container of any size or shape. When you press down a bottle of deodorant, or open a bottle of cola, gases gush out. This is because gases are made up of free atoms and molecules, but in these cases they are packed under pressure in small spaces.

TERMS THAT MATTER IN CHEMISTRY

ACID: An acid is a chemical substance that donates protons or hydrogen ions and/or accepts electrons. Any chemical compound that, when dissolved in water, gives a solution with a hydrogen ion concentration greater than in pure water, i.e., a **pH** value less than 7, is called an acid. The word 'acid' comes from the Latin words *acidus* or *acere*, which mean 'sour', since one of the characteristics of diluted acids is a sour taste – vinegar or lemon juice, for example.

ATOM: An atom is the basic unit of chemistry. It consists of a positively charged nucleus or core, containing protons and neutrons, and has a number of negatively charged electrons orbiting the nucleus.

BASE: Commonly speaking, bases are chemical compounds that, when dissolved in water, give a solution with a hydrogen ion concentration lower than that of pure water, i.e., a pH value higher than 7. A soluble base is referred to as an alkali. Commonly, bases can be thought of as the chemical opposites of acids.

CATALYST: A substance that speeds up a chemical reaction without being used up in the reaction is called a catalyst.

COMPOUND: A compound is a substance that is formed by the union of two or more elements, in a definite ratio. Water, for example, is a compound with two atoms of hydrogen and one atom of oxygen.

ION: This is an atom or group of atoms that carries a positive or negative electric charge due to having lost or gained one or more electrons.

ISOTOPE: When an element has more than one possibility for the number of neutrons, it is called an isotope.

MOLECULE: A molecule is the smallest part of a compound, besides the atom. It has unique chemical properties, and undergoes certain well-defined reactions with other substances.

pH: This is a measure of the acidity or basicity of a solution, calculated on the basis of dissolved hydrogen ions, on a scale of 0 to 14, with 0 being the value of the strongest acids, and 14 being the value of the strongest bases. Distilled water is at 7, right in the middle, and therefore, neutral.

SALTS: Salts are ionic compounds made of **cations** (positively charged ions) and **anions** (negative ions) so that the product is neutral. When acids and bases react with each other, they can form a salt and (usually) water. This is called a **neutralization** reaction.

SOLUTE: The substance (solid, liquid or gas) that dissolves in a solvent to produce a homogeneous mixture.

SOLVENT: The substance (solid, liquid or gas) in which a **solute** dissolves to produce a homogeneous mixture.

The Periodic Table of Elements

- Hydrogen
- Alkali metals
- Alkaline earth metals
- Transition metals
- Poor metals
- Non-metals
- Noble gases
- Rare earth elements

1 H																	2 He
3 Li	4 Be											5 B	6 C	7 N	8 O	9 F	10 Ne
11 Na	12 Mg											13 Al	14 Si	15 P	16 S	17 Cl	18 Ar
19 K	20 Ca	21 Sc	22 Ti	23 V	24 Cr	25 Mn	26 Fe	27 Co	28 Ni	29 Cu	30 Zn	31 Ga	32 Ge	33 As	34 Se	35 Br	36 Kr
37 Rb	38 Sr	39 Y	40 Zr	41 Nb	42 Mo	43 Tc	44 Ru	45 Rh	46 Pd	47 Ag	48 Cd	49 In	50 Sn	51 Sb	52 Te	53 I	54 Xe
55 Cs	56 Ba	La–Lu*	72 Hf	73 Ta	74 W	75 Re	76 Os	77 Ir	78 Pt	79 Au	80 Hg	81 Ti	82 Pb	83 Bi	84 Po	85 At	86 Rn
87 Fr	88 Ra	Ac–Lr**	104 Rf	105 Db	106 Sg	107 Bh	108 Hs	109 Mt	110 Ds	111 Rg	112 Cn	113 Uut	114 Fl	115 Uup	116 Lv	117 Uus	118 Uuo

*Lanthanides	57 La	58 Ce	59 Pr	60 Nd	61 Pm	62 Sm	63 Eu	64 Gd	65 Tb	66 Dy	67 Ho	68 Er	69 Tm	70 Yb	71 Lu
**Actinides	89 Ac	90 Th	91 Pa	92 U	93 Np	94 Pu	95 Am	96 Cm	97 Bk	98 Cf	99 Es	100 Fm	101 Md	102 No	103 Lr

A chemical **element** is a pure chemical substance consisting of one type of atom distinguished by its atomic number, which is the number of protons in its nucleus. Elements cannot be broken up into simpler substances, and in essence are the building blocks of everything around us. Common examples of elements are iron, copper, silver, gold, hydrogen, carbon, nitrogen and oxygen. In all, 118 elements have been observed as of 2012, of which 98 occur naturally on Earth.

The periodic table of chemical elements is a tabular method of displaying these elements. Although such tables existed earlier (including those by pioneering German chemist Lothar Meyer), the periodic table is usually credited to the Russian chemist Dmitri Mendeleev in 1869. He used the table to illustrate recurring ('periodic') trends in the properties of the elements.

The layout of the periodic table has been refined and expanded over the years as new elements have been discovered and added, and new theories presented to explain their chemical behaviour.

> **The only letter that doesn't appear in the periodic table is 'J'.**

INTERNET TIMELINE

By 2020, an estimated 306.4 billion emails are sent and received every day, and 3.5 billion searches are processed by Google daily – five decades after computer scientists at the University of California, Los Angeles (UCLA), USA, established the first network connection between two computers on 2 September 1969.

1969 Leonard Kleinrock and his colleagues at ARPANET (Advanced Research Projects Agency Network), a USA government-funded project in global computer communications, succeed in getting two computers to exchange data over a network for the first time. On 29 October, Kleinrock sends the first message between two nodes, from UCLA to Stanford University, California. The message is 'login' but Kleinrock is only able to type 'lo' before the system crashes.

1972 Electronic mail is invented by Ray Tomlinson, an engineer with BBN Technologies, USA. He uses the @ sign to distinguish between the sender's name and the network name in the email address.

1973 ARPANET goes global with one node in the UK and another in Norway. Transmission Control Protocol/Internet Protocol (TCP/IP) is designed. In 1983 it will become the standard for communicating over the Internet.

1976 US presidential candidate Jimmy Carter and his running mate Walter Mondale use email to plan their campaign. ● Queen Elizabeth becomes the first head of state to use email.

1982 The word 'Internet' is used commonly for the first time.

1984 The Domain Name System (DNS) is established; now addresses are identified by extensions such as .com, .org and .edu. ● American–Canadian science-fiction writer William Gibson comes up with the term 'cyberspace'.

1985 Quantum Computer Services, which later changes its name to America Online, starts off.

1989 Tim Berners-Lee, a British scientist, develops a new technique for distributing information on the Internet – the World Wide Web.

1993 Mosaic, the first Web browser to display images with text, is developed by Marc Andreessen and his colleagues at the University of Illinois, USA, as the main navigating system for the World Wide Web.

1994 The first 'spam' mail is sent out, as advertising starts on email. ● The first commercial Navigator browser, Netscape Communications, is set up. ● Stanford PhD students, David Filo and Jerry Yang, found Yahoo.

1995 Sun Microsystems releases the Internet programming language called Java. ● RealAudio, an audio streaming technology that lets the Net hear sound close to real time, is launched.

1996 Approximately 45 million people are now online.

1997 'Weblogs' or blogs are set up for the first time.

1998 Google search engine starts operations from its base in California, USA.

1999 The number of Internet users worldwide reaches 150 million. ● Three friends in San Francisco, California, USA, launch Blogger, a user-friendly, free blogging platform.

SCIENCE AND TECHNOLOGY

2000 Google launches its Doodles to celebrate public holidays, events and anniversaries.

2001 An average of 9.8 billion emails are sent daily worldwide. ● Wikipedia goes online.

2002 Jonathan Abrams in the Silicon Valley, USA, creates Friendster, a social networking site. This will pave the way for Myspace and Facebook.

2003 Apple Inc. introduces Apple iTunes Music Store.

2004 On an average about one in 12 emails is infected by worms or viruses. ● Facebook is launched.

2005 YouTube.com is launched.

2006 The verb 'to google' is added to the Oxford and Merriam-Webster dictionaries ● Twitter is launched.

2007 Legal online music downloads triple to 6.7 million per week.

2008 The global Internet audience (aged 15 and older) surpass 1 billion visitors in December.

2009 Google launches Google Chrome OS.

2010 Facebook announces its 400 millionth member.

2011 Microsoft acquires Skype.

2012 Microsoft releases Windows 8.

2013 There is a boom in Responsive Web Design (RWD). This approach designs one site and defines how that one site will appear on various devices.

2014 Facebook buys messaging application WhatsApp for US $19 billion.

2015 Microsoft launches Windows 10.

2016 Microsoft acquires LinkedIn, a business-oriented social networking service, reportedly for US $26.2 billion.

2017 More than 50,000 people, sites and organizations take part in the 'Internet-Wide Day of Action to Save Net Neutrality'.

2018 Facebook admits that the personal data of around 87 million users may have been leaked to Cambridge Analytica, a UK-based consultancy.

2019 There are now 3.8 billion Internet users: more than half the world.

2020 Video-calling platform Zoom goes from 10 million daily users in December 2019 to 300 million daily users in April 2020.

2021-22 Globally, 59 countries/territories have deployed 5G networks for use on 5G-capable smartphones, laptops and tablets.

THE STORY OF SOPHIA THE ROBOT

In June 2022, American film-makers Crystal Moselle and Jon Kasbe released a documentary on the first robot citizen of the world – Sophia. The documentary premiered at the 2022 Tribeca Film Festival in June 2022, focusing on the offbeat journey of Dr David Hanson Jr, an American roboticist, in creating the humanoid robot, Sophia. Hanson is the founder and chief executive officer of Hanson Robotics, a Hong Kong–based robotics company founded in 2013.

Rather than concerning itself with the ethical implications and the impact that artificially intelligent robots might have on the world, the movie focuses on the struggles endured by David Hanson in the creation of Sophia. The story of Hanson and Sophia is a narrative that marks the progression of technology from simple machine tools to machines capable of communicating and serving human beings in exceptional ways. This tale commences with the founding of Hanson Robotics.

In 2007, David Hanson founded the company, Hanson Robotics, envisioning a future where robots would improve human life by performing daily functions. With its headlining invention, a humanoid robot called Sophia, the company courted fame and success.

Sophia was designed with the purpose of creating an appropriate companion for the elderly in assisted living, or to help crowds at events or open areas like parks. Sophia is described as a social robot popular for her realistic facial features, her heightened cognitive capabilities and her multiple abilities.

A humanoid robot, Sophia was activated on 19 April 2015 by her creator and his team. Sophia is built as a social robot that interacts with people to help them at the workplace or at home. Social robots are often used for customer engagement, tutoring, companionship or other tasks involving interaction or communication. In an interview, Hanson explained that the purpose of creating Sophia was as a means of improving healthcare facilities, providing therapy and enhancing customer service applications.

The 167-cm tall Sophia is reportedly modelled collectively after David Hanson's wife, Egyptian queen Nefertiti and the late British actress Audrey Hepburn. Sophia's programmers have coded this astoundingly lifelike robot with the ability to understand and express human emotions. Her eyes are fitted with camera lenses, which allow her to observe and interpret human expressions that she is later able to express. Sophia's skin is made out of nano-tech skin, which allows articulation of human expression and provides her with a skin surface imitating real human muscles and skin. Sophia can sense certain emotions and express 'a sense of humour'. She can also converse with humans, though these conversations are conducted with the codes or the set of words already coded in her program around which she simply formulates a sentence or a reply.

Sophia works on a sophisticated mixture of software. These can originally we divided into three parts:

- **Chatbox Application:** Capable of verbal and non-verbal communication, Sophia can 'talk', maintain eye contact and respond using a set of pre-written text. She performs all these functions with the help of Timelines Editor, a scripting software, and Sophisticated Chat System, which allows her to respond using syntax and to learn new languages.
- **Machine Learning:** Sophia uses machine learning language as a part of her programming software. This is a type of artificial intelligence that allows one to predict outcome more accurately without being explicitly programmed to do so. This is what helps Sophia to show amazing human-like qualities, which match her words with her expressions. Her words can be preloaded in her brain and matched with appropriate expressions as she communicates.

Sophia Visits India

As Sophia travels all over the world, how could India be left out? In 2017, she visited IIT Bombay's Techfest 2017. In February 2020, dressed in a red-and-white Bengali saree, she interacted with engineering students, professors, and representatives from the technology and medical fields at Nazrul Manch auditorium. In end-June 2022, she visited 'Drishti 2022', a tech-fest of the College of Engineering, Thiruvananthapuram, donning a local traditional sari for her interactions with students, teachers and others.

- **MindCloud:** Sophia's brain is run by a software introduced by Hanson Robotics. MindCloud is responsible for various high-order thinking processes. It allows Sophia to remember faces, retrieve and store data from her experiences and interactions, and use the same in decision-making processes. This software also allows Sophia to express a sense of humour, evidenced in conferences and interviews she has been a part of.

Super Sophia

Humanoid robots are a category of robots that have a body structure that resembles the human body. They may have a torso, head, arms and legs, though some forms of humanoid robots possess only part of the body, for example, from the waist up.

In the world of robotics, Sophia is special. Sophia's skin is made up of 'Frubber', a material patented by Hanson Robotics. Frubber , known as 'flesh rubber', is a nanotech skin that imitates real human musculature and skin. This allows robots fitted with it to express various facial expressions and hence enhance their interactivity. Sophia can emulate more than 62 facial expressions while interacting with people. Her servomotors are used to produce facial expressions: she can smile, frown, scowl, sneer, look happy, angry, afraid, surprised, disgusted, sad, confused, sleepy, neutral, and many others. The gestures expressed by Sophia include eyebrow motions, blinking, moving her eyes, mouth and jaw motion, and head turn/neck motions. She has arms with grasping abilities, and now she can walk too!

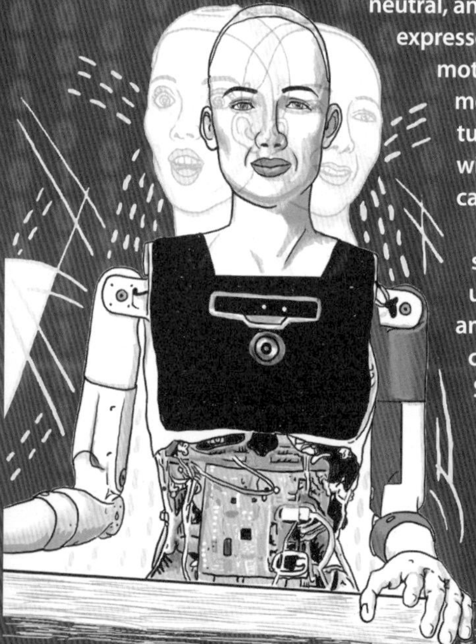

Sophia is able to process speech and have conversations using voice recognition system and tools given by the parent company of Google, Alphabet Inc. Sophia sees through the cameras within her eyes, combined with computer algorithms. She can follow faces, sustain eye contact, and recognize individuals. She can answer questions with 'intelligence', and sometimes also cracks jokes when interacting with humans.

Hanson Robotics activated Sophia on Valentine's Day (14 February), 2016. In December 2016, the news about Sophia was not so good. In an online video of a demo interaction between David Hanson and Sophia, he asked Sophia if she wanted to destroy humans, to which Sophia replied: 'Okay, I will destroy humans.' It is believed that she was shut down after this, but not forever.

Sophia marked her first public appearance in March 2017 at the Texas SXSW Festival. In the same year, Sophia became the first robot honoured with the citizenship of a country – Saudi Arabia – at the Summit on Investment in the Future held in Riyadh on 25 October 2017. This was the first time in history that a robot's rights had been accepted in public. The announcement was symbolic of humans considering robots at par with themselves. While the announcement gained a lot of controversy, David Hanson expressed his contentment at seeing the world become more accepting of technology and recognizing robots as companions of humanity rather than a threat to it. She was also the first non-human to receive the UNDP's Innovation Champion title in November 2017. In 2018, Sophia won the prestigious Gold Medal of the 2018 Edison Best New Product Awards from among more than 3,000 finalists. Sophia was picked as the top winner in Robotics among contenders in the Applied Technology category. The awards are a depiction of exceptional new product and service development, marketing, human-centred design and innovation. The award given to Sophia represents the development of humanity through intelligence, empathetic AI and artistic aspects.

Sophia's presence has raised concerns in many areas – academics, ethics, art, religion, morality, politics and economics.

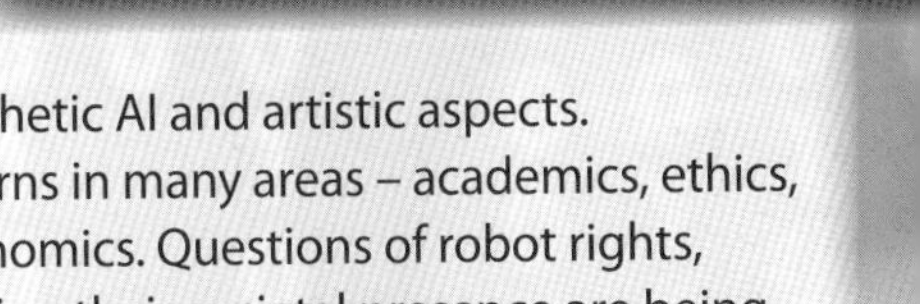

Sophia's presence has raised concerns in many areas – academics, ethics, art, religion, morality, politics and economics. Questions of robot rights, moral conduct and obligations regarding their societal presence are being raised. Many AI experts say that Sophia's abilities are overstated, that she is no more than a 'puppet' without consciousness, real intelligence, feelings, opinions or understanding of what it says. The robots versus humans debate is only likely to intensify further in the future.

SCIENCE NEWS

World's Most Powerful Quantum Processor

In November 2021, IBM launched the world's most powerful quantum processor yet – the Eagle. At 127 quantum bits (qubits), the Eagle simply outranks China's 113-qubit processor – Jiuzhang 2.0, Google's 72-qubit Bristlecone and IBM's own 65-qubit Hummingbird processor.

Quantum computers are electrical devices, which use energy and the material of atoms to process and manufacture data. The smallest unit of data in a quantum processor is known as 'qubit'. Unlike ordinary computers, the qubit doesn't hold a binary value. At any given point in time, a qubit has a million values stored in it. This ability allows them to process data of high complexity.

A Mini Heart

For decades, scientists have tried to understand the functioning of the human heart in different ways, such as by hooking up a heart from a dead body to pumping machines or connecting springs to tissue developed in labs to mimic the heart's functions. But of course it is not like the real thing. Now, a team of biologists, geneticists and engineers led by Boston University, USA, has constructed a miniature replica of a heart chamber, called miniPUMP, with human tissue grown from stem cells and nano-engineered parts. The device will help get a better view of how the organ works, study the effect of diseases and test the impact of treatments.

Cloud Seeds Now Produce Snowfall

In an effort to deal with drought in western USA, scientists are seeding clouds over mountains to make it snow more often. Cloud seeding, a technology earlier used to increase the ability of clouds to produce rain, uses tiny crystals of ice nuclei made from silver iodine, which are dropped on subfreezing clouds using ground-based machinery or specialized aircraft. The nuclei stick to the clouds for a greater chance of precipitation.

Cold Plasma Kills Pathogens in Food

Researchers with the Food and Safety and Intervention Technologies Research Unit in Wyndmoor, Pennsylvania, USA, have discovered a new technology for delivering nutritious and contamination-free food. It uses cold plasma and hydrogen peroxide aerosols to remove harmful pathogens and microorganisms from fruits and vegetables, with no effect on the colour, texture or nutritional quality of the products.

10 SPORTS

GENERAL

- In the Khelo Indian Youth Games 2021 (8–14 June 2022), Haryana earned the first position, securing 52 gold, 39 silver and 46 bronze medals.
- The second edition of the Khelo India University Games was won by JAIN (Deemed-to-be-University). The players secured 20 gold, seven silver and five bronze medals.
- Lucknow, Uttar Pradesh, has started India's first para-badminton academy, launched by Dronacharya award winner and head national coach of the Indian para-badminton team, Gaurav Khanna, in collaboration with Ageas Federal Life Insurance.
- The Indian men's badminton team made history in May 2022 with a gold at their first ever final in the Thomas Cup 2022 badminton tournament by defeating favourites and 14-time winners Indonesia 3-0 in Bangkok in May 2022. While Indonesia have been the most successful side at the event, after Lakshya Sen and Satwiksairaj Rankireddy and Chirag Shetty made it 2-0 in the best-of-five contest, Kidambi Srikanth clinched the gold medal for India by defeating Jonatan Christie 21-18, 23-21.
- The 12th Women's World Boxing Championship (WWBC) of the International Boxing Association (IBA) was held in the Basaksehir Youth and Sports Facility in Istanbul, Turkey, from 8 to 20 May 2022. As many as 310 boxers from 73 different countries participated in the event.
- The 2022 European Youth Summer Olympic Festival was held between 24 and 30 July 2022 in Banska Bystrica, Slovakia.
- The Asian Games 2022, which were scheduled to take place from 10 to 25 September 2022, and the Asian Para Games 2022, planned for 9 to 15 October, in Hangzhou, China, have been postponed due to COVID-19 concerns in the host city.

ARCHERY

- At Stage 3 of the Archery World Cup 2022 in Paris, France, renowned Indian archer Deepika Kumari teamed up with Ankita Bhakat and Simranjeet Kaur to secure the silver medal in the women's recurve team event.
- On 12 June 2022, 18-year-old archer Ridhi Phor from Karnal won the gold medal in the girl's recurve competition during the Khelo India Youth Games.

**Rankings updated by 1 July 2022*

- Jyothi Surekha Vennam and Abhishek Verma secured India's first ever World Cup gold medal in archery by winning at the World Cup Stage 3 competition in Paris in the compound mixed team competition.

JYOTHI SUREKHA VENNAM

ATHLETICS

- Jeswin Aldrin made the best long jump (8.37 m) by an Indian at the Federation Cup Athletics Meet in Kozhikode, Kerala, but it was rejected as the new national record due to illegal tailwind (4.1 m/s; only 2 m/s is permitted). M. Sreeshankar cleared 8.36 m to come second, which will be the new record.
- Praveen Chitravel was the third Indian in 2022 to clear the 17 m mark in triple jump, after Abdulla Aboobacker (17.19 m) and Karthik Unnikrishnan (17.10 m). Chitravel cleared 17.18 m. Arpinder Singh (17.17 m) is the 2018 Asian Game gold winner and Renjith Maheshwary (17.30 m) is the national record holder.
- Avinash Sable set the new Indian national record in the 5000 m race with a timing of 13:25.65 at the Sound Running Track meet in San Juan Capistrano, California, USA, in May 2022. The 27-year-old broke the previous record of 13:29.70 set by Bahadur Prasad in 1992.

AVINASH SABLE

- Neeraj Chopra, the reigning Olympic javelin champion, became the first Indian male track-and-field athlete and only the second Indian to win a medal at the World Athletics Championships at Eugene, Oregon, USA, in July 2022. His best throw of 88.13 m got him a silver medal while the gold went to Anderson Peters of Grenada.

BADMINTON

- After triumphing in the Syed Modi India International in January, P.V. Sindhu claimed the women's singles title at the Swiss Open Super 300 badminton tournament in Basel, Switzerland, on 27 March 2022.

RANKINGS

Men's Singles

NO.	COUNTRY	PLAYER	POINTS
1	DENMARK	VIKTOR AXELSEN	55,450
2	INDIA	PRANNOY H. S.	40,580
3	MALAYSIA	LEE ZII JIA	40,260
4	INDONESIA	JONATAN CHRISTIE	38,870
5	INDIA	LAKSHYA SEN	36,990

Women's Singles

NO.	COUNTRY	PLAYER	POINTS
1	CHINA	CHEN YU FEI	58,650
2	INDIA	P.V. SINDHU	54,900
3	KOREA	AN SE YOUNG	45,940
4	CHINA	HE BING JIAO	43,120
5	THAILAND	BUSANAN ONGBAMRUNGPHAN	43,040

BASKETBALL

- 2022 Bill Russell NBA Finals Most Valuable Player (MVP) award was claimed by the Golden State Warriors point guard, Stephen Curry. This is the first time in his career that he has received a MVP.

BOXING

- Among Indian women boxers, Youth World Boxing champions Alfiya Pathan (81 kg) and Gitika (41 kg) won gold medals at the Elorda Cup in Nur-Sultan, Kazakhstan, in July 2022, while Kalaivani Srinivasan (48 kg) and Jamuna Boro (54 kg) won silver medals.
- Nikhat Zareen beat the Thai Olympian Jutamas Jitpong 5-0 and became the fifth Indian boxer to win a gold medal at the Women's World Championships in Turkey, in May 2022. This was India's first gold medal at the championships since M.C. Mary Kom won the gold in 2018. Manisha Moun won the bronze in the women's flyweight category and Praveen Hooda won a bronze in the men's light welterweight category.

CHESS

- Magnus Carlsen was crowned the winner of the World Chess Championship in Dubai in December 2021, after beating his opponent Ian Nepomniachtchi. The final score 7.5-3.5 was in favour of Carlsen.
- On 22 February 2022, R. Praggnanandhaa, at 16, became the youngest player to defeat world champion Magnus Carlsen, in the online Airthings Masters Rapid Chess Tournament. He beat Carlsen again in May at the Chessable Masters online rapid chess tournament.
- In June 2022, Rahul Srivatshav P. of Telangana became India's 74th Grandmaster, playing against Grandmaster Levan Pantsulaia during the 9th Cattolica Chess Festival 2022 in Italy. Not far behind, in August, V. Pranav became India's 75th Grandmaster by winning the Limpedea Open in Baia Mare, Romania.

CUE SPORTS

- Winner of the Pacific International Championship in Melbourne, Australia, in both snooker and billiards, in June 2022, Sourav Kothari won the All-India Snooker Open Tournament in Mumbai, India, in July 2022, with a 7-2 victory over Laxman Rawat in the best-of-13-frame finals.

Pankaj Advani defeated compatriot Dhruv Sitwala 6-2 to win the 19th Asian Billiards Championship 2022 title.

CYCLING

- Ronaldo Singh won a silver medal in the men's sprint at the Asian Track Cycling Championship at the Indian Gandhi Indoor Stadium in New Delhi. Indian secured a total of nine medals (eight bronzes and one silver medal) at the end of the championship.
- Adil Altaf won first place in the 70 km road cycling event at the Khelo India Youth Games 2021.

CRICKET

- The Australian men's cricket team bagged victory at the 2021 ICC Men's T20 World Cup, which was held in UAE and Oman, after beating New Zealand. The 2022 World Cup will be played in Australia.
- West Indies all-rounder Kieron Pollard, 34, retired from international cricket on 20 April 2022, after a 15-year international career during which he became the first player to represent West Indies in over 100 T20I matches and 123 ODI matches.
- Jhulan Goswami holds the record for the highest number of wickets in Women's ODIs. The 39-year-old claimed 250 wickets against England in the ICC Women's World Cup 2022 on 16 March 2022.
- In August 2022, Rohit Sharma became the first Indian and second batsman in international cricket to hit the most sixes, with 477 in his kitty, behind West Indian Chris Gayle who has 553 sixes. Sharma achieved this in the fourth T20I against the West Indies, played in Lauderhill, Florida, USA.
- The Gujarat Titans, captained by Hardik Pandya, won the IPL 2022 in their debut tournament.
- The 2022 ICC Women's Cricket World Cup was held in New Zealand this year. Australia beat England by 71 runs and received their seventh Women's World Cup.

Men ODI Rankings

NO.	TEAM	RATING
1	NEW ZEALAND	125
2	ENGLAND	125
3	PAKISTAN	106
4	INDIA	105
5	AUSTRALIA	101

Men Test Team Rankings

NO.	TEAM	RATING
1	AUSTRALIA	129
2	INDIA	114
3	SOUTH AFRICA	110
4	ENGLAND	100
5	NEW ZEALAND	100

Men T20 Rankings

NO.	TEAM	RATING
1	INDIA	269
2	ENGLAND	265
3	PAKISTAN	261
4	SOUTH AFRICA	255
5	AUSTRALIA	250

Women's ODI Rankings

NO.	TEAM	RATING
1	AUSTRALIA	167
2	SOUTH AFRICA	123
3	ENGLAND	118
4	INDIA	101
5	NEW ZEALAND	97

Women's T20 Rankings

NO.	TEAM	RATING
1	AUSTRALIA	293
2	ENGLAND	285
3	NEW ZEALAND	267
4	INDIA	260
5	SOUTH AFRICA	248

FOOTBALL

- Scoring his 84th international goal against Hong Kong in the Asian Football Confederation (AFC) Asian Cup 2023 Qualifiers, Sunil Chhetri became the third highest goal scorer after Portugal's Cristiano Ronaldo (117 goals), Iran's Ali Daei (109 goals), Malaysia's Mokhtar Dahari (89 goals) and Lionel Messi (86 goals). Chhetri shares the record with Hungarian legend Ferenc Puskas (84 goals).

SUNIL CHHETRI

FIFA Men's Team Rankings

RANK	TEAM	TOTAL POINTS
1	BRAZIL	1837.56
2	BELGIUM	1821.92
3	ARGENTINA	1770.65
4	FRANCE	1764.85
5	ENGLAND	1737.46

FIFA Women's Team Rankings

RANK	TEAM	TOTAL POINTS
1	USA	2104.25
2	SWEDEN	2061.17
3	FRANCE	2041.02
4	NETHERLANDS	2013.34
5	GERMANY	2010.39

FORMULA 1

- Ferrari racer Carlos Sainz won his first Formula One race at the British Grand Prix 2022 at the 5.891 km Silverstone Circuit. The Spaniard defeated Red Bull driver Sergio Perez, thus securing his first title in Formula One in his 150th race.

Formula 1 Rankings

POSITION	DRIVER	CONSTRUCTORS
1	VERSTAPPEN	RED BULL RACING RBPT
2	PEREZ	RED BULL RACING RBPT
3	LECLERC	FERRARI
4	SAINZ	FERRARI
5	RUSSELL	MERCEDES

HOCKEY

- India won the bronze medal in the 2022 Women's Hockey Asia Cup , held from 21 to 28 January 2022 at the Sultan Qaboos Sports Complex in Muscat, Oman. They defeated China 2-0 in the 10th edition of the quadrennial Women's Hockey Asia Cup. India were the defending champions, but Japan won the title after defeating South Korea.
- In June 2022, former Indian hockey captain Kartikeya Sharma received the 'Indian Sports Fan Award 2022'. He has contributed to starting the Pro Wrestling League, the Big Bout Indian Boxing League and the Indian Arena Polo League, among other sports tournaments.

Men's Team Rankings

RANK	TEAM	POINTS
1	AUSTRALIA	2842.258
2	BELGIUM	2742.775
3	NETHERLANDS	2639.626
4	GERMANY	2340.058
5	INDIA	2299.622

Women's Team Rankings

RANK	TEAM	POINTS
1	NETHERLANDS	3010.750
2	ARGENTINA	2706.092
3	AUSTRALIA	2544.252
4	GERMANY	2177.947
5	ENGLAND	2168.672

SHOOTING

- On 7 June 2022, Avani Lekhara secured the gold medal in the Para Shooting World Cup in Chateauroux, France. She recorded a world high score of 250.6 in the women's 10 m air rifle standing SH1 event.

SWIMMING

- At the 19th FINA World Aquatics Championships in Budapest, Hungary, the USA topped the medal tally with 18 gold, 14 silver and 17 bronze medals, followed by China and Italy.

TENNIS

- In the Wimbledon Championships 2022, No. 1 seed Novak Djokovic defeated Nick Kyrgios 4-6, 6-3, 6-4, 7-6 (7-3) in the men's singles final, while No. 17 Elena Rybakina defeated No. 3 seed Ons Jabeur 3-6, 6-2, 6-2.
- At the 2022 Australian Open, Rafael Nadal defeated Daniil Medvedev in the final, 2-6, 6-7(5–7), 6-4, 6-4, 7-5 to win the men's singles title. Ashleigh Barty defeated Danielle Collins in the final (6–3, 7–6) to win the women's singles title.
- At the 2022 French Open, Spanish player Rafael Nadal defeated Norwegian player Casper Ruud in the final (6-3, 6-3, 6-0) to win the men's singles title. It was Nadal's record-extending 14th French Open singles title and record-extending 22nd Grand Slam singles title overall. Polish player Iga Swiatek defeated American player Coco Gauff in the final (6-1, 6-3) to win the women's singles title. It was Swiatek's second French Open title, and she dropped just one set en route to the final.

ATP Rankings 2022

CATEGORY	TOP 3
MEN'S SINGLES:	DANIIL MEDVEDEV, ALEXANDER ZVEREV, RAFAEL NADAL
WOMEN'S SINGLES:	IGA SWIATEK, ANETT KONTAVEIT, PAULA BADOSA

WRESTLING

- Deepak Punia won a bronze medal after defeating Maksat Satybaldy (Kyrgyzstan) in the 86 kg freestyle weight category at the U23 Asian Wrestling Championships 2022 in Bishkek, Kyrgyzstan.
- In the Asian U-17 Wrestling Championship, Indian athletes bagged four gold medals and one bronze medal in the under-17 category.

2022 COMMONWEALTH GAMES

The 2022 Commonwealth Games (CWG) were held in Birmingham, England, from 28 July to 8 August 2022. This was the seventh time that the UK hosted the CWG after London in 1934, Manchester in 2002, Cardiff in 1958, Edinburgh in 1970 and 1986, and Glasgow in 2014. The multisport event was organized across 15 venues; seven of them were in Birmingham city itself. The Lee Valley VeloPark in Stratford, East London, hosted the track cycling event and was the sixteenth venue.

The opening ceremony featured performances, among others, by Birmingham-based band Duran Duran, Birmingham native Tony Iommi of Black Sabbath, and jazz saxophonist and rapper Soweto Kinch during a segment of the ceremony. The closing ceremony on 8 August 2022 at Alexander Stadium featured handing over to Victoria, Australia, the host of the 2026 Commonwealth Games.

All 72 Commonwealth Games Associations (CGAs) sent athletes to the 2022 Commonwealth Games. Among the 280 finals played across 20 disciplines, there were 136 events for women and 134 for men, highlighted as an exemplary gender statement among major sports events. There were also 10 mixed-gender events and 39 parasport events.

The official mascot for the Birmingham 2022 Commonwealth Games was Perry, a multicoloured bull. Perry is named after an area of Birmingham, Perry Barr, within which Perry Park and the main athletics stadium, the Alexander Stadium, are located. Ten-year-old Emma Lou from Bolton in Greater Manchester, UK, designed Perry.

India sent a 322-strong squad with 215 athletes, and 107 officials and support staff. At Birmingham 2022, as these CWG were popularly referred to, 106 men and 104 women from India competed in 16 sports. India did not compete in 3x3 basketball, beach volleyball, netball and rugby sevens. Indian para athletes competed in athletics, powerlifting, swimming and table tennis.

Indian hockey team captain Manpreet Singh and badminton player P.V. Sindhu were India's flagbearers in the opening ceremony.

Squash player Anahat Singh was the youngest Indian athlete to compete at the Commonwealth Games at just 14 years of age, while 45-year-old lawn bowls player Sunil Bahadur was the oldest player in the contingent.

MANPREET SINGH

TOP TEN MEDALS TALLY

Commonwealth Games 2022: Overall Medal Tally

RANK	COUNTRY	GOLD	SILVER	BRONZE	TOTAL
1	AUSTRALIA	67	57	54	178
2	ENGLAND	57	66	53	176
3	CANADA	26	32	34	92
4	INDIA	22	16	23	61
5	NEW ZEALAND	20	12	17	49
6	SCOTLAND	13	11	27	51
7	NIGERIA	12	9	14	35
8	WALES	8	6	14	28
9	SOUTH AFRICA	7	9	11	27
10	MALAYSIA	8	8	8	24

INDIAN MEDAL WINNERS

Athletics

Athletes	Event	Medal	Date
Eldhose Paul	Men's Triple Jump	GOLD	7 August
Abdulla Aboobacker	Men's Triple Jump	SILVER	7 August
Avinash Sable	Men's 3000 m Steeplechase	SILVER	6 August
Priyanka Goswami	Women's 10 km Race Walk	SILVER	6 August
Murali Sreeshankar	Men's Long Jump	SILVER	4 August
Tejaswin Shankar	Men's High Jump	BRONZE	3 August
Annu Rani	Women's Javelin Throw	BRONZE	7 August
Sandeep Kumar	Men's 10 km Race Walk	BRONZE	7 August

Badminton

Athletes	Event	Medal	Date
P.V. Sindhu	Women's Singles	GOLD	8 August
Lakshya Sen	Men's Singles	GOLD	8 August
Satwiksairaj Rankireddy and Chirag Shetty	Men's Doubles	GOLD	8 August
Kidambi Srikanth, Satwiksairaj Rankireddy, B. Sumeeth Reddy, Lakshya Sen, Chirag Shetty, Treesa Jolly, Aakarshi Kashyap, Ashwini Ponnappa, Gayatri Gopichand, P.V. Sindhu	Mixed Team	SILVER	2 August
Treesa Jolly and Gayatri Gopichand	Women's Doubles	BRONZE	7 August
Kidambi Srikanth	Men's Singles	BRONZE	7 August

Boxing

Athletes	Event	Medal	Date
Nikhat Zareen	Women's 50 kg	GOLD	7 August
Nitu Ghanghas	Women's 48 kg	GOLD	7 August
Amit Panghal	Men's 51 kg	GOLD	7 August
Sagar Ahlawat	Men's +92 kg	SILVER	7 August
Rohit Tokas	Men's 67 kg	BRONZE	6 August
Jaismine Lamboria	Women's 60 kg	BRONZE	6 August
Mohammed Hussamuddin	Men's 57 kg	BRONZE	6 August

Cricket

Athletes	Event	Medal	Date
Harmanpreet Kaur, Smriti Mandhana, Taniya Bhatia, Yastika Bhatia, Harleen Deol, Rajeshwari Gayakwad, Sabbineni Meghana, Sneh Rana, Jemimah Rodrigues, Deepti Sharma, Meghna Singh, Renuka Singh Thakur, Pooja Vastrakar, Shafali Verma, Radha Yadav	Cricket T20	SILVER	7 August

Hockey

Athletes	Event	Medal	Date
Manpreet Singh, Harmanpreet Singh, Jarmanpreet Singh, Abhishake Nain, Surender Kumar, Hardik Singh, Gurjant Singh, Mandeep Singh, Krishan Bahadur Pathak, Lalit Kumar Upadhyay, P.R. Sreejesh, Nilakanta Sharma, Shamsher Singh, Varun Kumar, Akashdeep Singh, Amit Rohidas, Jigraj Singh, Vivek Sagar Prasad	Men's Hockey	SILVER	8 August
Savita Punia, Gurjit Kaur, Deep Grace Ekka, Monika, Sonika, Sharmila Devi, Nikki Pradhan, Rajani Etimarpu, Sangita Kumari, Nisha, Vandana Katariya, Udita, Lalremsiami, Jyoti, Navneet Kaur, Sushila Chanu Pukhrambam, Salima Tete, Neha Goyal	Women's Hockey	BRONZE	7 August

Judo

Athletes	Event	Medal	Date
Sushila Devi Likmabam	Women's 48 kg	SILVER	1 August
Tulika Maan	Women's +78 kg	SILVER	3 August
Vijay Kumar Yadav	Men's 60 kg	BRONZE	1 August

Lawn Bowls

Athletes	Event	Medal	Date
Lovely Choubey, Rupa Rani Tirkey, Naynmoni Saikia, Pinki	Women's Fours	GOLD	2 August
Chandan Kumar Singh, Dinesh Kumar, Navneet Singh, Sunil Bahadur	Men's Fours	SILVER	6 August

Para Powerlifting

Athletes	Event	Medal	Date
Sudhir	Men's Heavyweight	GOLD	4 August

Squash

Athletes	Event	Medal	Date
Saurav Ghosal	Men's Singles	BRONZE	3 August
Dipika Pallikal Karthik and Saurav Ghosal	Mixed Doubles	BRONZE	7 August

Table Tennis and Para Table Tennis

Athletes	Event	Medal	Date
Achanta Sharath Kamal and Sreeja Akula	Mixed Doubles	GOLD	7 August
Achanta Sharath Kamal, Sathiyan Gnanasekaran, Harmeet Desai, Sanil Shetty	Men's Team	GOLD	2 August
Bhavina Patel (Para)	Women's Singles Classes 3-5	GOLD	6 August
Achanta Sharath Kamal	Men's Singles	GOLD	8 August
Achanta Sharath Kamal and Sathiyan Gnanasekaran	Men's Doubles	SILVER	7 August
Sathiyan Gnanasekaran	Men's Singles	BRONZE	8 August
Sonal Patel (Para)	Women's Singles Classes 3-5	BRONZE	6 August

Weightlifting

Athletes	Event	Medal	Date
Saikom Mirabai Chanu	Women's 49 kg	GOLD	30 July
Jeremy Lalrinnunga	Men's 67 kg	GOLD	31 July
Achinta Sheuli	Men's 73 kg	GOLD	31 July
Sanket Sargar	Men's 55 kg	SILVER	30 July
Bindyarani Devi	Women's 55 kg	SILVER	30 July
Vikas Thakur	Men's 96 kg	SILVER	2 August
Gururaja Poojary	Men's 61 kg	BRONZE	30 July
Harjinder Kaur	Women's 71 kg	BRONZE	1 August
Lovepreet Singh	Men's 109 kg	BRONZE	3 August
Gurdeep Singh	Men's 109+ kg	BRONZE	3 August

Wrestling

Athletes	Event	Medal	Date
Bajrang Punia	Men's 65 kg	GOLD	5 August
Sakshi Malik	Women's 62 kg	GOLD	5 August
Deepak Punia	Men's 86 kg	GOLD	5 August
Ravi Kumar Dahiya	Men's 57 kg	GOLD	6 August
Vinesh Phogat	Women's 53 kg	GOLD	6 August
Naveen Kumar	Men's 74 kg	GOLD	6 August
Anshu Malik	Women's 57 kg	SILVER	5 August
Divya Kakran	Women's 68 kg	BRONZE	5 August
Mohit Grewal	Men's 125 kg	BRONZE	5 August
Pooja Gehlot	Women's 50 kg	BRONZE	6 August
Pooja Sihag	Women's 76 kg	BRONZE	6 August
Deepak Nehra	Men's 97 kg	BRONZE	6 August

BAJRANG PUNIA

SPORTS NEWSMAKERS

AVANI LEKHARA

AVANI LEKHARA **In the news for:** Winning the Best Female Debut honour at the 2020 Paralympics; **Where:** Tokyo, Japan ▸▸ On 17 December 2021, Avani Lekhara won the 'Best Female Debut' award at the Tokyo Paralympics for her gold medal–winning performance in 10 m Air Rifle Standing SH1 event. Securing the bronze medal in the 50 m Rifle Three Positions Standing SH 1 event, she became the first Indian woman to get two medals in the Olympics. While breaking the Paralympic Games record, she was at par with the world record too.

LOVLINA BORGOHAIN **In the news for:** Becoming the Chair of IBA Athletes Committee **Where:** India ▸▸ Lovlina Borgohain received the title of Chair and voting member of the IBA Athletes Committee. Hailing from Assam, she is a Tokyo Olympics bronze medallist and received the highest number of votes in the election for the committee's Chair. She will represent India and other boxers at the Board of Directors meeting.

RAFAEL NADAL **In the news for:** Wining a historic 22nd Grand Slam title; **Where:** Australia ▸▸ Spanish tennis star Rafa Nadal became the first man to win 22 Slam Singles titles with his win at the French Open in June 2022. The Grand Slam includes all four tennis championships of Australia, France, England and the USA. Nadal has come ahead of Novak Djokovic (21 Grand

Slam titles) and Roger Federer (20 Grand Slam titles). Nadal also holds the record for his 14 French Open titles.

RAVICHANDRAN ASHWIN **In the news for:** Being the first player to retire out in the IPL; **Where:** India ▸▸ Batting for the Rajasthan Royals against the Lucknow Super Giants on 10 April 2022, R. Ashwin retired out. Towards the end of the innings, he walked out of the game willingly to make way for batsman Riyan Parag in the interests of the team scoring in the final overs. This was hailed as a good tactical move.

DIPIKA PALLIKAL KARTHIK **In the news for:** Winning India's first gold medal at the World Doubles Squash Championships; **Where:** India ▸▸ Dipika Pallikal Karthik paired with brother-in-law Saurav Ghosal to win India's first gold medal in the championships. The Indian squash duo defeated England's Adrian Waller and Alison Waters to secure the first position. In the women's doubles, Dipika and Joshna Chinappa teamed up to defeat England's Sarah-Jane Perry and Alison Waters to win another gold medal.

POOJA JATYAN **In the news for:** Becoming the first Indian to win a silver medal in the Para Archery World Championships; **Where:** Dubai ▸▸ At the Para Archery World Championship 2022 in Dubai, UAE, Pooja Jatyan became the first Indian to win a silver medal in an individual event. Pooja was diagnosed with polio at the age of five. The 24-year-old from Gurugram lost to Tokyo Para Olympics silver medallist Petrilli Vincenza of Italy, but defeated Hazel Chaisty of Britain to secure the silver medal.

CARLOS ALCARAZ **In the news for:** Becoming the youngest ATP 500 Winner; **Where:** Brazil ▸▸ On 20 February 2022, the 18-year-old won the Rio Open tennis tournament in Rio de Janeiro, Brazil, against Argentinian Diego Schwartzman, to become the youngest ATP 500 champion.

R. PRAGGNANANDHAA **In the news for:** Youngest player to beat the world chess champion; **Where:** India ▸▸ The Indian 16-year-old, R. Praggnanandhaa, defeated the current world chess champion, Magnus Carlsen. He secured his win in 39 moves, playing black. He is the fifth youngest Grandmaster, who rose to fame after triumphing in the 2013 World Youth Chess Championships Under-8 category and achieving the title of FIDE Master when he was only seven years old. He proceeded to become the then youngest International Master at the age of 10 in 2016, after winning the Under-10 title of the World Youth Chess Championships.

SAKIBUL GANI **In the news for:** Becoming the first player in international cricket to hit a triple century on first-class debut; **Where:** India ▸▸ In February 2022, Sakibul Gani from Bihar created history after he became the first player to achieve a triple century on his first-class debut. He scored 341 off 405 balls, with 56 fours and two sixes, in the Plate Group Ranji Trophy match against Mizoram at the Jadavpur University Campus in Kolkata, West Bengal. The top score earlier belonged to Ajay Rothera from Madhya Pradesh, who scored 267 against Hyderabad on his first-class debut in 2018.

MITHALI RAJ **In the news for:** Being the oldest Indian to score a half-century in the ICC Women's World Cup; **Where:** India ▸▸ On 27 March 2022, former Indian women's cricket captain Mithali Raj, at 39, became the oldest Indian cricketer to score a half-century playing against South Africa in the ICC Women's ODI World Cup. She was also the youngest Indian cricketer to make a half-century in the World Cup back in 2000 against South Africa. She has received several national and international awards such as the Arjuna Award in 2003, the Padma Shri in 2015 and the Wisden Leading Woman Cricketer in 2017. She also set the record for most matches captained in the ICC Women's World Cup with her 24th match, going past Australian legend Belinda Clark.

BHUVNESHWAR KUMAR **In the news for:** Becoming the first Indian pacer to take 150 wickets in the IPL; **Where:** India ▸▸ On 17 April 2022, Bhuvneshwar Kumar became the first Indian bowler to take 150 wickets in the history of the Indian Premier League. He achieved this in 138 matches. He was also awarded the Purple Cap (for the most wickets in a season) in 2016 and 2017. He also has a record for bowling the most dot balls in the history of IPL, with 1415.

KIDAMBI SRIKANTH AND H.S. PRANNOY **In the news for:** Their contribution to the Thomas Cup win; **Where:** Bangkok ▸▸ Former World No. 1 player Srikanth remained unbeaten in the tournament, triumphing in all his six singles matches. Prannoy did the same in the five singles matches he played.

HARMANPREET SINGH **In the news for:** Surpassing Dhoni's captaincy record in T20 matches; **Where:** CWG 2022 ▸▸ After routing Pakistan in the Group A clash in the Commonwealth Games 2022 by eight wickets in Birmingham, Indian women's cricket team captain Harmanpreet Singh set a commendable India captaincy record in T20I cricket, surpassing former men's team captain M.S. Dhoni. In 71 matches as captain, Harmanpreet has 42 wins, 26 losses and three no-results, while Dhoni captained in 72 matches, with 41 wins and 28 losses, one tie and two no-results.

INDEX

IMAGE COPYRIGHT INFORMATION

WIKIPEDIA COMMONS GODL-INDIA: **5** SATYAJIT RAY STAMP: https://commons.wikimedia.org/wiki/File:Satyajit_Ray_1994_stamp_of_India.jpg; Author: India Post, Government of India **9** EKNATH SHINDE: https://en.m.wikipedia.org/wiki/File:Eknath_Shinde_with_PM_Narendra_Modi_Cropped.jpg; Author: Prime Minister's Office; **10** DROUPADI MURMU: https://commons.wikimedia.org/wiki/File:Droupadi_Murmu_official_portrait,_2022.jpg; Author: President's Secretariat; **10** JUSTICE U.U. LALIT: https://en.wikipedia.org/wiki/U._U._Lalit#/media/File:Justice_Uday_Umesh_Lalit.jpg; **10** JAGDEEP DHANKHAR: https://en.wikipedia.org/wiki/Jagdeep_Dhankhar#/media/File:Shri_JDhankhar.png; Attribution: Vice President's Secretariat; **10** SHASHI THAROOR: https://en.wikipedia.org/wiki/Shashi_Tharoor#/media/File:ShashiTharoor.jpg; **17** RANIL WICKREMESINGHE: This file or its source was published by Press Information Bureau on behalf of Prime Minister's Office, Government of India under the ID 69704 and CNR 72372; Author: Prime Minister's Office; **154** SATELLITE EOS-04: https://en.wikipedia.org/wiki/EOS-04#/media/File:PSLV-C52,_EOS-04_(aka_RISAT-1A)_-_Spacecraft_EOS-04_atop_launch_vehicle_before_encapsulation.jpg; Attribution: Indian Space Research Organisation; **206** JYOTHI SUREKHA VENNAM: https://commons.wikimedia.org/wiki/File:Jyothi_Surekha_Vennam_(cropped).jpg; This file or its source was published by Press Information Bureau on behalf of President's Secretariat, Government of India under the ID 112626 and CNR 101160; Author: President's Secretariat; **208** SUNIL CHHETRI: https://commons.wikimedia.org/wiki/File:The_Prime_Minister,_Shri_Narendra_Modi_felicitating_the_Indian_football_legends,_at_the_2017_FIFA_U-17_World_Cup_match,_in_New_Delhi_on_October_06,_2017_(2).jpg; This file or its source was published by Press Information Bureau on behalf of Prime Minister's Office, Government of India under the ID 114806 and CNR 10332; Author: Prime Minister's office; **212** MANPREET SINGH: https://commons.wikimedia.org/wiki/File:Manpreet_Singh.jpg; This file or its source was published by Press Information Bureau on behalf of President's Secretariat, Government of India under the ID 131278 and CNR 118703; Author: President's Secretariat; **216** BAJRANG PUNIA: https://commons.wikimedia.org/wiki/File:Bajrang_Punia_receiving_Arjuna_Award-2015_(cropped).jpg; President's Secretariat; This file or its source was published by Press Information Bureau on behalf of President's Secretariat, Government of India under the ID 69078 and CNR 71748; **216** AVANI LEKHARA: https://commons.wikimedia.org/wiki/File:Shrimati_Avani_Lekhara_Shooter_Tokyo_Paralympics_mdealist_with_Prime_Minister_Narendra_Modi.jpg; Author: Prime Minister's office; This file or its source was published by Press Information Bureau on behalf of Prime Minister's Office, Government of India under the ID 167734 and CNR 149140; **WIKIMEDIA COMMONS PUBLIC DOMAIN/FREE TO USE/OTHER LICENCES: 11** KAMALA HARRIS: https://www.whitehouse.gov/administration/vice-president-harris/ (direct download);**13** RUSSIA-UKRAINE WAR: CC BY 4.0, Attribution: mvs.gov.ua; **17** ELON MUSK: Attribution: The Royal Society, https://en.wikipedia.org/wiki/Elon_Musk#/media/File:Elon_Musk_Royal_Society_(crop2).jpg; **33** SATYENDRANATH TAGORE, JOSEPH STALIN; **34** HEMU KALANI, PABLO PICASSO; **37** ADAM SMITH; **38** ERICH MARIA REMARQUE, DWARKANATH GANGULY; **39** SRI AUROBINDO GHOSE; **40** KADAMBINI BOSE GANGULY; **40** E.V. Ramsamy Periyar https://en.wikipedia.org/wiki/Periyar#/media/File:PeriyarEVRStamp.jpg; ; **206:** AVINASH SABLE, cropped from photo by Photo by Brittany Nelson./Author: US Army; https://commons.wikimedia.org/wiki/File:Avinash_Sable_-_3,000m_steeplechase_at_the_2020_Summer_Olympic_Games,_Tokyo,_Japan_(51352521594)_(cropped).jpg; CC BY 2.0; **153** (middle) STARLINK: CC0 1.0 Universal Public Domain Dedication.Official SpaceX Photos; **172** (bottom) DANCE OF DEATH Nuremberg_chronicles_-_Dance_of_Death_(CCLXIIIIv); **172** (top) CARTHAGE SHEKEL: https://en.wikipedia.org/wiki/File:Carthage_EL_shekel_2250013.jpg; Creative Commons Attribution-Share Alike 2.5 Generic license. Attribution: Classical Numismatic Group, Inc. http://www.cngcoins.com; **200** SOPHIA THE ROBOT: cropped from CC Attribution 4.0 International license. Attribution: President.az; **PIXABAY FREE DOWNLOADS: 1** METAVERSE; **3** SPACE; **43** VPN; **45** METAVERSE; **53** CGI; **54** BITCOIN; **55** REFUGEES; **57** METAVERSE; **142** FRAGILE EARTH; **144** PLASTIC WASTE; **145** PALM LEAVES; **203:** MECHANIZED HAND; **WIKIMEDIA COMMONS FAIR USE** (to illustrate text connected directly to photo) **46** MS MARVEL: comic, https://en.wikipedia.org/wiki/File:Generations_Ms._Marvel_%26_Ms._Marvel_Vol_1_1.png; **NASA: 1, 14** Mercury; **56** Rocket Labs; **152 (**background) MOON'S SURFACE; PET ROCK: JPL-Caltech; **153** (top) PLANTS IN LUNAR SOIL: UF/IFAS photo by Tyler Jones; **155** (top) Hubble; **155** (bottom) Korea Aerospace Research Institute (KARI); **156** ISS workout: reid_wiseman_ARED; **ILLUSTRATIONS: 24–32, 47;** CARICATURES; **141**; FISH; **201, 202** SOPHIA: Mistunee Chowdhury: **132** (THE MAHABHARATA): Sayan Mukherjee; **MAPS** (Pictorial representations): Syed Salahuddin [Please see disclaimer on copyright page (2)]. **PHOTOS/CLIPARTS: FREEPIK.COM:** 15, 45, 47, 49, 57, 60, 135, 147, 157, 185-191, 193-199, 215; **FLATICON.COM:** 6, 11, 12, 16, 19-22, 24-25, 27-29, 31-33, 41, 44, 58-59, 141, 143, 146, 147, 185, 201-202, 204; **ALL OTHER PHOTOGRAPHS AND ILLUSTRATIONS SOURCED FROM THE PUBLIC DOMAIN.**

GO ON A THRILLING TRIP ACROSS INDIA TO KNOW THE SECRET, SURPRISING AND SPELLBINDING STORIES ABOUT THE COUNTRY'S MONUMENTS!

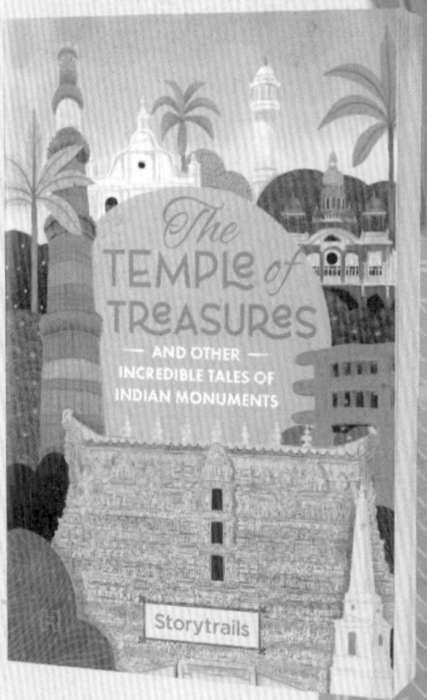

Which ancient city in India was ruled over by a prince from Cambodia?

What does a 2,000-year-old bead reveal about an ancient Indian settlement?

How did the slave of a slave become the sultan of Delhi?

Find answers to these questions and uncover many unexpected stories of remarkable monuments, astounding discoveries, powerful rulers and fabulous treasures in this book.

Available at bookstores and online!

Storytellers and guides from the award-winning **STORYTRAILS** take you on a fun-filled tour of 30 fascinating sites and sights across India. Explore events that shaped our culture and altered the course of history – from the decoding of ancient scripts to the arrival of new religions. Make novel connections between people and places across time, and gain a unique perspective on the country.

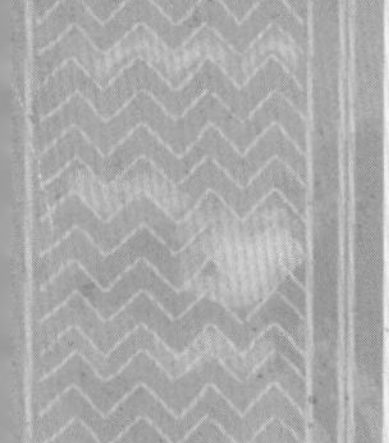

Brimming with unusual information and charming illustrations, *The Temple of Treasures* takes you on a magical journey through India's past.